reborn

BY CRISTINA COSTANTINO

Copyright © 2019 LIVE::LOVE::WHOLE

All rights reserved.

ISBN: 978 – 0 – 692 – 95539 – 0

REBORN

Dedicated to our love.

REBORN

PROLOGUE — The Fall: Another Time

1	The Fall: This Time	Pg 2
2	Stumbling Forward	Pg 18
3	When Help Came	Pg 34
4	First Lessons Learned	Pg 48
5	The Weight a Spirit Carries	Pg 62
6	Seeing Patterns	Pg 80
7	The Weight of Fear	Pg 94
8	Finding Reason	Pg 110
9	Time Spent Telling the Truth	Pg 122
10	Lifelines	Pg 134
11	Shifting to Trust	Pg 144
12	Continuing to Persist	Pg 158
13	An Isolated Program	Pg 170
14	Cutting Old Cords	Pg 182
15	The Start of Our Story	Pg 192
16	Facing Darkness	Pg 200
17	Struggling to Stay the Course	Pg 212
18	Creating a Clear Beacon	Pg 222
19	Stomping Out Fear	Pg 230
20	The Power of Dreams	Pg 252

REBORN

THE MIXED TAPE

SIDE A:
MISS YOU – The Rolling Stones
TANGLED UP IN BLUE – Bob Dylan
HURRICANE - MS MR
DARK PARADISE – Lana Del Rey
TRANSATLANTICISM – Death Cab for Cutie
SHELTER FROM THE STORM – Bob Dylan
NEVER HAD NOBODY LIKE YOU – M. Ward
STOLEN DANCE – Milky Chance
THE WOODPILE – Frightened Rabbit
IT'S THUNDER AND IT'S LIGHTNING – We Were Promised Jetpacks
TOO CLOSE — Tribute to Alex Clare
RUN – Snow Patrol

SIDE B:
DFW – Citizen Cope
RADIOACTIVE – Imagine Dragons
SHORT MOVIE – Laura Marling
SMOKE AND MIRRORS – Imagine Dragons
COMIN' BACK – Citizen Cope
BLEEDING OUT – Imagine Dragons
IT WILL COME BACK – Hozier
LITTLE TALKS – Of Monsters and Men
BACK THEN – Citizen Cope
COMING DOWN – Halsey
LOVE LOVE LOVE – Of Monsters and Men
HURRICANE WATERS – Citizen Cope
I BET MY LIFE – Imagine Dragons
TAKE ME TO CHURCH – Hozier
IT'S TIME – Imagine Dragons

REBORN

PROLOGUE
THE FALL – ANOTHER TIME

Hanging from the cliff, grasping the hand of the love my heart had told me I could count on to hold me, I looked up into the terror in his eyes and felt the magnitude of his fear resonate deep within me. Stretched across the rough surface that was just out of my reach, his strength was the only thing keeping me from dropping through the air that was pumping life into me and down into the unknown, waiting below to take my life away from both of us. Tearing my gaze away from his, I glanced over to my right and saw the little boy he was gripping as tightly as me, his small hand wholly hidden in his father's larger left one. With two legs swinging and one arm dangling, time stood still, and the world was silenced as a sense of peace overtook me.

    The terror that had filled me moments earlier, a combination of my man's and mine mixed up inside of me, was pushed out by a deeper knowing that rose, telling me the ending to this story had already been decided. It was a knowledge that wasn't backed by any facts, but nonetheless, I knew I had a debt that required payment, and had already agreed to sacrifice myself, if it became necessary, to save this child. Looking back into the eyes of the man I was linked to, that I had and would love across time, I mouthed the words – "Let Go."

With my hand opening wide, the weight of gravity pulled me down towards the end of that life's cycle, and with my faith in his strength failing the both of us, he lost his grip on me. As I left him, his hand, which had been my lifeline, instantly grabbed the other. With all of his strength, he yanked his son up close to his heart, and rolling over, pulled him down to lay on the safety of his chest, securing two arms in a tight bear hug around him.

With eyes staring straight up, through the atmosphere and into the universe above, his mouth opened wide to howl out the pain that was tearing through everything inside of him, including the faith in a love he'd believed could surmount anything, which was lost to him for the rest of that life. The sun met his anguish with its brightness, and the universal understanding of this epic scene, the theme of which had been repeated across centuries, was mistaken as indifference by him.

This was my life, and I saw it from the perspective of the one dangling, even though I had no memory of what came before or after that episode. It came to me as a vision. Not before, so there was no forewarning to change the course of that disaster, but hundreds of years later, after this man and I were pulled apart in the new life we'd met in. One that came after countless others held their own disastrous endings for us and for the unconditional love our souls were trying to seed into this world.

Only, in this latest life, our separation, which hadn't come from the killing of either of us, had triggered me correctly, and I'd taken the path that was our purpose. The vision came at a time when I was becoming despondent and needed a reminder of the terror causing this man, whom I knew loved me, to take so long to find his way back to us.

This is where our story of separation continues, and where I intend for it to end.

REBORN

REBORN

CHAPTER 1
THE FALL – THIS TIME

Rushing down a path lined with benches, I ran out into an open square of pavement and tried to weave through the people flowing in front of and around me. The brightness of the city's lights, combined with the noise of music blasting and skateboarders crashing, hammered me. With my hand held up to my temple, I shielded my eyes in an attempt to both hide the tears I felt coming and protect my senses, which were raw with grief and couldn't comprehend how this much happiness could still exist while my world was crumbling. The noise crashing down kept me from hearing the call of my name that was coming from the mouth I'd just kissed, what I'd thought was a final goodbye, a few moments earlier.

His hand shocked my mind when he grabbed the side of my hip that was just within his arm's reach. Jolted, not expecting to turn and see him, my heart jumped with joy. Hope that he'd changed his mind flared up and gave a moment of relief from the grief I was trying to run from. Reality returned in an instant, and I hid my face in his chest as he wrapped both of his arms around my body, which shook with sobs as he gripped it tightly. Tears gushing down from my eyes, I looked up into his, and with his tall frame hunched so he could get closer, saw up close the regret that clouded them. His words, which I would hear on repeat from that moment forward, filled my head – "The only reason this is happening is because of that little boy."

Nodding, I knew. We stood there for what seemed like an eternity, completely engulfed in one another and surrounded by people who had no idea of the magnitude of emotions we were experiencing. After I stopped shaking, and the tears stopped streaming, he laid his next line on me – "I need you to walk away first. I can't do it."

My voice declared what I knew to be our truth then. This wasn't the end, and we would be together again in the future. Nodding, he knew. I walked away, and a sense of calm overtook me. Somewhere deep inside a sixth sense, one that I'd never known existed, unveiled that this is what had to happen. Our separation had to start so it would reach its end and we could be reunited.

I wish that confidence had lasted, but it would prove to be fleeting and my faith in our truth, which had come from a higher plane, soon faltered. With the loss of that faith, I would lose myself, entering a period I could only explain as a crisis of existence, and that only received the credit it was due with the universal label I came to learn once I started healing – The Dark Night of the Soul. That darkness didn't happen instantly. First, we were both given a lifeline of short-lived false hope.

It came as a shock in a message I wasn't expecting. A few days in and it was already over between them. The wife who'd left him months before we'd met, only to ask to return when she'd sensed the happiness my presence was bringing, hadn't been able to let go of what she'd felt. A day after her return, which had been orchestrated for the sake of the small son they shared, she cracked into the phone that still held our romance in its message history.

Despite her knowing he'd been seeing other women, and his request that everything done while separated be forgotten, to give their family a chance at success, she went searching for what would end their marriage. Reading every word exchanged, which laid out the love that had surfaced between us, was too much for her to take in, so she turned her pain around and struck him with it.

Calling while he was working, she called him out for cheating, and with all of our details lined up in front of her, she was able to pretend someone had been following him everywhere. I felt the invasion of our privacy with his re-telling of this scene, but unaware of how much shame was hidden within him, had no idea how much this attack had crippled him. I felt the change in him though, and a fright of his newfound chill sent me reeling. Trying to hide it, I took in what he shared. The momentousness of the dissolution of their marriage had set in, and he was reeling. He needed to give it the time it deserved to culminate and would keep his distance from me until then.

I heard him, and I understood him, but I didn't listen to him. What followed was six weeks of what felt like the worst torture, since I'd yet to experience our real separation, and the person I'd been while with him started to disappear. It occurred with a steadiness I didn't have the power to stop. The words I couldn't resist sending came from a heart full of understanding for his situation, but this man, struggling under the obligation he'd been pulled back into and his newfound terror of being seen doing something deemed wrong, felt the pressure of every ounce of my need. We both watched my confidence, which had seemed strong when we'd met, wilt with every message I sent that grew in its grasping nature.

Unable to step back and reinstate the certainty of his return, which I'd felt at the moment of his exit, I kept trying to find reassurance by pulling his presence back into my life. He was replying, but every message took longer to receive than the previous. This change in a man, who in the recent past wouldn't have blinked before responding and had always sent three messages to my one, was too quick a reversal for me to follow. None of his words spoke of the battle he was going through, but I felt everything. The rollercoaster of his emotions was mirrored inside of me blow-by-blow, and it was devastating.

The highs brought a certainty that he would soon be free enough to be mine, and I'd see that confirmed in one of his sporadic calls placed in secret or in a message showing a list of new apartments he was viewing. The lows dropped me to the depths of despair and made me question how I could ever matter next to the woman he'd spent 14 years of his life with and who had born him his son.

The days dragged by slower than I could have ever imagined possible and even though the horoscope I read monthly warned to change the actions that were leading to disaster, I kept moving forward on the same track. I was helped along by the moments of hope he gave, which distracted me from the fate that was looming. His request that upon his return he pay for the image of an owl I'd been inspired, months before we'd met, to get inked on my body as a symbol of patience and wisdom, was heartfelt and provided comfort. His words of gratitude for the patience and understanding I was showing him were deeply appreciated by me, but the revulsion I felt over my inability to stand back and stop messaging was infecting the line between us. My plea that he not forget the real me while this email impersonator existed was met by his promise that it didn't bother him. But neither knew he was lying to both of us.

Flashes of strain showed through and hinted that the weeks it was taking to find his new home were filled with more strife than I was aware of, but I didn't understand the degree to which it was impacting him. He shared bits that revealed I was an issue that hadn't been let go of, but I didn't probe for more details than he was able to volunteer. When he told me she accused him that someone out there already loved him, I felt for her and silently questioned his statement. Knowing all the messages exchanged by heart, I knew our mutual love shone through in them and couldn't help but wonder if she'd thrown it in his face that he'd already found someone to love. It didn't matter since I knew the truth was we both loved each other.

I did what I could for him and spent my time wishing I could do more. Every word I sent or said fulfilled the promise I'd made earlier, while he'd been deciding on the future of his life, and I tried to soften his strain by speaking to him with nothing but kindness. His gratitude for it showed he wasn't receiving any elsewhere. Then he relayed the news that was going to cause further interference. His wife was setting him up in his new life by paying the fees for his apartment. I understood why he needed this help she was offering. His work as an actor had been spotty, and while he'd come close, it still hadn't brought him sustained success, so his wife's career had paid for their life. Trying to change that for the sake of their family, he'd gotten a job as a producer, but it had been too little too late for them.

Without asking for details, since I didn't want to invade the privacy I didn't have rights to, I took it in without too many questions and didn't mention the truth I felt. The strings tied to this act, which I was sure had more to it, were that I wouldn't be allowed to enter his new life. Keeping silent, I decided it wasn't my place to speak on the subject since I wasn't the one who had a son that needed a second home to grow up in. I left it without voicing my belief that this would turn his new home into a replica of the couch he'd slept on for the three years between when his son had joined them, and she'd left him. It would just be a larger version pretending to be something different. Hoping I was wrong, but knowing I wasn't, I understood this was something that would have to be lived through.

I pushed my thoughts, that were full of terror, away as much as possible, and he made it easier with his efforts to keep us close, as much as he was able to with the blocks that created a new boundary between us. The flurry of messages he sent, frantic to reach me the afternoon I was feeling my first bouts of anger at the situation, came as a surprise since I'd given him no indication of what I was feeling. Reassured, I was reminded of the man whom I knew cherished my feelings. The call that came on another afternoon, one when I was out walking, sat me down on a nearby bench with the label 'for couples' marked on it, and warmed my mind with his words – "This will all be a blip someday soon." We were both misguided in thinking that 'soon' would be after the last two weeks of his life in their married home were over.

The signs screamed at me to realize what was happening, but I resisted. I kept hearing how he still hadn't packed the boxes that were sitting in the hall, waiting for his possessions. Unaware of the implication that action held for him, I took in that he was having a hard time leaving his home, but my desire for him to be free of its binds outweighed my understanding of the strain he was under. It seeped through though.

First, in the two songs he sent over one random afternoon. Both tore through my heart as I learned, through their lyrics, that he was straining to put one foot in front of the other. Feeling trapped in the corner of a burning building, he needed to be rescued. Then, the second came on the night a surprise call came through after he'd wandered aimlessly for hours while pondering his new life, the thought of which he admitted didn't come with any sense of joy. His battery dying, he was forced to hang up but promised to call back once he powered up. Instead of a call, a little while later, I received a short good night text, and my heart plummeted under the weight of what I could feel was coming. Sensing my fear in the short reply I'd sent back, he called quickly to relay with adamant force – "I'm not rejecting you!"

Wanting to cheer his spirits and support his efforts, I found a small card with a single hand raised in a high five, and I mailed it to his work with the message that he deserved credit for making it through something so difficult. Not wanting him to grieve in deafening silence on the days ahead when he'd be in his new home alone, without his son, I then sent him a small speaker. It was identical to the one that had once played music we both loved to listen into the lyrics of while we wrapped our arms around each other in every nook of my apartment. Shocked by what he called a gracious gift, he wrote in response that he loved both it and my magnanimous spirit, but the hollowness I felt behind his lengthy message stuck with me longer than the words I'd read.

Not stopping where I should have, I went on to purchase and send tickets to a live show being held two weeks after the move to his new life. He voiced his joy and questioned how I could have known he'd recently been thinking about bringing live music back into his life. I repeatedly re-read every word he sent and ignored the voice inside that knew what he really needed was time and space to grieve the loss of his marriage. I couldn't manage to give him that, not when my need to help him through this transition was beating my senses.

As the day of his departure neared, the terror I felt grew. My memory of us as a couple had become fuzzy, and I couldn't envision how this new life together, with him in a home this other woman had rights to, was going to play itself out. Worried that I would have to be kept hidden, anxiety-filled every moment and pushed out all remnants of my confidence entirely.

That's when a message came through that wouldn't be understood by me for months to come. While wandering the streets during one of my lunch hours, I crossed to stay on the side soaked in the sun, and a woman handing out flyers took pity on me. She saw the energy clouded around my body clearly and proclaimed – "This pain isn't yours. Your life will be filled with happiness and laughter again, someday." Handing over a note with her rates for a psychic session, she invited me in with the words – "Let me help you." Tempted, I was reminded of a similar stranger that had spoken the truth she saw on the side of another street on a different day.

It happened while we'd been out walking together one morning before our separation. My man and I had crossed this other woman's path as she was sat in front of a shop that held a sign professing her to be psychic. She'd taken one look at us, with my two arms wrapped around his right one, our eyes gazing at each other and lips stretched wide with laughter, and she'd declared loudly for everyone to hear – "That's real love." Her words hadn't surprised or embarrassed me, despite it having been only a few weeks into our relationship. Confident and glowing, we'd continued on with our day, which we'd both thought was one of many to come that we'd be spending together.

Cracking under the loss of that and all the other moments of pure happiness we'd shared, I needed help, but since the rate listed on her card was low, I doubted the validity of her services, so I set her words aside. Then the end, unaided, came. Choosing to move out of reach, the days before and of his move, I tried to protect myself from rejection by putting up a barrier of geographic distance.

Wishing I could be the one to aid him in shouldering the weight of those boxes, I was jealous of the friend that was going to be there for him and knew that no matter what, I wasn't going to be asked to help. Wanting to be invited over immediately, I knew the only safety I had, from sitting and watching a phone that wasn't ringing, was to not be there to hear the silence. So I booked a trip to visit a friend that had moved to the other side of the country, to live in her home state of Texas.

While there, I did the only thing I could do for him, which was something I'd never done before, but that came naturally. I focused my energy on him and sent the strength of my support early in the morning two days before his impending move. He was spending it packing, and with his son off for the weekend, so he wouldn't have to watch what his father was doing, I imagined he was feeling alone and devastated. Elation filled me later that day when he messaged that the sound of music, played out loud on his new speaker, was aiding him beyond measure. Telling him what I'd sent earlier, he confirmed it was indispensable. I left him to it and went on with my weekend, feeling a brief respite from the heaviness of his problems; the weight of which had grown daily.

While away, in this state filled with vast open areas of nature, my friend and I left the city she resided in to spend some time visiting her father, who lived in a remote location that could only be gotten to by taking a road the neighbors had built together. We spent two days enjoying the emptiness that surrounded the ranch he and his wife lived on. With nothing but open space for miles in every direction, I felt myself lighten up, and while there was no way I could forget the situation, I felt clear of the torture my man was going through.

With a clearer head, some confidence came back, aided along by a few neighbors who gathered together one evening. As everyone packed in on a porch to share the moonshine brewed by the ones whose country shack we were visiting, they began reciting some of their history. It was kicked off with a folk song sung by an old man whose big belly was covered by bibbed overalls. Stomping his foot on the wooden floor he'd built, he belted out a tune that filled my heart with happiness.

Then, the large woman by his side, who had a formidable appearance, spoke of how he'd sung that to her early on while he was making her his second wife. Which led the wife of my friend's father, who was also a second, to add that the 10 years he'd spent with the first wasn't comparable to the decades they'd since spent together. Their stories felt like a personal message delivered straight to me, one intended to soften my doubt that I still did, or ever could, matter to my man.

With so much genuine companionship surrounding me, I felt grateful for the moment I was experiencing that was such a departure from what had become my existence. I then left the porch that was barely lit, so my friend and I could walk a few feet into the woods that surrounded it and get a closer look at the deer browsing nearby. While standing there, I looked away from them and was struck by the site above. Littered with more stars than I'd ever seen, the black sky was completely lit up.

Staring in awe, a profound energy entered me, and I felt driven to take my friend's hand as pure happiness radiated throughout my being. I could sense something bigger connecting all of us and knew there was more out there that I'd never tapped into. It shot straight to my core, and I felt in an instant that everything was going to be alright. Ethereal in nature, the memory of that moment would stay with me forever, even once the feeling faded.

Returning to the city that was full of pain, the night that followed the day of my man's move, brought me back into his tortured mind. In the darkest hour, a shock of fear riddled my body awake with the gravitas of what had happened that day, and I sensed I was losing him to it. Picking up the phone lying by my side, I sent a message fueled by the fear I felt for what lay in the future.

Trying to keep my senses about me, I sent a hope that he and his son were doing alright. The words were casual, but the fear behind them was palpable. His annoyance, which I felt behind the words he sent back the next day, came as a shock since that emotion was one that had never been exchanged between us before. The pressure of my desire to move forward together, countered by the weight of his obligations, and infused with the fear he felt for himself and his son's future, had become too big a burden for him to continue to balance.

Having felt the truth for weeks, I would hear it falter out of his mouth two days later, when we saw each other again for what felt like a first date with someone who wasn't a stranger. Shock filled me as he walked up; I barely recognized the withered man who stood there. Without understanding the feeling clearly, I instantly knew his soul was no longer rooted within his body.

His gaunt frame made him look like a victim that a disease had infected. My compassion rose as our arms reached out for the briefest of hugs and our lips the lightest brush. Sitting down opposite one another, I didn't realize what was happening, at first, as he began to try to end us. But my ability to read him kicked in quickly, so I squelched the hope that it was finally time for us to start back up.

The feelings he couldn't explain led him to ask if I felt obligated to make something of us, since I'd waited for what (at that point) seemed like forever. Taking in his words, without seeing the mirror he was holding up to himself, I let him know there wasn't the tiniest bit of me that felt that way about him. Then I heard him question himself as he reasoned that everything about me was a step up from where he'd been. Hating the comparison, even though it was in my favor, I came to understand what was happening and voiced the thoughts he couldn't articulate clearly now that we were sat face-to-face.

I understood deeply, as I explained quickly, that he couldn't think about being connected to me when he'd just stopped being connected to his wife, and I knew he needed to stand on his own before we could stand together. Confirming that what I'd said was exactly how he felt, he added his wish to become as strong as he thought I was. My intent had been to take the pressure of moving forward too soon off of him, and I went on to ask that he not make any decisions, not right after the biggest move of his life.

With my calm compassion beating away the grasp of fear, I saw him start to recognize me again, and he wavered. His hand raising to touch his heart, he explained the feelings he held for me were still there, but the overwhelming nature of what his life had become was exhausting. He had no idea how to be happy while so much pain shrouded his senses, and now that his time with his son had been halved. The stress of his situation was underlined by his cell, which wouldn't stop interrupting us with short bursts of shrill ringing. Picking it up to put it back down just as quickly, each call, which was only identified by a row of zeros, was cut off before he could answer.

The repetition kept breaking his concentration until the call finally came through, and he spoke to an administrator at the school his son was starting his first day of Pre-K at the next morning. That taken care of, we exchanged a few more words before a message pinged in from his son's mother. The triviality of her words about dishes being done by a new helper, right when he was trying to give me his focus, triggered him, and he sarcastically questioned if he was being followed. Not wanting to continue to pull him in two directions, I suggested he give her a call from the curb, so he could have a private conversation.

By the time he returned, I'd paid the bill for the drink each we'd had in the hour we'd been sitting there, and we stood to leave. Walking a few short blocks in the same direction, our steps, which had once easily fallen in line, kept being separated every few feet as he walked to the right of every tree we crossed. Not wanting the people walking towards us on the narrow sidewalk to be separated, he was moving away from me so they wouldn't have to be inconvenienced by us. When it came time to fully part, I hugged him goodbye and felt the pounding of his heart against my chest, as mine pounded its feelings back. Pointing out the strength of both, he said he didn't feel it, and I feared he was no longer in touch with his heart or mine. Reaching up to kiss him, he quickly jerked his head back. Without reacting, I let him know that a hug was enough. I reminded him to take the time he needed to bounce back to himself before we let go of each other and turned to walk in opposite directions down the same road.

Dejected, but refusing to let go of my belief in the strength of what I knew still existed between us, underneath all the pummeling pain, I spent the next day hoping our separation would only last a short while longer. The message that came at the end of that day's work slammed into my mind and tore straight through my faith. He did what he had't been able to in person – he ended it. Admitting he would never find anyone like me, he listed out all of my qualities that couldn't be replaced. But from my kindness to my sensuality, none were able to surmount his current situation.

Overwhelmed by what was at hand, he wanted to focus all of his attention on the little boy whose life had been shattered. Beyond that, he had something important that had to be done, and he stated it with firm clarity – "I have to learn how to be alone." My heart sinking, it surged slightly as he thanked me for showing him what real, satisfying happiness was and that no one should ever settle for anything less in life. Knowing neither of us could replace what we'd shared with anyone else, I took that to mean he wouldn't be able to ever settle for another woman, so there was still a chance for us. His closing line explained he couldn't give me what I deserved at that point in his fractured life and that gave even more hope, which I needed, that he would come back once it was repaired.

Setting my despair aside and drawing on the compassion I felt, my words back met his with the love I held for him. Without any grasping, I let him know how much I understood the pain he was under and guaranteed him that happiness would return in time. From weeks to months, I knew it would get easier and understanding he needed to live free during that time, of everything including the obligation that came with me waiting, I promised I would't do that. But I went on to add that I wouldn't give up the hope I held in my heart for us.

I ended by referencing, without a direct mention, the time right before his wife had come back, when he'd asked if he could call me, possibly years in the future, once what they were doing for their child came to its end. Repeating the same thing I'd told him then, I let him know that the door would always be open if he wanted to reach out when this difficult period ended. I only asked for one promise – that he not let fear stop him. With no reply, I didn't know if he'd made it, but I knew that if he had, then it was done silently, to not keep me dangling in limbo any longer than I already had been.

REBORN

REBORN

YEAR ONE

REBORN

CHAPTER 2
STUMBLING FORWARD
MONTHS 1-2 OF YEAR 1

The shock of our ending was followed by what felt like a solid steel wall slamming down in-between us. A sense of it overcame me the moment I woke, the morning after the night I spent trying to comprehend what had happened by re-reading the finality in his words repeatedly. With the link between us completely blocked, I was left with a chasm of emptiness inside. Struggling to get up, a dark cloud surrounded me and followed my every move. It clung close during my morning routine, which was done with dread for that day and all the others that lay ahead. It held on throughout the walk south, from where I lived on the East Side of New York City to my office in Soho.

My pain, too fresh to be suppressed, smacked me in the face with every corner I turned. There was no avoiding it. A sign attached to every bus shelter, calling out for others to come be entertained by the story a movie had chronicled, was screaming its message at me – THIS IS WHERE I LEAVE

YOU. Everywhere I turned, this reminder spiked my despair, and I couldn't stand it. Head down to avoid seeing what I couldn't forget for a second and shoulders stooped by the weight pressing me down, I stumbled forward.

Everything, every day, became dulled by the daze of this suffering. All desire left me. Food, which I'd always relished, was something I could no longer bear to touch. I tried to pretend I could manage, but nothing anyone said, who was either under or above me at work, registered. I took in and put out the bare minimum, which was all I could do to continue to survive. The fear of being alone with my sorrow was overwhelming and forced me to get up and go to work every day just so I could be in the company of my colleagues. But the pain followed me everywhere. I continued to walk with it past that sign which spent the next month jumping out in front of me no matter what route I took.

The friends I'd made at the work that was new were kind to me and listened to my sorrow no matter how many times I repeated the same words to them. Leaning on them was the only thing getting me through the days that led to the dark nights I'd no choice but to endure alone. Lying in a ball on my couch, from the moment I got home until the moment I went to bed, I curled up with the pain that clouded my eyes with a steady stream of tears. With no idea how to make it end, I tried to distract myself from it by calling on good friends – from those long ago to those more recent – but with no ability to talk about anything else, I didn't call too much, not wanting to burden anyone. They took every call made and said what they thought might help, but sleep handed over the only relief available, for the few hours a night I managed to get any.

Knowing this had to end, I hung on to hope, and that word became my mantra. When my eyes sprung open in the deadest hour of every night, and my heart was slammed with a fresh dose of remembering, I drew on that word to see me through to the morning. Looking for a visual to sustain me, I tapped the little screen I slept with and found what I needed. Hundreds of illustrations depicting – **H**old **O**n **P**ain **E**nds. Swiping continuously, I kept my eyes trained on that message until drowsiness returned and sent me back for another hour of freedom from the pain pulsing up from the remote depths within. This became my routine, night after night.

The loss of this man, whose love was the purest I'd felt in all 37 of the years I'd lived before he'd entered it, had sent me over the edge and it was like I'd lost myself right along with him. The hours we'd spent together were the happiest of this entire life, and my heart knew it would be impossible to replace them. I'd never felt that way before him, so this led my mind to believe all happiness was a thing of the past.

The humor he'd constantly sprung on me brought lightness into every moment we'd shared, and lightened me up more than I'd ever thought was possible. It felt like the joy, which came with the smiles that had never ceased while together, would forever be a distant memory, never to be recaptured in this life. The way his eyes had seen through to every side of my personality and had shown how he truly appreciated the beauty he was seeing, had enabled me to effortlessly shine out the brightness I hadn't known I was hiding. As that brightness retracted, it was replaced by a terror that said I would never see those sides of myself again. There seemed no way out of this darkness that was eating me alive and cutting my life off from everything that had radiated with goodness.

Happiness wasn't the only thing the two of us had shared. We'd both held an innate understanding of what the other needed and a desire to give it without any concern for what we were receiving in return. As well as a deep knowing that what we shared was real, something that would last far into the future. Seeing this man give us up, and seemingly forget the connection entirely, shook me to the core. My heart wilting, while my body melted, I struggled to find an answer to how this could have happened, and my mind raced back over the memories that didn't add up to the reality I was living.

Not when he'd both felt and fought for it before I'd been able to open myself up to it. He'd first sent his feelings over in a tirade of morning messages on a Saturday after our first three dates held back-to-back in one week. Just out of a short fling that had singed me, I'd asked the night before for a break from what we were doing, which had felt too sudden. I wasn't sure I was ready for how quickly we were moving, even though I'd answered his question of what I wanted, on our second date, with my truth – love. But I wanted to close the other door more firmly before fully opening this one, which was obviously leading to that with him. His fear of losing what we were starting sent him into a panic, and he let me know exactly how he was feeling. What we shared was different, and he knew we would miss out on something major if we lost it.

Pulled from what I needed, I took it in, and despite telling him to see if he still felt the same in five weeks time, I pushed away what I thought I needed. Instead of keeping my distance, I suggested we spend the next day together. Our journey to a local beach, which took a ferry to get to, was filled with signs I wouldn't understand until the days grew colder.

While sat on the deck, he'd pointed to the young couple a few seats over, who shared our same coloring, and proclaimed – "That's us at 18." Then, while walking across a wide field of green after docking, we both noticed how, despite a gap, the younger version of us mirrored every step we took. Only, ours brought us closer to the small white chapel, which looked like it'd come right out of the vision I'd once had of the perfect place to get married. Struck by the resemblance, I was then left speechless when he started and then quickly stopped himself from asking a question. One that seemed plucked from the memory I'd just had and was going to suggest this was where we would get married.

Walking away from that, we set ourselves up to lie down next to one another. With no idea of what he could handle, he did what I wanted and spent the day scorching his white skin red as we lay a few feet from the ocean. With his arm propping him higher, his blue eyes gazed down at me and showed everyone around us that he was completely enamored. With happiness leaping inside, between, and off of us, under the bright stare of the sun, that's the day my heart opened to his, and everything between us skyrocketed.

Our parting after that exchange, on a corner that held an

exit to the subway we'd taken, was cut short by the surprise greeting of a friend that lived a few blocks away from me. Giving him a quick peck, I turned to walk away with her, and he lamented in a message sent later that night that it'd been too abrupt an ending. Foreshadowing hidden in the moment, I'd seen nothing but brightness ahead.

Our joy hadn't changed his situation, which I'd known all along was complicated, and I saw him struggle with it in brief flashes, but there was never anything but blissful ease between us. Even after he told me his wife had requested to return for the sake of their child. Torn, knowing that what was between them as a couple was over, he spent weeks debating what to do and spoke of it candidly. Wanting the happiness we shared to continue, his desire for our future battled the biology that was driving him to give his son a whole family to grow up in.

On one night in particular, his torment led him to ask me flat out – "What should I do?" A deep knowing rose from somewhere inside and relayed that our relationship couldn't be the reason behind his decision. Following my instincts, despite my desire to help him, I let him know he had to decide this alone. Whatever he chose needed to rest on what he wanted for his life, with or without me in it. I tentatively went a tiny bit further than I thought I should and pointed out that it was hard enough for a boy to grow into a man who knew how to be in a loving relationship, even harder if he didn't have love surrounding him to act as his teacher. His son needed to be in a home filled with love, even if it wasn't between the two that were his parents. My man, crushed under his duties as a father, had listened intently and respected every word I'd said, but the weight of his son's pain had eventually outweighed everything else entirely.

With all that love and understanding having once flowed so easily between us, the crash that had dropped me from the highest peak of my life's happiness was wreaking chaos on my spirit. Despite repeating the rationale that this had to be done for both himself and his son, my belief in his feelings for me, which I'd recently felt deeply and trusted in beyond a shadow of a doubt, was under an intense attack. Turning my heart and mind against one another, my faith in everything, including myself, was shattered.

If I couldn't count on what I'd believed in so deeply, then how could I count on anything, or anyone, ever again? My heart had told me this man would never hurt me and yet his actions had, so how could I ever trust anyone else not to? How could I trust my own instincts? It was September, and while the sun was still fooling everyone into thinking it was summer, I felt frozen and could see nothing but endless dark days stretching out ahead.

With the daily numbing of grief getting the better of me, a voice in my head, one I didn't recognize, suggested there was a way to stop feeling. The desire to go out and sleep with 10 men in one week overcame me. Shocked by the urge to do something I never had or would do, I shoved it aside and tried to find a better answer. Which led me to send the man who still felt like mine an urgent cry, despite the previous words sent that were perfect in their compassionate nature. Telling him I'd given up too easily, I tried to mirror the time when he'd convinced me to not take the time I'd thought I needed away from him. My plea, unlike his, was met by failure.

Two days without a reply and the heart that had already been broken was crushed. Laying those words and that guilt on him, he immediately responded and explained he wasn't trying to ignore me. The transition of his life was as overwhelming as he'd expected, and he was trying to do what was right by his family. Waiting until I honestly felt it, I tried to take back the guilt I'd ladled by letting him know it was the situation, not him, that had crushed me, and I hoped whatever he was doing was working.

Feeling powerless, I turned to the only thing that gave me any semblance of control. I distracted myself from the pain pumping through my heart by swiping my fingers left on the photos of as many men as I could per second, while my eyes gave them the briefest glance and my mind threw out one negative comment after another. The addiction to this app was the only thing that gave me any respite, through its numbing repetition, during my waking hours. I used it everywhere, even in meetings, to try to keep myself from feeling the pain tormenting my senses. A few swipes managed to go right instead of left, and that's how I found another way to distract myself.

With a look I recognized since he resembled many of the men I'd dated before I'd met the one who glowed brighter than all the rest, a new man's weathered face grabbed my attention. Attracted to his rugged look, I'd always liked men who carried a shadow of a beard that was sprinkled with grey on cheeks that were gauntly chiseled. Even though friends had commented that the overall look was skeletal in nature. Having no idea of the pain that shadowed him, which equally matched my energy, I agreed to meet up. With all of my thoughts numbed by what I couldn't escape, he seemed nice enough to hang out with but every second with him was spent with the shadow of my man looming just over his shoulder. I thought it was evident in the way I couldn't bring myself to meet his eyes, no matter how often he squirmed his head around to try to capture them, but he was oblivious.

Despite the lack of a deeper connection, we had interesting enough conversation, so I kept agreeing to meet back up. But after each meeting, spent with him while thinking of the one I'd rather be seeing, the pain slammed back through me. Seeing him couldn't stop that from happening or stop me from searching for answers. With all the well-meaning advice from friends not cutting it, I turned to the woman who wrote the horoscope that had once tried to warn me. Paying for an answer to one question, I asked if she could see if my love would return in time. Unable to see why he was staying away, she told me the one thing she could see clearly – "Trust in your love. No one can come between it."

Her words helped briefly, but I'd already lost my grip on the trust she decreed was imperative. Instead of spending time searching for that, I agreed to take a day trip with the weathered man, so we could hike the area around a town aptly named Cold Springs. Waiting for him on a corner the morning of, I picked up a call from a friend that had once seen and agreed that what I'd shared with the other man was exceptional, and I told her what I was doing.

Every fiber of my being fighting it, I spoke about my internal struggle. Despite my heart knowing that greater happiness could exist, my mind was trying to convince me that this way was better. Being with a man that made you content, in measured doses, seemed a good safeguard against being crippled by pain if you were with, and then lost, someone you loved dearly. As I explained this to her, my senses kicked in, and I put in a request – "Just stop me before I walk down the aisle with him."

Getting in his truck when he pulled up, which I gave him looked cool in its old-school appearance, my eyes were immediately drawn to the cassette player built into its front panel. As we pulled out, he asked if I'd brought my mixed tape with me, and his words hit like an arrow to the heart. Hearing the voice of the one I wanted, I heard again what he'd told me on the first date we'd gone on – "You deserve to have a hundred mixed tapes made for you." I turned to look out the window and mumbled an unintelligible response to this man I wanted nothing from. But the next hour was spent making good conversation, so the ride was more than bearable, and I was able to slightly set aside the agony that afflicted me.

After arriving and while enjoying our walk along the main street of the quaint old town his truck had taken us to, I was struck again. As we passed a building containing stalls selling other people's junk, he felt guided to point out the board games on display in front of it. Asking if I wanted one, I couldn't believe my ears or my eyes. No matter where I went, I couldn't enjoy a moment without a memory.

Pulled back into the recent past, I thought of my real man's extensive board game collection. One that had taken him to a conference, full of other enthusiasts, on one of the weekends we'd been in separated limbo. The one that had led me to suggest he convert an alcove in the new apartment he'd landed into his game room. Reminded of the man I loved, I went back to comparing him to the one in front of me who could never stand as tall by my side.

The rest of the day was uneventful. Other than when on

our hike to find a waterfall, which led us in the wrong direction and eventually stopped us at a stream that trickled by, he kissed me for the first time. I let him. Aware every minute that, even though he was good at it, no part of me felt anything other than a shallow physical attraction to him. Letting it go on for as long as he wanted, but not caring if it continued, it eventually ended, as did our hike.

Our conversation hit a lull as we sat to eat in the chilling sun, so I questioned him about the letters inked on the arm that was waving them in front of me with every mouthful. Not wanting to go there, he said he'd save that story for another time. I let it go since I hadn't really cared in the first place.

Returning to the city, I watched as he pulled me closer to ride all the way back sitting snuggled up against him and thought how we looked like a couple that had decided to be together. Not sure when that decision had been made, I felt powerless to stop it. Then, just like every other time he'd left me alone at the door to my building, the pain rose back up, so as soon as I crossed through I tried to take back control by returning to my furious swiping.

The attempts to keep myself from focusing on what was going on inside didn't stop with him or with those swipes. Pulling myself out of the fetal position, I filled my time with as many activities as I could manage to get through. Walking through each in the haze of pain that had become my existence, I met up with one friend after another, hoping my time with them would make it evaporate. They all showed up, but none could take away the pain.

I struggled to walk through an over-crowded museum one afternoon with the friend that had always been able to see me better than any other and had always given sage advice. All she could see or say that day was that the weight I'd lost wasn't healthy. She couldn't see why I was suffering to the point of extinction. I tried to stay in the sun across another day, one filled with boutique shopping with the friend whose strong opinions had always guided our friendship, but neither the sun nor the shopping was soothing, and my anger came up to strike out at the wife that had torn my love apart.

Not understanding where it was coming from since up to then I'd felt nothing but compassion for this woman's situation, I raged. My indignation at her for having come back to a man she'd no longer wanted, one that she couldn't leave to have his own happiness, singed every ounce of compassion I had. There was no denying the truth he'd shared, that she'd admitted – her fear of him being happy while she wasn't, even years after they separated, was something that scared her. Screaming this out in the most subdued voice possible, I struggled against the person I didn't want to become. The rant only lasted a few minutes and then my pity for everyone that had been hurt by what happened, including her, returned, and I went back into the haze of pain that was my new reality.

Only, someone above was looking out for me, and they started working on waking me out of this stupor by forcing out all the distractions that were keeping me from facing what needed to be done. It began when the man I was seeing came over on a night I was considering letting him in further. I still couldn't bring my eyes to look into his, but part of me had started to enjoy the ease of his presence. I liked the way he kissed and that there was no one threatening to take a picture of it, so maybe, in time, I could grow to feel something deeper while his lips were pressed against mine. Those were the thoughts running through my mind as we lay on the couch together. Then he interrupted them to say that since we'd reached this point, it was time to share his story.

Hearing difficult information that would change everything was something I'd grown used to, so with resolve set, I listened to what he was ready to lay down. Despite the enormity of it, he relayed it all in a matter-of-fact tone. The initials on his arm belonged to an ex who had taken her own life. There was more. Her death had followed that of their child, who had been growing inside of her. It didn't end there. He'd been her last call. That one he'd missed, but he'd gotten the call the next morning questioning her absence from work, which had led him to find her hanging.

Despite knowing that everything he'd said was horrible, I took it all in and felt nothing. He went on to add – "I'm dead inside." Wanting to feel again, he'd been working across the 18 months since she'd changed the course of his life with someone who was trained to help. He'd recently decided it was time to take matters into his own hands and was dating multiple women, trying to find one who sparked anything in him.

Mouthing a few words of compassion, I went on to add that I'd just come out of something that, while in no way close to his tragedy, was emotionally difficult. For the first time in my life, I wasn't capable of feeling anything for anyone, so it seemed fine by me if we continued dating. I didn't tell him the full extent of what I was thinking. I liked that since neither of us was able to feel anything, I wouldn't have to feel any guilt over using him as a distraction. He agreed with what I did say, but I knew he hadn't understood me and would continue to test his ability to feel out on me whenever we were together. That didn't matter since I was sure nothing more than the superficial feeling of skin touching was going to be possible for either of us.

I knew because I could feel how different laying next to him felt compared to the man who was the best I'd ever been with. This weathered man had the skill I enjoyed, but my man and I had that as well as something indescribable. We'd connected and brought each other total bliss on a soul-level. We'd both felt it when we'd been together, and the depth and intensity that came with it had been the best kind of shattering. With no way to explain it, even to myself, I knew I'd gone higher than was humanly possible every second we'd been together. This wasn't that, but knowing it wasn't possible to re-create it with anyone other than the one I couldn't have, I settled for it.

Then, his pain tried to settle itself on me. The next day at work, after telling his story to the boy who always shared his dating stories, I felt a new heaviness come down on me. Knowing there was something wrong with this story, the boy in front of me stared in shock. His blunt words asked a serious question – "What's wrong with you? No, seriously? Why do you keep attracting men going through so much trauma?" Feeling the poignancy in his words and the weight of the death that surrounded me, I momentarily sunk under what felt like too much to handle. All of a sudden life was even more unbearable than it already had been, and it seemed like the physical weight of both of these men was resting on my shoulders.

My mind debated ending it with this weathered man, but my fear of being left without any distractions got the better of me, so I didn't remove myself from his painful story, the one that was keeping me from facing my own. I was wobbling but continued down this path that was set to bring my life back to where it'd been before love came along. Then, with a hard push, I was forced to hit rock bottom when another win was taken away. It had entered my life the same week my man had, and like him had been full of possibilities. A new job with people I both liked and respected. But the desire to create something better, which was a bond between all of us, had blinded me to the truth.

I'd joined them after leaving an agency that had followed in the tracks of the previous two, which had all nearly destroyed my love for this advertising career I'd poured my heart into. The hope that it was possible to do good work that I believed in, without being worked to death, had been nearly extinguished. Reigniting the dream I'd once had for this work, the joy I felt in the laughter all of us shared, while trying to drum up new business, lifted my days higher than I'd experienced in ages. Adding to the laughter instigated by my man at night and on the weekends, when he'd been there, the two together had brought the feeling that I finally had everything I'd ever wanted. Unfortunately, none of us had a firm foundation to stand on.

Those who'd hired me hadn't done it on purpose. They hadn't known what was coming. Promising that they were stable, they'd only been able to give me security for a short time before their parent company pulled the rug out from under them. With business faltering, and unable to grow as expected, the decision was made to merge with another company and let everyone who loved working together go. Losing this job, which was helping to distract me, was yet another blow I could have seen coming if I'd been more discerning.

My life had been littered with other bouts of unemployment, each chosen by me at times when I couldn't take any more of the heavy lifting I'd been doing, but I'd sworn I would never again experience the fear that came from a lack of financial support. The terror of not having an income, coupled with the loss of the people who were keeping me from the solitude that scared me, was devastating.

Leaving work at the end of the day the news hit, I was forced to face another fear. Headed to meet a friend whose strong opinions I'd always let silence mine, I ran right into him. The golden man whose light was fractured almost missed me but faltering, unsure what to do, I'd held out my hand to wave. He stopped, and we stood there awkwardly, facing each other on the opposite side of the square where we'd once held each other. Scared to look straight at him, I stared at my feet as he finished putting on the sweater he'd been hurriedly pulling out of a bag, which made me think it had just been purchased to be worn wherever he was headed.

Unable to answer the question of how I was doing, I mumbled a response. Then he made a heartbreaking mention of the jacket I was wearing. It was one that someone before me had worn to war, and he asked if I was headed there myself, involuntarily. Backing away from his presence, which I was struggling to recognize as the man I loved, I stumbled, and his arms reached out to guide me away from the hot dog cart I almost tripped over. He then reached both arms around to give me the briefest of hugs, done without our bodies touching, and I quickly turned mine around to run from his.

Home, after the drinks that hadn't made me feel any better, I was struck by what had happened before them. Unable to find refuge from the pain exploding inside of me, I fell lower than I had been and wrapped my arms around bent knees, as I sat curled up in the corner of my apartment closest to the exit. I couldn't stand to be anywhere else since every other spot held a memory that was attacking. Seeing the ghost of us as a couple everywhere, the love and laughter we'd shared bombarded my senses with their absence.

With my body pressed against the door in an attempt to keep from crumbling over completely, even it held a memory. I couldn't escape a scene from the morning we'd realized it had been left unlocked all night. Voicing, with a serious tone that was meant to draw laughter, that we were lucky no one had come in to rape and murder us, he'd laughed at the remark we'd both naively thought was cute in its ridiculousness.

Any chance of making him laugh gone, my eyes filled with tears of anguish as I avoided staring at the couch to the left of my corner, which was riddled with images of more happiness than I could handle. A shadow of a memory showed us sitting on it one night close to his departure. When his arm had pointed up to the open vent located too high on the wall for me to reach and in a quiet voice full of trepidation, he'd questioned where the cover, which he said had been there recently, had disappeared to. His intent was to scare me into thinking a spirit had taken it off to create a portal it could come through. Punching his arm, I'd laughed off my fear, while crying out for him to stop since I was the one that had to sleep there, on my own, after his departure.

The fear of either my death or dead spirits coming for me was the least of my worries in that moment, as I cowered under the pain pummeling my heart. I couldn't bring myself to lay down with it, not in the bed that now only felt the tossing and turning of sleepless nights. The bed that had once been lucky enough to hold us up as we'd held each other across every night once spent in it together. The one that had witnessed, on our last night, my focus being momentarily pulled away from his body. Lyrics had broken through our bubble to warn that I'd never be able to let him go since once true love was found it continued to live on forever. Laughing off the impending pain, I'd paused what we were doing and skipped forward to the next song while telling its singer to stop speaking directly to me.

Alone in the corner I was stuck in, and with no ability to skip the pain I was feeling, I closed my eyes in an attempt to hide from the torment, and all memory of our love was pushed out. Grief turned to rage, and I sent him a message that didn't come from me. Fear had taken over, and my wounds yelled at me that he was supposed to be there so I wouldn't have to go through this ordeal alone. That was the energy that drove the words he didn't respond to. The ones that claimed I was no fool and hoped he was enjoying the date he'd been rushing to. Fear had convinced me that that was the only reason he would have been throwing on a new sweater while walking hurriedly down the street.

Feeling its power, anger whispered in my ear louder. Why stop there? Demand that the speaker, sent when love existed, be returned immediately. Another woman had no right to listen to music being played on it while with him. Especially not when music had left my life entirely. Unable to listen to any since his departure, out of a fear that lyrics of love or heartbreak would trigger more pain within me, the image of him using it with another woman squeezed the life out of my heart.

Staggering under the thoughts that were trying to kill me, I wrenched myself away from self-destruction and voiced the truth I knew, instead of the illusion fear was trying to instill. I reminded myself I'd known his situation from the beginning, and I should have known better than to continue. I wouldn't worsen things, for either of us, by spewing more pain out at him. He had enough that had been piled on already.

I said as much in an apology, sent to remove the negative energy I couldn't bear to leave hanging in the air between us, a week later. His response, which came back quickly, said there was no need since he understood everything. But I didn't, and my wounds flared back that I couldn't grasp why this was happening. Then, just as quickly, I followed up to say – "It's ok. This is my pain to get through. You have your own, and I won't bother you with mine again." I'd hit bottom, and there was nowhere for me to go, so I started my struggle to rise.

REBORN

CHAPTER 3
WHEN HELP CAME
MONTH 3 OF YEAR 1

With nowhere to turn, I knew there was no lower level to drop to, and even though this one had been the lowest yet, there had been plenty of other drops spread across this life, so I started to wonder why I kept dropping. That's when I met her. The woman, with hair bleached and buzzed short, I went to when I needed to get mine trimmed. She took one look at me and saw the sorrow radiating off my body. Then heard my story of loss, triggered by her question of how life was going. Reciting verbatim the words I'd memorized with repetitive reading that had been exchanged in our final messages, she told me people didn't talk to each other like that. The depth of feeling embedded in our words to each other had come through in my telling of them. With a fleeting second of confidence, I agreed with her statement and confirmed that what we'd shared was real.

Offering what she thought might be helpful, she mentioned another woman. One who had helped her in the past by predicting her future while reading how the stars and planets had been lined up at the exact time and place of her birth. With the need for answers burning through all of my thoughts, I took the outside help being handed over. Leaving her that day feeling uplifted, this would be my way with this woman across the year that followed. What she trimmed would fall to the floor as she worked, while my words would fall freely, updating her on the progress I was making on the path I would come to understand had been planned out before my birth.

While I waited for the day that would bring me answers, I let the man who was dead stay in the wings of my life. We didn't see each other often; just enough to occupy me and satisfy him, but seeing him was a diversion that wasn't helping. The pain was still agonizing and would come on and overwhelm me when I least expected. One of the worst bouts came two days after the day of my birth, which I'd tried to fill with some happiness by going away for the weekend. Hoping to divert myself with a friend who lived in Toronto, I failed, and every step I took across the four days spent there was shadowed by the one whose life was no longer tracking with mine.

The pain flooded over and into me the instant I opened my eyes one of those mornings there, and it brought on a deadly fear for my life. The idea that there was no way out and no hope for happiness to ever return was all I could think of as the terror petrified every cell of my being. Not wanting to further burden the friend lying to my right, who had listened to enough already, I reached out to an old friend for help. She'd always been one who mothered me, and I felt an urgent need for that kind of help, even though her recent answer to a similar call had delivered the hurtful words – "He already told you he wants nothing to do with you." My fresh plea screamed that I couldn't take this much longer and didn't know where it would lead. Despite the despair in every word, I didn't receive an answer until much later since her real mothering duties were keeping her busy and had already started to pull her out of my life. Having eliminated some of the pain by writing it out, I struggled to rise, while still questioning everything, and went on trying to pretend that I was normal.

Then it came time for the call that would change my life. Having given her both my name and his beforehand, I was hoping to hear that the stars knew he would return eventually. This woman who read the stars for a living told me what she saw about that, as well as a lot of other vital information. Beyond what she said, what would stick with me was how I felt as she spoke. Everything relayed resonated on levels that went deeper than my pain and higher than my mind's logic.

I couldn't explain it, but I felt how I already knew every truth she laid out. Which made sense since she informed me that I was extremely psychic, which was exciting to hear, despite it being the one thing she said that I found hard to grasp. Then, without admitting she was, she told me what her psychic mind picked up on while she read how closely our stars were aligned.

He'd given no indication that I'd played a part in any of the choices he'd made, but I felt the fact her words stated when she relayed that he wanted to separate me from this time to keep me from being labeled as the reason for his family splintering. Back when he was speaking to me, his words about his soon-to-be-ex-wife had never once been disparaging. Yet I knew this stranger knew what she was saying when her compassion leapt over the line as she voiced how badly he had, and still was, being battered by her. Then she reminded me of the ultimate truth since buried underneath layers of anguish, as she declared – "The only reason he's not with you is because of that little boy."

She went on to say that he might look happy on the surface, and those around him weren't the wiser, but the exact opposite was true. Not sure how he could be faking it to anyone, I imagined he was using his sarcasm as a shield, but wouldn't come to find out for a while how true her words rang. Then, calling up what I'd felt clearly as the slamming of steel, she pointed out that he was curled up inside of himself, with his arms tightly wrapped around his body. He was trying to block his pain by blocking out his feelings, including those for me that he'd once handed over generously.

He could no longer hear nor understand anything I said. Not on this plane, but I could reach him on another. Our stars, which were totally intersected, showed her how close we were connected in all facets of life, and how I could use my energy to both reach and heal him. Struck by memory, I thought back to one of the last dinners we'd had together, and what he'd told me towards the end – "Use your energy to bring me back to you."

When they'd been spoken, I'd known nothing more about energy than that people said you could manifest the man you wanted by writing out a list of his attributes. His statement had come right after I'd shown him the list that matched him completely, written a week before he'd shown up in my life. Not having believed in it when I'd written it, I felt and believed in what she was telling me wholeheartedly.

Then the piece of information came through that I'd been waiting to hear. She saw him returning, ready to commit to me, exactly one year from the month he'd left since he was determined to stay away until every emotional stage of separation had ended. At that moment it felt like an insufferable amount of time, but also seemed accurate since I'd once told him – "Best case scenario, I get you back in a year. Worst case scenario, never."

Now that he'd shut me out of his life, that prediction, which could replace the promise he hadn't voiced, became the lifeline I needed. Then I asked her about the possibility of me conceiving life. The question sprung from the memory of a prediction that had entered my mind as a teenager. Having thought, up until then, that I wanted five children, I'd been struck by the knowledge that told me, out of nowhere – "Your path to a happy family will be different from everyone else's." From that day on, I'd lost all desire to have even one child. Hesitating in her answer, she voiced what I'd already felt, which didn't bother me in the slightest – "You had children in other lives. This one isn't about that for you."

Her prophecies almost entirely overshadowed what would prove to be the crucial piece of information that she provided.

Without an explanation, she made an off-hand comment. I was meant to do something I'd avoided in previous lives; become involved in the metaphysical. Not understanding it as the words were spoken, the one word took root, and I looked up its meaning a few days after our conversation.

What I read, defining it as the study of that which exists outside of human perception, was vague and meant nothing to me, so I had no idea how to do what she'd mentioned, but I didn't forget the word or the fact that there was a way for me to reach him. It didn't take long for my first attempts to commence. While laying in the dark of the early hours, I stumbled my way closer to him the only way that was left open. With eyes closed, I did what had come naturally that morning I'd been on the other side of the country, while he'd been struggling to pack up his belongings. I directed my energy his way. Sending a stream of pink light, which she'd told me was a healing color, I intended for it to reach and alleviate the suffering I knew he was under.

While it streamed, I had my first vision. I saw a man, one I'd never seen before, staring and smiling benevolently. He said nothing, but I felt the love shining out from his features. This man, whose existence I couldn't understand or explain, looked like he knew me and was pleased by my action. His features were crystal clear and the kindness exuding from his face, which was bearded the same gray as the close-cropped hair on his head, stayed with me for the rest of that day, like a photo pristinely preserved in my head. With no idea of who he was, I wondered if he was the dead father of the man whose light I refused to let fade. I didn't know, and it didn't feel quite right since this man looked more like a prophet than a father, but either way, I knew he approved of what I'd done.

My decision was made. If I had the power to alleviate my man's suffering, and I'd felt I did in that moment, then that's precisely what I intended to do. With no idea of how it worked, I could feel it did in the way my body throbbed while the light surged out of it, so I decided to keep moving it towards him whenever I could. I wanted him back, but even if this didn't help with that, I would do it since there was no world in which I would leave this man to suffer, not if I had the power to stop it. No matter what happened between us, I wanted him to live as healed a life as possible.

With approval from this soul that was watching over us, I kept sending my light, and it grew stronger. Emboldened by my actions, I decided to take it one step further. On a night like every other, I closed my eyes with the thought of him ever-present, and that's when I had the idea that I could help by trying to speak to the woman battering him. Turning my light in the opposite direction of where his body lay, I sent a white beam towards her while my mind apologized for the pain our love had caused.

I promised that if I was to re-enter his life, I would never try to erase what they had meant to each other and would always respect her position as his son's mother. She answered with rage, and the white light I sent exploded back towards me in shards of electrifying red and blue hues. Within an instant, my man's spirit appeared by my side to lead me away from the negative charge that had struck and back to a peaceful space, which existed in the universe I was only just beginning to understand.

Wanting to learn more, I went to a bookstore and walked down a row that marked the titles on its shelves as spiritual. The one I was meant to read drew my hand straight to it, and picking up what promised to tell everything about a soul's purpose, I bought my new bible.[1] Every word on every page resonated and told me what my heart already knew, which my mind had forgotten.

The most essential piece came first. My soul, along with those of all the people I encountered in this life, had chosen every experience we shared before incarnating, to support each other in learning valuable lessons. This news was earth-shattering and completely changed my perspective on everything. Realizing I wasn't a victim of what I'd experienced, not when I was a driving force behind all of it, I resolved to understand every lesson my soul had intended.

Then the words explained that whatever emotion was experienced by the ego, which was always combating the soul out of its fear of extinction, could be traced back to either love or fear. One or the other was what led every action, or reaction, that a person executed. If performed unchecked, patterns were constructed and circumstances manifested from the emotions that existed in one's subconscious. Taking that further, it was possible for a person to see their own feelings and patterns in anyone they brought into their life since everyone was a mirror.

That's when I realized that every moment of those weeks of limbo had been led by fear. Overcome with it, I'd manifested exactly what I'd feared the most. Going back further, I knew that when we'd first come together, we'd both been high on the life changes we were making, and the desire for something better had drawn us together, but our unhealed wounds had still been there, hidden, waiting to trigger our actions. Even if his wife hadn't returned, the patterns that had led our lives up to that moment, still unchecked, would have eventually pulled us apart just like it did them.

I read on in amazement and learned that it didn't matter how well an action was disguised, even from the one performing it, the emotion lying behind it would always be felt by the recipient. Turning to every 'helpful' word I'd sent my love during his period of transition, I could see they had all carried a grasping pressure that weighted them with the condition that he let me hold on to him, which had only served to push him away.

I pondered intently as the author explained that everyone had the power to find a balance that couldn't be rocked by anything, as well as to create their own personal happiness since it already existed inside of them. Both were things I desperately wanted, that I'd never been able to hold on to, and were non-existent at that point in my life. I'd already felt, keenly, that I needed to learn how to be happy despite anything and not because of something, and I was finally getting the guidance I needed on how to do that.

The book, which wrote of these worldly goals, also outlined what could only be considered otherworldly. It spoke about senses that existed beyond the five, and the author's words, which were channeled from the angels and guides that exist above us, opened my mind. Thinking back, I realized I'd been sensing every emotion my man was experiencing, first when we were solid in our love and then when he'd begun to undergo his torture, which had equally shaken me to the core.

These words that should have sounded like insanity made more sense than anything I'd ever heard, and I knew I wasn't just learning, but re-awakening a knowledge that already existed inside of me. I started furiously scribbling in the margins, charting my recent life against what I was reading, so I could understand myself more clearly. The joy I got in this knowledge, that was helping me tap into an inner-happiness I'd never known existed, helped pull me out of my dark well of despair. They gave me a purpose. That's not to say the pain disintegrated, but there was a new meaning to my life, and it was growing with importance.

I finally understood that everything was of my own creation and to change the course of my life I would have to look into the mirror each one of my life's experiences was holding up for me, so I could see what needed healing. Otherwise, anything new I brought into my life would be a manifestation of the negative, unconscious feelings I'd suppressed and would lead to my past repeating itself. My intent was set. I was going to heal everything.

I still went about my days as I had before, and I didn't tell everyone what I was learning, but to some, I told everything. Not sure if they believed or humored me, I didn't care. I felt the truth, and I wanted to share the excitement it was bringing me. The days left at work had been extended but were dwindling, and when they ended, I planned on entering this other world more fully. In the meantime, I hadn't pulled myself out of everything set up to distract my mind from my heart's sadness.

I asked the dead man, the one I was barely seeing, over to help me hang the decorated head of a dead steer on the wall of my studio. Thinking we could transition into friendship, I wanted his help with what had been too heavy for me to manage alone. Left unattended since its arrival, it was sitting in the box that had shipped it over from the state I'd visited to try to escape the rejection I'd felt coming. He came and did what I asked with determined focus, and no laughter or joy shared between us. Afterward, I let him lead us to spend some time, for the last time, exchanging a few feeling-less kisses, despite my earlier intention of keeping us in the friend zone.

Knowing it would lead nowhere and wanting to focus on the healing my eyes had been opened to, I knew I wouldn't see him again after that day. Once he left, I made the conscious decision to not date anyone for however long it took to get healthy, but I still wasn't ready to entirely cut out the thought of dating. Despite knowing there was only one man I wanted to be with, I couldn't commit to not seeing anyone else for the entire year before our separation was prophesied to end. What if he didn't return? Or once he did, he came with stories of other women he'd been with? The thought of that was too painful to endure, and the only thing that seemed to make sense was that I have a story to compete with his.

Not able to see the festering wound of unworthiness that underlaid this train of thought, I still had no idea how much healing needed to be done or how long it would take to get through. But I felt my natural ability to do it come through right after that skull went up as decoration. When I laid myself down to sleep, the first night it was hanging, fear rose, triggered by the hatred I felt directed straight at me.

Emanating off the wall, it took a good while before I could override my fear and jump out from under the covers I'd pulled up to hide under. After taking down the skull that I sensed had once been male, I moved him over to the other side of the room and covered him with blankets. With his energy blocked, I buried myself back under my own covers. My fix worked for the night, but I knew I couldn't keep him there, like that, for longer than one.

Putting him back up the next morning, I was drawn to place one hand on each cheekbone and start speaking to him. Bathing his skull in the light I'd started to use, I felt his energy shift as my words apologized for the wrongs that had been done to him. I asked that he let go of the bones that were keeping him stuck and let his spirit leave this plane that had stripped his pride. Then saying I honored him, I promised if I felt his unhappiness again, I would find a way to bury him. Satisfied I'd done what I could, I felt his spirit lighten and making the wrong choice, even though it no longer affected him, kept his bones on display in the home I was attempting to bring light into.

With this reminder of death ever-present, the healing I'd initiated was working, but darkness still had its hold on me. Its grip, when tightened, brought up an excruciating amount of the pain that was still buried in my heart. It came up on a day that initially felt exactly like one of the days when my man and I had been a couple. With the steel block disappearing for a few hours, I was shocked I couldn't send my love a message or see him that night, both of which felt natural. I stumbled through those feelings while sitting at the desk that wouldn't be mine much longer. Walking out of work, I forced myself to go to the gym that had once been a staple of my day, instead of returning home to resume my curl on the couch.

Running like a demon was chasing, I focused my eyes forward and stared at absolutely nothing. Then my gaze was drawn far to the right, to a screen hung at the end of a long row of them. In the split-second my head was turned towards it, the scene on it showed a man speaking to a woman. Barely able to decipher the sub-titles, I read the message intended for me – "I will call you my girlfriend, but I'm not ready yet. It has to be on my time." Showering after, the water drenched my body as I leaned against a wall to the left for support. My face straining up, my voice cried out to anyone in the universe listening, hurling out the question that was killing me – "Am I supposed to wait? But he doesn't want anything to do with me! Please help me!"

As I walked home, the help I'd cried for came. Turning a corner, it gave a hard nudge to my chin. My head was instantly forced to turn to the right awkwardly while my body continued walking straight, and I saw the poster that told me – "I never stopped loving you." Elated, the way I'd been directed to see it removed all doubt, and I knew this was a message sent to give me hope.

Content, I walked a few steps forward and was drawn to stare into a boutique window. Lit up brighter than its neighbors, it spotlighted rows of shirts that were all identical in nature. The pattern, cut, and tight roll of each sleeve tied these shirts, which were the only type my man wore, to the message I'd just been handed. The sight came with a sense that told me I was right.

What I'd seen was convincing enough, but 10 minutes later, right before I reached home, whoever was helping gave another nudge. This time my head was pushed to the left, prompting my eyes to stare directly at the empty table we'd once occupied while enjoying a meal we'd eaten as the rays of the morning sun enveloped us. The one we'd shared after our first night spent together.

Grateful for these signs, I went home to lay myself down on the couch and revel in the magnitude of what I'd experienced. Only, what had started wasn't finished. Up to then, I'd felt our energy connect whenever I'd instigated it, but as I lay there, not asking or trying for anything, it flooded over me. As if no time had passed since our days spent together, I felt everything profoundly while the moments of happiness we'd once shared played themselves out before my eyes like a movie. Watching, they bombarded my heart with our love.

I relived the morning we'd paused on a corner to say a second goodbye since the kiss we'd exchanged moments earlier had been preemptive. In that flash of time, we channeled the innocence of children as he showed me how twisting the flesh above my elbow, which was something that made me cringe, was, in fact, painless. Laughing with relief, I high fived him goodbye and turned to enjoy the day ahead, with total confidence that we would see each other later that night.

Then came the moment after we spent a Sunday evening together, before he left to go home for the night. Stretched out on the couch, with my head on his seated lap, I felt deeply how the new show, which I'd turned on for us to start watching together, was an unbearable distraction from his presence. Turning my body around to snuggle in closer to his turned that moment into another one that was driven by our insatiable passion for each other. Consumed by it, he reached the core of my soul during the intimacy of that exchange.

All the memories came from the time when we'd thought we were ready to start a life together, so the memory of the night we went to the movies was especially poignant. Having sat ourselves down too early, we were asked to leave for a short time so the space we were in could be cleaned of what had been strewn there previously. Standing at the door together, he waited patiently, even though we both voiced a concern that we'd lose our prime seats, and I brought a laugh to his lips by posing myself in the stance of one set at the starting line, ready to race back for them.

That memory was to be followed by the evening that turned spontaneous after I tapped into his anxiety and knew he felt as trapped as a caged animal. He'd just walked through the door a few moments earlier and was quietly sat on my couch while I walked around in sweats. Feeling his need to escape, I quickly changed and provided one. Suggesting we go to a part of the city we'd never been to together, we walked there, and he immediately lightened up. Stopping on the way to hug me, he questioned himself out loud – "Should I tell her about you?" Still in the midst of making his life-changing decision, I responded it was his call to make but added that no matter what he chose, everything between us would only ever reflect pure happiness.

Finding a cozy little bar that resembled a speakeasy, we exchanged my couch for another, and after a couple of drinks, which we drank while laughing, he went to use the restroom located behind us. Without turning, I sensed him looking at me, wondering if I would check out the man seated to my right. Feeling how it would hurt him, I kept my eyes down since his feelings were the only thing that mattered. When he came back, I used my finger to draw what I was feeling profoundly on his arm – I love you. The happiness in his eyes met mine, and I knew he loved reading my message.

Then, the last memory surfaced. It showed the two of us standing on the side of a street an afternoon that had brought the end closer. We were hugging a final, lingering goodbye before we had to turn and walk the different paths we each had to traverse. Whispering my love for him, he'd hesitated for a moment and then told me his truth in return, which I'd already felt – "Just because I'm not saying it, doesn't mean I'm not feeling it. I won't say it until I can commit to you."

As the memories surfaced, it felt as if he was sitting there, reliving each one of them with me. Once they wrapped up, we started a conversation held via our senses. Knowing I was reaching him, I told him I understood why he had to stay away and go through this period on his own. Feeling the beauty of his presence embrace me, my mind's eye was blinded by the golden light that infused and surrounded him, and I knew without a shadow of a doubt that I was staring straight into my love's soul. Overcome, I couldn't help but continually whisper in awe – "You're so beautiful."

Then, trying to help, I asked that he not get distracted by other women, but find what I'd seen, which existed inside of him. Pulling away, I felt him shudder and heard him feel – "I can't be controlled." My words rushed to declare my sorrow, then proclaimed I didn't want to do that and for him to do whatever he deemed necessary. He softened, but with the magic of the moment over, his spirit faded, leaving behind the energy of his crippling desire to contact me.

It was strong, and I was shocked he could resist it, so I checked my phone a hundred times that evening, positive a message was coming. Knowing it was his feelings and not mine I was sensing, I had no urge to reach out because it felt like we'd just spent a completely satisfying evening together. I felt the love we'd shared again, and I vowed to hold on to the certainty of that feeling, but the challenges ahead and the wounds still inside would make that a difficult vow to uphold.

Despite the continued absence of his physical presence, I glowed from that experience for weeks after. Then a friend from work, one originally from India, returned from a visit there and gave me something else to hold on to. Wanting to help, she'd offered to visit a temple while on her trip and ask a Hindu priest to chart my life. Without telling him anything other than my name and birthdate, he'd told her what I looked like, how I'd once lived, and exactly what I needed to hear.

The flowing dark hair, high forehead, and beauty mark he'd seen on my face were described as if he was looking at a picture that hadn't been placed in front of him. Then this man, who saw me clearly, saw the boy who had controlled me before I broke away from him in my late twenties, the one this friend knew nothing about. He also saw my future, the one that included the man who would come into my life upon the resurrection of his own and would be dedicated to me from that moment forward. Hearing about the love I wanted returned to me, the joy it sparked was deepened by his next revelation. Having told her she was too young a soul to carry the truth of my existence, I didn't hear everything he'd seen, but one thing voiced clearly was that I'd just started down my path to becoming a healer.

CHAPTER 4
FIRST LESSONS LEARNED
MONTHS 4-5 OF YEAR 1

With life at my office reaching its final days, I was looking forward to starting the work I'd lined myself up for. But before I got to it, there was something I was driven to do. I messaged the golden man I couldn't see in person but was still seeing clearly in my mind's eye. Letting him know I didn't expect a response, I sent my hope that with the recent passing of his son's birthday and the holidays nearing, he was doing alright. He responded in the heartfelt way I recognized and surprised me with an apology for the pain he felt he'd caused. The reason he gave for his actions came as no surprise. He knew he'd be a fool if he didn't take advantage of this period of personal growth and self-development. While he put himself through that, he was also doing his best to stay in the light.

I understood and told him the pain had triggered my own transformation, so there was nothing for him to be sorry about. Believing that would be the end of it, the surprises continued when he replied with a question – "If it's ok to ask, what do you mean?" So I went into it a little bit and told him I was looking inside of myself and at the course my life had taken, to uncover what was weighing me down and keeping me from connecting to my own inner-happiness. He reminded me of the man I loved when he expressed how beautiful and inspiring he considered that to be.

Then he pricked my heart by using the word 'disintegrated' in reference to what we'd once shared. Knowing his head was still scrambled by pain, I didn't take offense or tell him what I thought – that his life had disintegrated, not us — because I knew that I was jumbled up in that for him. Attempting to reset the track running in his mind, I told him that what had happened, while justified, was not a judgment on what had or could exist between us again one day. I went on to declare that despite there being no guarantee of what would be at the end of this path, for either of us, I would remain open to everything, while always keeping the door open for him. Then I left him to the healing I was happy to know he was doing, and I returned to my own.

With a date set for the end of my office job, which would launch the start of my more profound work, I was rattled by an offer that came in for a short-term contract with a company I could see was close to shutting its doors forever. Told a decision needed to be made quickly, my fear of living without an income tried to steer me, but my intuition railed against it since I could feel that this position would deaden my senses. Asking for 24 hours to consider their offer, I heard what my answer should be later that night. Waking me, the word "NO" rose up from somewhere deep inside and screamed out that I couldn't work there for any amount of time, under any circumstance. I instantly knew that the consequences for my soul would be far worse than it would be for my finances.

That negative notification was instantly followed by a completely different sense. An affirmation, which came up from where it was deeply embedded in my bones, confirming that my golden man and I belonged together. Unable to ignore either, since the sensation both brought was intense and all-encompassing, I continued to leave him to heal and turned down the company that would take me away from the same course.

After those choices were made, and once my last day was behind me, stripping away every other distraction came easy. My new routine, which didn't include any television or works of fiction, started every day off early. I woke by seven, promptly walked one block over, exchanged a few words with my café's barista, and then sat myself down on a stool with an open book on the counter in front of me and a pen poised in my hand. I added more layers of marks to the pages I was reading over more slowly for the second time, then marked up one book after another, all of which I found in the same section as that first title. Sipping my coffee – I read, pondered, scribbled, and then paused to think over everything I'd read and written, repeatedly.

I then brought all the words that were sparking my being awake one block over to sit on a park bench I'd made mine. Randomly chosen, it seemed fitting since once I sat down, I noticed a plaque dedicating it from one lover to another after his death had parted their lives. Staring up at the trees around me, I would spend an hour to two, no matter the weather, taking in the nature around me and thinking over how I'd lived, what I was learning, and why everything had played itself out across my life as it had. It was on one of those mornings that I received a message from my man's spirit.

Feeling like reintroducing some music into my life, I opened my playlist and noticed a song I didn't recognize, one I'd never purchased. Hitting play, I heard that he'd had to leave because everything happened too close together. Not able to give me what I deserved to receive, even though I'd given him so much, all he could do was go off to release what was gnawing away inside of him. Marveling at the miracle, I listened to what had been sent to drive what I already knew even deeper.

From that moment on, different songs were brought to me periodically, to speak the words he couldn't, while the points relayed in each of those books of wisdom taught me something different. One opened up the mind of a Buddhist, so I could understand how meditation would calm mine.[2] Another taught the four things a person needs to know to be happy – the one that stood out the most told me to not take anything personally since everything everyone did had nothing to do with anyone other than themselves and their own wounding.[3] Then there was the book written by a doctor who taught how external control over circumstances, garnered through force, couldn't compare to the authentic power one had once choices were made with no attachment to their outcome.[4] The former was what I'd always tried to attain, and the latter was my new objective.

While I gained the wisdom these words brought my mind, I learned how to perform other helpful practices for my body and spirit. After taking a test that showed how congested mine were, I took an online class that explained which type of energetic power center each of my chakras was aligned to and guided me through exercises to help clear them of the negativity blocking the flow of positive energy within me.

Connected, but done as a completely separate endeavor, I added yoga to my workout routine. Done three times a week, this practice, that I'd once condescendingly considered nothing more than stretching, became a rigorous routine I refused to miss. Those hours released my stress and made room for the positive energy I was trying to bring in to my life. My early attempts at both were weak, and not much seemed to change as a result of either, but then my senses started to pick up on what I hadn't been open to before my world had been shattered.

Without knowing it was the man who couldn't speak to me, I started to hear him. Awakened three times in the dead of night by the screams I thought were coming from the street below my window, each experience was identical in nature, despite the weeks that separated them. I felt the terror pulsing through the man whose voice repeatedly begged, with a frantic energy that grew in intensity – "Please. I just want to go home." Unable to see him, I sensed him running forward blindly while glancing back periodically. Not hearing the person

I felt sure must be chasing him, I was positive he was being held at gunpoint since the fear, which shuddered out of him with every word, was visceral.

The morning after the third waking, I came to realize these were the only times I'd ever heard anything that sounded so threatening on the street I'd, by then, lived on for a full five years. That's when I connected it to the work I was doing and knew this new form of hearing was a result of the clearing I'd just done on the sixth of my seven chakras – the third eye, which is linked to psychic vision. Despite understanding that I was picking up on the torture my golden man was enduring, I knew there was nothing I could say to him that would help him get through it. The only thing I could do was figure out how it was even possible that I was able to hear him.

Driven to pick up a new book, I learned about the clair senses and realized which of these skills came naturally to me – clairvoyance, clairaudience, clairsentience, and claircognizance.[5] There were others, but these were what made sense considering what had been happening. I could, in varying degrees, see, hear, feel and know things I had no reason to believe were true, except for the super-natural quality that came with them, which I could only equate to a hyper-saturated scene in a movie.

His screams weren't the only thing that woke me. The pain still came with an acute intensity that was beyond anything I'd ever sensed before. At this point, it was subsiding for most of each day since my work had started to clear out what was on the surface, but the pain that lay deeper rose each night to shock me awake. Assured that he was healing his life, I stayed intent on doing the same, so I could free myself from this agony and give us a chance to come back together. I knew there was no way he could return, a changed man, to the same person I'd been. We had to be a match for each other's new vibration, which was another bit I was learning.

It was something that everyone knew, but the importance of which was lost on the masses – like attracts like. It explained why he and I had met when we both had the hope that came with a big change in life. It didn't help explain why we weren't together any longer, but I reasoned that our energy had become too damaged by the pain that had grabbed and dragged us both backward, and we weren't able to continue moving forward together carrying the weight of so many wounds. I'd always thought the sorrow strewn across the life I'd lived up until then had been resolved, but my lessons were showing that all I'd ever done was run from what had hurt me. Finally facing mine, I trusted he was doing the same, even though I had no idea of what he was actually doing.

But, I was sensing more than enough to understand his situation. The pain I was experiencing that had been, and at times still was, beyond measure, wasn't mine alone. Not when it hit out of nowhere and pulled me out of a moment of happiness. There were dozens of times it happened, but one, in particular, was especially disempowering.

It came at the tail end of an afternoon I'd taken off to briefly reunite with an old friend I hadn't seen since college. Spending the afternoon and early evening reminiscing, laughing, and loving the reinstated connection, I walked home with what had become a lighter step. Then the pain hit out of nowhere. It swept over me and spread quickly, wiping the smile straight off my face. A new-old feeling told me there was nothing left to live for, and it quickened my pace with a driving need to get back to the couch I could curl myself up on.

The books changed, and the lessons deepened, but the pain never lifted for long. The answer as to why it wasn't was one I still couldn't find anywhere I looked. I got that what we'd shared was incomprehensible in its goodness and was coming to understand why I felt and knew things I had no reason to, but why this man and I were linked so closely was something I'd yet to understand fully. There'd been two men before him that had meant enough to cause a lot of pain when they exited my life, and while each experience had been painful, neither was close to the depth of this one, had lasted as long, nor riddled me with their feelings.

That answer eluded me, but other messages kept arriving. After another morning spent reading, writing, and pondering, I went for a walk through the park that had turned icy and a song started to play, all on its own, from the phone in my pocket. It tried its best to warm me. A man sang out that even though I wasn't able to hear his voice, he was always beside me. This kindness that I knew had been sent by my man's spirit beat away the sadness his missing presence was bringing me, albeit briefly.

Then, during a brief encounter with an old acquaintance, as I exited and she entered a subway platform, I heard about a fair for those interested in metaphysical matters. She was the only person I knew who was into them, so I decided that seeing her so spontaneously was a sign that I should go to it. Still nervous of the unknown, I worked up my courage and attended.

Signing up for two sessions, once there, I sat and impatiently waited for the first, which was a psychic reading. The hope I'd been handed by the last prediction I'd received was fading, and my wobbling faith needed reassurance. It came from a large black woman who stated quite bluntly, after telling me what I wanted to hear, that she would have no problem telling me if I should forget this man.

I believed her and found what I needed in her reading, which picked up on the exact same information that the previous one had. Only, she saw something that the other hadn't. Shown a silver circle, she said it told her that what the two of us had was unbreakable, which is exactly what I needed to know. Adding to that, she said he was moving incredibly slowly to ensure he created a solid foundation to build a life on and wouldn't return before he was 100% certain that he was ready.

Feeling better, I left her to walk over to my second session. One carried out with no words, but that would bring up an excruciating amount of emotion. With no idea what to expect, since it was my first experience with a healer, I'd picked one whose look I liked out of a line up of photos. Her mane of long brown hair and loose clothing gave her the appearance I thought someone who was a healer should have. As I lay on a table, usually used to massage out someone's tension, she proceeded to work me over. Never touching, she hovered her hands over each of my seven chakras, and I sensed shifting occurring deep within me. With eyes shut, I tracked every move she made through the throbbing sensations my body was experiencing.

With a tightening discomfort rising inside, she lingered over each area until relief flooded, as whatever she was helping release lifted. Then, without warning, she moved to my heart and what occurred there went well beyond discomfort. Pain tore through that fragile organ, as it had plenty of times before, and tears started streaming from the corners of my closed eyelids. She stayed over it the longest, and I felt relief when she finished, but already guessing it wouldn't last, she told me what she'd sensed after the session ended – "You have lifetimes of pain trapped in your heart."

Ready for more help, I asked what other services she offered and heard about the Akashic Records. Another name for the Book of Life, she explained it as an energetic record of every word, deed, or emotion ever felt by anyone, across every life they had ever lived. She could access mine to help release whatever I was carrying from my past lives that was ready to go. Wanting that done as soon as possible, she said she could fit me in after the holidays, so we booked a session for six weeks from that day.

With growing excitement over this new release, I felt lighter for a week after that session. The pain had finally, momentarily, left me entirely alone for the first time in five months. It returned, as expected, but now that I had this new tool available, I had more than hope to keep me going.

While I was navigating through these new experiences, I felt another slice of what my man was enduring. It came with a new set of screams that woke me out of another night's rest. The berating words I heard came out of the mouth of a small woman, whom I couldn't see, but could feel had descended from Asia and was in her late twenties. In my stupor, I thought she was in the same spot as the man I'd once thought was being held at gunpoint below my window. Knowing there was a man with her, even though he wasn't speaking, I didn't hear his side of the story, but from her perspective understood that he'd left her alone, somewhere unfamiliar.

They were in a relationship, which was evident by the familiarity I sensed after I heard them enter an apartment they lived in together. Without hearing the building door open or close, the slamming of an interior door shook me but didn't dull her as she continued to badger him for what he'd done, which she believed was incredibly wrong by her. Shocked that I could still hear them so clearly, despite the walls that separated us, the sense of them eventually faded, and the truth didn't come to me until I was fully conscious the next morning.

Waking to ponder the memory, with a mind that was fully functioning, I started to wonder how I could have possibly known that woman's age or ethnicity. Realizing the heritage I'd tuned into was the same as the woman who'd been my golden man's wife, I came to understand that the fight hadn't occurred in the year we were currently living in. I connected it to my learning that time wasn't linear, and everything was happening at the exact same moment. It was a difficult concept to comprehend, and I didn't have a firm handle on it. Still, it was clear, I was picking up on a fight that had happened over 10 years earlier. Linking it to what that first psychic had told me, I knew I'd caught a glimpse of what was occurring at that moment in the life of the battered man I loved.

Unable to help him directly, since he still couldn't hear me, I knew the only thing I could do was continue to help myself. With no job paying for my time, I lived on my savings and spent every day working on myself. Intent on healing every negative experience and emotion, which existed in the life that lay behind me, I wanted to release all of it, so I could change my life from that point forward.

Starting with the childhood that had been spent soaking in my parents' paralyzing fear of everything, while depending on the friend who had walked by my side through every second of it, I thoroughly analyzed the resulting co-dependent behaviors that stemmed from those early experiences. Before moving on to the boyfriend I'd once lived with, who'd manipulated me with his angry silences until he'd finally ended us by choking my cries quiet. Then I spent time considering the different bosses who'd all used terror to shove me back into the secondary, service role I'd chosen to inhabit, once I'd given up on my dream of working as a creative.

Putting what I was reading into practice, I started uncovering the root cause of every pattern, so I could change what was in me that had manifested every painful experience I'd lived through, and break the hold they had over my life. From the need to please and save others, so I would be deemed worthy of their love, to the desire to stay safely hidden in the shadows, I dug deep and faced every hard truth about myself.

Realizing it all stemmed from a fear of being rejected, since deep down I believed I was unworthy of the things I wanted, I was fully ready to be rid of what was holding me back from true happiness. My new pattern was working at doing just that – reading, self-analyzing, exercising, and clearing – and I did nothing other than one of those four, for 10 straight hours a day, for three consecutive months.

During that time, I read a second book from the same doctor and started to understand how to let go of the years of suppressed feelings that were propelling my patterns.[6] He understood that feelings were energy, and while talking about them was good, it would never release them. If they weren't taken care of correctly, they could become stuck, to then unconsciously lead every action or reaction one took.

His solution was to lay with your eyes shut and go inward while calling up a memory that was painful. Then, ask why. Again and again, he advised to keep asking, until the real reason for the pain was uncovered. Next, came his method for releasing. First, one had to sit back and become aware of where the negative feeling lay in the body. Each would bring physical pain to a different area. Without attaching, he advised to observe it and allow the pain to be felt, no matter how excruciating, until the energy lifted. Then move on to the next area in the body where the pain appeared.

Resolved to remove everything negative that had infected me, I spent hours at a time doing what he'd outlined. I wasn't pulling any punches, and I was willing to take as many as was necessary to eviscerate all negativity within me once and for all. Pulling up the most painful thought possible first – I imagined my man in love with another woman. I knew this jealousy was poison, and I wanted to be rid of the fear that thought brought me. With the image of him with an elusive her in mind, I kept my eyes closed as a visual of my physical heart overtook them.

Standing back, I watched, and felt, the torturous pain of a sharp blade stabbing a hundred wounds into it. Refusing to give up on the effort to free myself, I stuck with the process, and the stabbing eventually stopped. With the throbbing of each raw wound taking over, I continued to hold space for this release, despite the physical agony that pulsed through me with every ache. After what seemed like an endless amount of time, the slashes started to scab over, but I refused to take my focus away as they turned into less painful scarring, which ultimately led to the lifting promised, once they disappeared entirely.

I followed this up a few days later with another round. One that brought a vision of me sitting in the center of a room, surrounded by every man I'd ever felt anything akin to love for. Each was seated with a new woman, and none were paying any attention to me. While I sat alone and forgotten, I watched them gaze lovingly at "her" and felt my unworthiness spike with their lack of validation.

Soon the image transitioned to me lying on the floor, curled up in an attempt to protect myself as they all simultaneously started kicking my body. Sitting through the same process, the kicks, as well as the pain felt, eventually evaporated. Under no illusion that I'd released all of my feelings of unworthiness or the jealousy that erupted from it, I knew that a good chunk was gone and left the rest to be dealt with later. These were a few of many hours spent in a pain I was growing used to, but at least with this method, I knew an end to it would come, and once there, I could regain more of my personal power.

Midway through the second of those three months came the day of my Akashic Reading. Having entered my records beforehand, we sat to discuss what my new healer had found, but before that, I was told how difficult they had been to get into. Unlike anything she'd experienced with anyone else, all she could see at first was her own reflection, since there was a thick mirror set up around my field to provide a form of protection.

Permeating my life, it hid me, while projecting out to everyone I met whatever it was about themselves that they wanted to see in me. So everyone saw what they liked, and I stayed safe from any stabs of dislike. Throughout the hour she spent in them, she had to continuously remove the panes that kept coming back up, so she could get to the information and clearing I needed.

Reading from the pages of notes that had been scribbled, she was able to tell me a primary trait I already knew about myself, which had gotten me into trouble plenty. Set by my soul to aid in my life's purpose, I'd come into the world programmed to tell the truth, no matter the consequence. Luckily, my secondary trait, which was almost as strong as the first, was compassion, so my truth generally came with a soft edge to it. Laughing sharply, I let her know how valid her words were since I had plenty of stories of when the truth had led my actions and, ultimately, my downfall. Working in tandem, these traits had consistently driven me to tell people what they didn't want to hear, but that I thought was in their best interest to know, even if it made me look bad in the process.

Then, confirming what I'd already read, which was that every person in the world has a team of guides, teachers, and angels that looked out for them, she added that I had one she'd removed because of his negative nature. Attached to me since I was a child, he'd been drawn to me by my feelings of immense guilt, which I'd always joked came from a combination of my Italian heritage and Roman Catholic upbringing. His attachment had amplified all of that guilt, handed down through my ancestry, from the moment he'd latched on to my life.

Both pleased and shocked, I asked her exactly which day she'd accessed my records. Considering that two days earlier, I'd spontaneously felt a massive flux of guilt release out of my system, I wanted to know if it was connected to this guide's removal. So much of it had dissipated that the next day, a situation with my mothering friend, which would have typically brought up a ton of it, had triggered none. She confirmed her work had occurred on the same day as that flux.

Happy that this guide was gone, we moved on to the truth about two of my past lives, which had come up so she could remove the karma from them that was affecting me in this one. As she spoke, I stifled a laugh and questioned if what she was saying had come out of a romance novel. The first had occurred 21 lives before the current one, and in it, I'd agreed to be the concubine of a ruler. Wanting to feed my family, I'd succumbed to his desires and contracted myself to his every whim, even though it'd brought me pain, not pleasure. The vows of allegiance I'd been forced to voice had placed a collar around my neck, and it was still squeezing, trying its best to silence my words. Connecting that experience to this lifetime, I admitted I consistently, despite fighting against it, lost my voice whenever it was positioned against anyone, especially a man, in authority.

Excited for that to be lifted, she returned to my guilt. Some of it was linked to an experience had 13 lives earlier. Living in a culture, most likely Samurai, that prided itself on honor, I'd broken its societal boundaries when I'd fallen in love with someone who wasn't the person I'd bound myself to in marriage. We'd both succumbed to our feelings, but my guilt had gotten the better of our love when the other half of my binding had found out about us. Out of fear of the societal disgrace it would bring upon my family, I'd decided to sacrifice our love. My spouse and I had vowed to keep it a secret so our family's honor wouldn't be ruined. This was another contract that needed to be cleared, so my voice could be freed of its silencing impact.

Asking if the man I loved in this life had been in either of those, the woman in front of me, who would become my personal healer across the year ahead, didn't know the answer. I could feel she didn't like the question, but set it aside, knowing no one could understand why I was hanging on to hope for someone who had rejected me. Sure that he'd been involved in the life that carried karma from a love triangle; I wasn't sure of the exact details, but it felt similar to a vivid dream I'd had right before the reading.

It was one of many he visited me in, even though through the majority he was either unaware of my presence or refused to turn his gaze in my direction. In this one, I watched from afar as he knocked on the door of a large home he'd recently lived in. Not recognizing his appearance, since in this life he was half a foot taller than most tall men and had Nordic features, in that one he looked Asian. There was a woman and two children inside, and I knew that they had been a family, but when the door opened the only thing that came out was a large, black grand piano.

Rolling towards him quickly, he turned to run down the hill that had led him up to the entrance, but he couldn't escape and was crushed when it ran him over. I understood the meaning immediately upon waking. Early on, in this life's relationship, he'd spoken of the lessons he was taking to learn how to play the piano and had described the experience as one that fed his soul. I knew this dream was showing me the soul-crushing experience he was living through. With a heart heavy for him, I knew he had to go through this on his own, to uncover his power, but I'd yet to realize how much more I was going to have to endure on this path I was set on.

CHAPTER 5
THE WEIGHT A SPIRIT CARRIES
MONTHS 6-7 OF YEAR 1

Soon a night arrived when a new fear paralyzed me, which I knew with certainty wasn't connected to the golden man living a short 10-minute walk away. The weight of a spirit's empty form shifting the mattress below him, as he laid himself down next to me, had woken me out of a night's slumber. As he pressed himself against the soft barrier of a pillow I'd fallen asleep holding, fear pressed down on me.

Eyes wide open, I stared into the darkness above, too afraid to look over to the right. Unsure of what would be worse – to see or not to see what I could feel was laying there next to me. The knowledge of his presence was deepened by an awareness of his thoughts. His belief that he was going about his nightly routine, and that he belonged there, came over me. Knowing, without any words spoken, that he had no desire to hurt me lightened my fear of him. Then the weight lifted as he left me as alone as I'd been when I first laid myself down earlier that night.

Waking up to the light, my mind had no doubt of what had been felt in the dark. I knew instinctively that both the raw grief over my missing love and my efforts to lighten that load had triggered a sense for what had always been there, that I hadn't been open enough to feel before. Unsure of what to do about him, I set the experience aside. But with our connection made, his first visit was quickly followed by a second. He came the night that followed the day I'd bought and hung a small circle of wood, its interior wired with mesh stringing that resembled a spider's web, over my bed to catch my dreams.

Not knowing until later that the stones woven into those strings could protect me, they kept him out, but his sorrow at being barred called out and woke me. The illuminating light engulfing my window made its shades transparent and gave me a clear view of his shadow hanging there while watching me. Feeling the false safety of a protection that I didn't know wouldn't last, I turned away from him and with fear subsiding, slipped back into the dream he'd interrupted.

I spoke of him to the one helping me heal my energy, but she couldn't see him clearly amongst my lifetimes of wounds and karmic patterns still to be dealt with. The only thing she was sure of was that he was someone I'd known in a past life. Thinking she'd cut off his access by closing a portal he was using to enter my home, she left me with the same sense of security the stones had managed for one night. Fear turned itself around and became a story that came out with laughter. Told from a heart that believed this being, who I was sure hadn't been out to hurt me, was gone. But while I shifted my focus back to the heavy lifting of healing my heart, he waited patiently and then spirited back in quietly, so he could continue to watch everything.

While he did that, I kept saying no to any opportunity that came up to return to the career that had once deadened me, and turned the dial up on my new regime. The pain that wouldn't stay away for long drove me to expand my search for a solution, and I found a small center that focused on healing people's energy by teaching different methods in weekly workshops.

This is where I learned what was happening to me – I was waking up. Seeped in material slumber, unaware of my connection to the universe around me, I'd been living disconnected from my soul. Following the plan that had been laid out before my birth, the pain of our separation had triggered a search for answers that had put me on a path to re-awaken, to rebirth. Made up entirely of energy, I was more than my everyday experiences; I was a soul that had a path to follow.

Despite this knowledge, the pain of our separation was still palpable, and I knew I needed a lot of help, so I took a course that would certify me to do a version of energy work called Reiki on either myself or other people. Thinking this was something I would enjoy doing for money, I was looking for a career to replace the one in Advertising that had numbed my soul. It was in this weekend workshop that I was surprised by the words that came out of the mouth of another member when she approached to ask if I knew I was incredibly psychic. Laughing, I'd heard. She saw a silver ring of light circling my head, which represented this to her, and she'd only ever seen it as strong on a few other people. Not sure what to do with the gift I still couldn't control and that only came to me spontaneously, I set her words aside with all the other unanswered questions I had about who I was.

After completing that certification, I moved on to a few other workshops and realized just how much saving I needed before I could start helping anyone else. One that brought a shocking new insight came on the weekend that brought the day couples are guided to show their love to each other. With mine unable to share his with me, I went to the place where I felt safe sharing. That's when I found out I didn't believe I deserved anyone to love me. Instructed to pair up, I sat in front of a stranger and with my left eye trained on hers, silently started repeating – "You love me."

Floored, a flash of emotions instantly cycled through my heart. Starting with an intense need to do something to warrant her love, it flipped to the deep pain of feeling undeserving of it, followed quickly by the revulsion that came with thinking I was egotistical for expecting it, to an embarrassing need to pull away from her, and then a fear of the responsibility that receiving it would bring. Hearing after that not being able to receive love was linked to not loving oneself, I decided to add the instructor's month-long workshop, with guided daily meditations, to my routine.

Told to set up an altar for them, I positioned it on one of the windowsills in my studio and layered its surface with various items I cherished that represented what I wanted to manifest. Amongst the gathering of symbols was an orchid, which represented desire, a ball made out of twigs that had paper butterflies woven into it, as a symbol of my hope for the rebirth of our love, and the book that was my man's favorite – *The Secret History* – gifted to me before his departure. In the center of it all was a photo of me by myself, which I'd been instructed to place there, along with a love note that I was to write to myself daily.

The first, which was intended to rewire our thinking, was to include the line we wanted to hear most from someone who loved us. Starting with the words we were given – "I love you because..." – I initially added qualities to it, such as kindness and compassion, before realizing that I was justifying why someone should choose to love me by caveating it with how I would act towards them. After shredding multiple attempts, I landed on the one that felt like what I should strive for – "I love you because you exist."

With those meditations and mantras added in before my daily coffee, reading, and bench sessions, which I pushed back by one hour, I then went on to include another six-week workshop into my already rigorous healing routine. This one was intended to help me learn how to trust myself by honing my intuitive psychic abilities. Excited for that, all of my endeavors were working together to drive a new happiness, which was coming up straight from inside.

I still missed the man I wanted, but felt ok with our separation, especially since I thought I knew when it would end. Walking through the winter sun, I could see the changes happening within me with every outward kindness that was becoming my new way of being, and I loved it. At times I felt a deep happiness overcome me, and in my mind's eye, I would fling my arms wide open and hug the city I was traversing. Feeling connected to this pure happiness that I'd never experienced on my own before, I was gentler to everyone I encountered.

The bitter edge of resentment, which had once lashed out at those I didn't care for, was disintegrating. It had silenced itself while the golden man's light was in my life, but now it was disappearing from my being entirely. The simplest, most tangible example was that a stranger cutting me off while walking, or while I stood in line waiting, no longer brought a tirade of angry insults to mind. Whereas before I would have glared at them over the perceived injustice, I now smiled and hoped that whatever was making them rush wasn't too serious.

This happiness was similar to what I'd obtained briefly while with my golden man, but in truth had lost before we ever met. The years of disappointment and struggle, which everyone goes through in varying degrees – with family, friends, relationships, and jobs – had taken their toll and succeeded in stomping down the innocent part of me that had once wanted nothing more than to give and receive love. Reversing the tide, that beautiful version of me finally had a chance to rise to the surface.

I could see the work I was doing was helping, but I had no idea that the happiness I was tapping into still wasn't set on a solid foundation, not yet. Like the high that comes after the first couple of workouts, I was feeling a surge from my actions but had a lot more left to learn. Luckily, the drive to work hard, which had nearly worked me to death when I'd done it for others, coupled with my ability to access the deepest regions of my psyche, were two skills that came naturally. My perseverance and determination, along with my sensitive nature, which had always caused me to feel every emotion deeply, had been programmed into me for a reason. This healing was my life's purpose.

All this knowledge was deepened in the first class of my new workshop. Having already come across the word in my studies, I learned more about what I'd never known I was before – an empath. Across my life, emotions had swung me high or low at a moment's notice, and I now knew it was because I was picking up, soaking in, and feeling the emotions of people who were either in my near vicinity or with whom I shared an emotional connection. With the ability to handle intense and difficult feelings, which the majority didn't possess, I was processing and releasing their emotions for them, especially the ones they were avoiding.

With new eyes, I glanced back at the fear, which I'd had as a teenager, that there was something wrong with me. I'd never understood why sudden bouts of extreme happiness or sadness would come out of nowhere to overwhelm me. Then I moved forward to think through the previous months of disorientating devastation. Realizing I'd taken on, and felt as if they were my own, every emotion that had dropped my golden man lower and lower, I understood I'd been living as if I was going through the same divorce he was. Relief flooded as I realized that not only was I not crazy, but I could learn how to manage these feelings when they came on and overwhelmed me.

The woman teaching us how to trust ourselves taught us a method to clear others' feelings out of our systems before doing anything else, so we could then tune into our own intuition more easily. Filling ourselves up with a white light drawn down from the universe, we showered ourselves with it. Then, once wholly engulfed, we used each breath to pull it in through our pores, so it could infuse our bodies with its cleansing power. Once in, our breath drew it up and out of our crowns, where it then proceeded to rain down around us, to circle back in through the soles of our feet for another round that ran through our entire bodies.

After a few cycles of this vertical whirlpool, which purified our energy, we let a ball of it grow in our heart chakras. Turning it pink, we pushed it out through our chests so it could expand and fill our auras with its protective glow. Then, locating where in our systems it still felt heavy, we turned that energy into a small, condensed ball and returned it to the person it had initially come from. We sent it back with our love and let them know we couldn't take on their feelings. I did this with my golden man and felt some relief as his pain left me. But that moment would always pass, and I would repeatedly take back the only thing he had to give.

Able to set it aside in the hours I spent focused on learning, I was eager to know more and asked if the faces of strangers, which I now regularly saw flash before my eyes when I closed them, was linked to another power. Having recently seen the back of a couple's head, from the view provided by the rear window of the pickup in which they were sat, I was curious to know what I was tapping into. Especially since not all the scenes were as lovely as them. The one I'd seen from my stance on the side of a porch that overlooked a distant field, where I'd seen a cross burning and knew a black man was being hung by white ones, had filled me with horror. A certainty that I'd been there and known the one swinging from that limb had brought on the shame and guilt of having been too afraid to do anything to stop it.

The answer to my question was noncommittal. I heard that it was possible that these were recollections of my past lives, or perhaps I was tapping into the memories of people around me. No one in this new world that I'd chosen to enter would tell me what to do or hand over any definitive answers since that would take away from my power, so it was up to me to find out. The reason behind and use of these abilities could only be uncovered and accepted by me, if and when I was ready.

That, along with the messages the universe continually sent through signs, was for us to decipher, since everything was unique to the receiver. We were only taught one universal rule we could live by – there are no coincidences. Meaning that everything seen that resonates is a message from those attempting to help us. This bit came as no surprise since I'd already read about, seen one, and come to believe in the guides, teachers, and angels looking out for me. As well as my own higher self – the pure part of me that exists in spirit form, didn't have any of the ego's hang-ups, and could channel my soul's greater knowing. Ultimately leaving me to make my own decisions, this group tried to guide me forward with the wisdom of what my soul wanted. Despite the cryptic nature of their messages, I thought I understood most of what they were trying to get through to me.

But theirs weren't the only messages I was receiving. During a walk to the gym located near the park where we'd once said one of our goodbyes in, my eyes were drawn to a sign that told me – "We deserve a longer life together." The smile that came with that was quickly wiped away as I fell forward. Catching myself before I landed flat on the ground, I turned around to see who had given the push I'd felt hit my back. No one. Not one living being was close enough to have touched me. Feeling it hadn't been done by anything friendly to me or to that sign's message, but unsure of what it meant, I righted myself and continued walking forward.

Back in class, we soon moved on to our innate abilities and tuned in to each other, so we could tell what we knew, felt, heard and saw about the other that ran deeper than our mind's logic. Stumbling through these first attempts, scared I wouldn't have anything to say to the stranger sat cross-legged in front of me, I focused in on them and voiced whatever came to mind. Unsure if I was right while doing it, I received confirmation that I was when I was guided to tell one woman – "Everything's going to be alright." In our post-tuning conversation, she revealed she was trying to make a life-changing decision, and this was the phrase she'd been saying to herself, on repeat, for the entire week leading up to that day. Ecstatic, I didn't fail to recognize I still needed validation from others to trust what I felt.

These teachings helped me understand the dreams and visions of my golden man that hadn't ceased, and I fully believed they were being sent to me as messages. There was no visible difference between the two, other than one was a vivid recollection I had upon waking, and the other came upon me while awake to send me somewhere else.

One of the dreams revealed an essential fact about why we were separated, which I hadn't been aware of before having it. He and I were seated in a room that had a table set center stage. It was strewn with cards and surrounded by a few people.

Seated close to me, I didn't recognize anyone other than him but knew everyone was playing the same game. Seeming to be completely ignoring me while watching everyone around us, his body was positioned in a way that shielded mine. He was keeping me hidden from a woman seated in the corner, who was throwing daggers our way. Deflecting her to protect me.

One of the visions confirmed what it was I was holding out for. Coming over me in the middle of an afternoon of introspective thinking, it started with a wash of purple light that wiped my thoughts clean. Then I was shown the version of us that would come to exist once everything within each of us was healed. On a night in the middle of a future summer, the sky was full of an explosive celebration of independence, and we were standing on a roof of the building we were living in. With arms circling each other, it wasn't what I saw, but what I felt, that moved me. The depth of his love and gratitude, for the time spent holding space for him, resonated off his being and touched me to the core of mine.

I believed in these messages, as well as everything I was learning, despite the doubt that crept back in with the pain that struck hard in-between them. Refusing to place blame on the man I loved, I understood him deeply and knew the loyalty and obligation he still felt towards the woman he'd once vowed to spend his life with was keeping him bound to her and away from me.

I inadvertently received confirmation of this through a guided vision I had while my intuitive instructor led us deeper, in the middle of one of our classes. While meditating, she prompted us to imagine a city and try to see everything about it clearly, while taking special note of what we had trouble making out. Then head into one of its shops and see ourselves in there while noticing whom we were with and what happened between us. After that, leave and take note of where we went.

The beauty of Paris popped to mind immediately. Its grandeur was easy enough to visualize, and I could even see the rough, pebbled texture of its buildings when a wall appeared in front of me. Looking like it could draw blood, I still ran my hand across its surface. Rough to the touch, but not painful, it looked like it would hurt more than it actually did. Stepping back, I looked over the city that stood for love and tried to see its rooftops, but I couldn't imagine what was at the top-end of any of the blocks spread out before me.

Then, appearing within a pastry shop in the form of a little boy, I was sat patiently, waiting for a sweet to be handed over. But the mother I was with wasn't happy with me, or the sister sat to my left since there'd been a massive fight between us. A strict disciplinary, she'd sided with her and refused to treat me, even to the smallest of glances. With a stern look, she avoided my gaze, even though in her heart of hearts, she knew it wasn't right to lay the blame on my shoulders.

Looking lost and forlorn, I sat there and waited, salivating for some sweetness and knowing she would eventually get over this feeling. Once it happened, as expected, she handed over precisely what I'd been hoping would come to me. The chocolate dipped, custard filled donut I sank my teeth into was as delicious in its sweet, decadent coolness as I'd anticipated. Finished with that, and with the sister having already gone off on her own, the two of us headed straight over to a nearby playground that I knew was going to bring us endless joy.

Coming out of that vision, I quickly jotted down everything I'd seen and then pondered its messages. I was instantly clear on everything and knew it was the truth that wasn't being spoken. Stuck between love and loyalty, my golden man still felt obliged to stay by the side of his son's mother, even if she was no longer his wife. Cutting off our connection with a severity that seemed like total indifference on his part had been rough on me, but he hadn't been trying to hurt me. The truth was he saw me as the one he had to stay away from, since being together had, and still might, hurt the family he'd made a vow to protect. This behavior matched the discipline of the man I'd been with, who wouldn't ingest an ounce of sugar, not even in a piece of cake on his birthday and wouldn't skip out on even one day's gym session. He couldn't see past his duty. And just like my inability to see the tops of those buildings, I was having a hard time seeing past everything blocking us, to what would come at the end of this journey, even though once we reached it we would experience nothing but joy.

These classes helped me see a lot of things more clearly and stopped me from doing one thing that had once felt right. I quit streaming my light over to my golden man, out of fear that I was crippling both of us by turning myself into his crutch. Listening to the woman instructing us, who was adamant in this belief, I cut off all the support I'd been sending. Using a butterfly as an analogy, she explained how the healing process must be handled. It was one of the few times she left no room for our own instincts or the possibility that some of us may be energetically different from others.

What she believed was that even if we could see what someone needed, it was imperative we leave them curled up in cocoon form until they were ready to transform; otherwise, risk clipping their wings and crippling their ability to soar. Still unsure of who I was or why we were connected so deeply, I stopped sending my light over and recommitted to not reaching out to him again, not until he'd healed his life enough, on his own, to choose if he wanted to take the path that led back to us sharing our happiness.

Despite all this newfound certainty, every day that passed without a word from him chipped away at my faith. It didn't help when fear got the better of me after I woke to the sound of him having sex with another woman. Thinking at the moment that it was someone living above me, I set it aside and returned to my slumber. Waking in the morning, I wondered why I'd never heard that sound before in all the years I'd lived there. That thought triggered the memory of what had entered my mind before I'd gone to bed, when I was neither thinking nor doing anything related to its meaning – "I've been alone for so long."

Not sure why I needed to hear either, I frantically flipped open my soul-bible and searched for an answer. The passage the book instantly opened up to reminded my mind that the universe will never do anything to hurt you, but will orchestrate events to bring up the negative feelings that have to be released. Forcing them to be felt and dealt with at the right time safely removed the power they held to trigger a negative exchange between two people, which might create more karma that would then need to be healed. I knew I had to heal the wound this experience had hit, so I wouldn't lash out and harm him if he came back with a story about another woman. But that was easier said than done.

Hating this jealousy that didn't match the person I wanted to be, I'd always known he would need to be with other women before returning, but hearing it still crushed me. It was the worst form of torture, and despite my understanding, it sent me spiraling. Struggling through the class I went to later that day, I stumbled home after, all in a daze similar to the one that had hit me early on in our separation. Unsure what to do, I wandered into a crystal shop a few doors down from the building I lived in, hoping to find a stone that would alleviate what I was feeling. Looking lost, I picked up and put down a good 20 before deciding on a couple.

As I stood at the counter waiting to pay, shoulders slumped and spine curved under the weight of this new burden, my appearance, which announced I was a victim, led him straight to me. He appeared next to me out of nowhere and after asking what stones I'd chosen, said he could prepare them for me if I wanted. With an intense need for help emanating out of every inch of my body, I handed them over without hesitation. The only thought to enter my mind was that this man, whose long gray hair and bushy beard made him look like he was somebody's grandfather, couldn't possibly have a malicious intent towards me.

After cupping them in both hands, as he wordlessly cast a silent spell over them, he gave them back and let me know that I had the weight of many resting on my back. Tears welling up, I nodded that I knew and let him lead us over to another part of the shop, so he could work more of his magic on me. Turning my body around, his hands pulled and pushed against my back, giving every indication that he was trying to remove what he'd sensed. Feeling lighter and grateful for it, I readily accepted when he offered more help. Not wanting it without giving anything in exchange, I agreed to pay for it and confirmed we could start that night.

After we left the shop, we aimlessly wandered the darkened streets for over an hour, while the full moon marked the sky above us with its pale light. Leading us to crisscross the city's streets, he spoke, and I listened intently, hoping to hear something that would lighten my load. He asked about the work I'd been doing, and while telling him about my first session at the spirit fair, I mentioned the name of the shaman who'd organized it. Scoffing, he knew her and warned to stay as far away from her as I could get.

Without explaining why, he said everything we ever spoke of was strictly confidential and never to be shared with anyone. He went on to advise I ignore everything anyone in the spiritual community said about the benefit of giving up material comfort. His way, which was confirmed by his appearance, was to drink the can of soda and skip the session of yoga. Nodding, despite disagreeing, I kept listening.

He moved on to other beliefs, more fitting to my life and explained something I should start doing. Pointing out that there was a power in my hands that would only come out if I fostered it, he tasked me to get a small book of blank pages and draw in it daily. Advising I not try to draw anything in particular, I was to start small, so the strength in this skill I had could grow naturally. Loving everything creative, even though I hadn't thought the natural ability to do it existed within me, I loved hearing this piece of news.

Then he voiced something I knew but didn't love. Without having said a word about it, he knew my childhood had been difficult, and that I hadn't felt like I fit into the family that raised me. My heart railed against his next suggestion, but I stayed silent. He warned to never go back to where they lived, not even for a quick visit. Switching gears, he started in on the man who couldn't hear my voice. His words registered a deep fear within me when he stated – "He was using you. Block his number so he can never manipulate you again."

Struck senseless, I didn't want to believe it, but I was still floundering from what I'd heard the previous night, and I didn't know what to believe in any longer. By this point, we'd wandered around in cold circles long enough to feel frozen.

Entering a used bookstore, to warm up, I then received the guidance I knew I should be listening to. Wandering its rows, my eyes became glued to a book sat on a shelf that grazed the ground. I couldn't stop staring as we walked by it and felt compelled to twist my head around, as my eyes stayed trained on one word in the title that stuck out – "Darkness."

We kept moving until it disappeared around a corner and he chose to pause in front of a display. Not hearing him, he kept talking while my eyes stared at the book positioned directly over his left shoulder. All I could register was the title, which told me – "Evil Walks At Night." Realizing I was being guided, I felt an urgency to get myself out of there quickly. Hurriedly handing him the money I'd promised to pay, I turned and made a beeline through the streets we'd just circled, so I could lock myself into the safety of my studio.

Baffled, I couldn't believe what I'd just done. I questioned how I could have listened, gullibly, to everything he'd said that, if done, would have completely isolated me. Aghast by my actions and scared to trust my thoughts, I wanted to know why this had happened. So I sent a message to the psychic who'd first read my stars, and she replied almost immediately. Telling me to throw away anything he'd either given or touched led to a mad rush out of my building, so I could trash the crystals he'd cupped in the bin on the corner. With that done, I reread the words that said he honestly thought he was helping but went on to warn that nothing he'd said could be trusted and to steer completely clear of him in the future.

Convinced, I decided to never go into that shop again. With hurricane force winds pushing me forward the next day, I counted my blessings as I passed it from across the road, refusing to even glance over at its entrance. Feeling a darkness descend as I hurried around the corner, I wanted confirmation that even if I ran into him again, I couldn't be manipulated, so I asked the healer I trusted to look into the situation. The timing was perfect since I'd already booked a session for the tail end of that same week.

She agreed to go into my records before our meeting, but this time only for a quick look. The focus of the session had been set to be similar to the first, an in-person clearing of my chakras. But because of this recent encounter, she would include this additional service. Since she was going in, I asked her to see if there were any curses aimed against my man and me coming together as a couple.

I thought there might be because of a strange feeling I'd had while riding an escalator in a different bookstore from the one I'd entered on the night I'd gone on my walk with the devil. Similarly, my eyes had become glued to the spine of a book that had declared clearly – "Someone Up There Hates You." Unable to look away, I'd been struck hard by the truth I'd felt in those words, and my head had twisted as my eyes continued to stare at them as I rode up to the second floor I was being delivered to.

Honoring my request to look into these two things, she'd checked in before our meeting and had uncovered what she'd been able to see. She told me all before turning to my chakras. The devil-man had, in fact, used his power to manipulate me. Connecting a cord of energy between his third chakra and mine, he'd been able to lull me into a more permissive state. She'd cut it so he could no longer wield this power over me and then went on to tell of another she'd seen and removed – one that connected me to my man. Shocked, I'd told her to remove anything that wasn't in my highest good, but couldn't believe that anything to do with him could be that.

Seeing my discomfort, she promised that if what we shared was a universal connection then it couldn't be broken, but this cord had been sucking my energy out and that hadn't been good for me. I understood the point, but still felt saddened by the thought that one more link to him had been taken away. Going on, she added that she hadn't seen any curses, but had cleared some heavy blocks sent my way by the woman I assumed was no longer his wife. Her pain was fueling a wish to keep me out of his life, which could be construed as a curse, but was created by nothing more than a natural form of negative thinking and could be cleared easily.

The chakra healing helped lighten my discontent slightly, but I still walked home feeling completely isolated and alone.

Thinking over her words, I hoped for the possibility she'd mentioned in passing. That the cut would be felt deeply by him and might instigate some form of contact. Arriving home, I sat myself down in the dark to ponder how I felt. Interrupted, I listened, amazed, as a song started playing out loud in the silence that surrounded me. With everything off, I questioned my sanity as I listened to the lyrics that pleaded for me to not walk away. It bellowed that there would be nothing left, except pain, if love were taken away.

The song faded out almost as soon as it'd faded in; then the ringing of a phone filled the silence left behind. Sounding as clear as if it was coming from the one lying on the couch next to me, I picked mine up to check its dark screen and saw nothing. Then sent a text to the guy living next door, to ask if it was his music I was hearing. Cordially, he'd given me his number one night after I'd asked that he turn down the sound of violence that was streaming out of the speakers his gaming system was attached to. Every other message related to sound had immediately prompted a "sorry" as he lowered the noise attacking my senses. This time neither came.

Walking out my door, I walked over to his and checked to see what I could hear. Nothing. Crossing the hall, I kept my ears open and heard the same at the other two doors sat next to each other, located 10 steps away from mine. Walking up the stairs, I then listened at each of the four doors to the apartments one floor above mine. Silence. I repeated the same on the floor that lay below mine and didn't hear a peep.

Realizing this was another sign sent to provide the hope I needed, I went to sleep in utter amazement of the life I was living. The next morning brought another surprise. A call from an unknown number had rung through while I'd slept. Not sure if my golden man had masked a call he hadn't been able to resist making, or if the universe had prompted a random caller's ring to reassure me that my man had felt the cut, I added this experience to the list of reasons I should continue down this path, while holding space for our love.

Soon, another message was delivered. This one came in two phases and used a sign to clarify a vision. Waking one morning, I saw it clearly in my mind's eye – a patch of ground was being dug up with a hand shovel. It was my hand holding the handle, removing layer after layer of what needed to be gotten rid of to get to the treasure that lay below. My instincts shouted that I was clearing away everything that had sullied our love and needed to keep going until I reached the end. Then, later that day, it was confirmed by a message written on a bus shelter. A new show was being promoted with the words – "Dig deeper." Knowing it was a directive sent to me from above, I was committed to doing just that.

REBORN

CHAPTER 6
SEEING PATTERNS
MONTHS 8-12 OF YEAR 1

Driving myself deeper, but still not believing I wasn't showing my friends who I was, the reality of this fact confronted me abruptly. A dinner that kicked off with joy, shared with my friend that had the strongest of opinions, turned into over an hour of strife, and ended with the severing of our friendship. It started with the description of a dream I'd had of my man, one in which he'd appeared to be an exhausted waiter trying to keep up with the duty of feeding everyone. This led her to tell me, out of nowhere – "You didn't like him as much as you think you did."

Shocked that she had the nerve to tell me, with total authority, how I'd felt, I did something new and countered her opinion. Initially, the words that voiced my truth back were spoken softly, but then her reply raised my ire. Having only met him once, she went on to group him in with all men and said – "There's no way he's spending the time you think he is healing himself."

With my voice rising to an octave that wasn't suitable for the environment, I fought her opinion of the facts. She refused to back down and raising her voice to meet mine, disagreed with everything I believed about the love I'd experienced. Matching her word for word, I didn't recognize myself. I'd always squelched my beliefs when they differed from those held by the ones I cared for, out of a fear that it would anger them. But that no longer felt like a path I could take. The collar had been removed, and I now had the ability to stand up for what I believed in.

The subject of the argument was irrelevant. It was her deciding what my truth was that I couldn't abide by. Unable to continue on with someone who felt she had the right to tell me how I'd felt, I let go of our friendship after that night, even though it'd been one I cherished. I chose myself over it and left her with her opinions. Walking away, I loved this new voice that had the strength to stand up for what I believed in, no matter the consequence.

Then, with my intuitive course coming to a close, something it'd kicked off brought me to the next phase of my healing. Re-reading an entry in the journal I'd been instructed to write in daily, I realized the words I'd used to chronicle an experience with my barista resembled a story. So I set aside reading the words of others and started to write my own. Keeping to my routine, I walked myself over to the same spot every morning but left the books of others behind. With a coffee steaming beside my laptop, I started typing.

With clear days ahead and a blank page in front, I began with a memory. Recounting the time I'd sat down to write a book with a pencil gripped in my pre-teen hand, I wrote of how I'd put it down after a few minutes since the story I'd wanted to write, about a girl going out to travel a hard road, had been too difficult to imagine out of nothing. After two pages of this memory filled the screen, I was struck silent and realized the story I'd tried to write then was the one I'd first had to live.

From that moment forward, the words, which came from

a place I hadn't been able to tap into before, consumed my life, and flowed out of me daily. They recounted every painful memory of the life that lay behind me, and with a new ability to analyze their meaning, I was able to piece together the patterns that had stuck my experiences, no matter the changing years or faces, on repeat. The hours disappeared and felt like minutes, as I wrote for both the pure joy it brought and to heal the wounds I was finally facing. The patterns I uncovered were universal in nature, and while my experiences were tough, they weren't any worse than what many handled and were far easier than what those that society defined as a victim endured.

My arsenal of books had changed my understanding entirely, and I viewed the events I was depicting from the perspective of the soul that had planned them. While there was no denying that a lot had been painful, and during this period of remembering, it was challenging to recollect even one event that had been happy, I could appreciate the role each had served. Seeing how everything had been orchestrated to knock me down so I would draw on my strength to stand back up, I had a new, empowered appreciation for my life. Happy, I was finally finding my true voice, one that had been squelched silent by so many that my soul had hired to trigger me so I would connect these dots, clear the patterns, and find my power.

Knowing that all the players were people I had karmic contracts with from previous lives, I decided to check in to one in particular. A broken boy I'd lived with in my twenties, whom I'd felt driven to save, while the weight of his wounds had silenced me. Leaving the city and friends I'd loved behind, in my early twenties, to live with him down south, I'd isolated myself in a life where his anger had been triggered whenever I'd voiced my feelings. Wanting to appease him, I'd eventually grown silent and lost myself in his shadow.

On the day I wrote about this move, that I'd chosen voluntarily, it felt like a hammer struck my head. Setting the words aside, I wandered the streets in a stupor. I saw so clearly, for the first time ever, that this decision had been a fork in my road, and how when I'd made it, I'd chosen to walk away from my happiness. Of my own making, I'd taken a path that had led my life to play out in what, at that moment, felt like the most painful way possible.

After five years that had been full of the continuous pain of living with him, I'd revolted, and that had eventually drawn his hands to wrap themselves around my neck, which led me to leave the life that had nearly destroyed my heart. I'd then proceeded to run straight into the arms of one unavailable man and crumbling company after another. Unconsciously, I'd been afraid to trust the choices made by the girl who'd chosen him, and I could only commit to things that were bound to fail, so I wouldn't risk becoming trapped by my loyalty to anything or anyone again. Having already seen this pattern years earlier, I now worked to release the energy around it, which I knew was keeping me stuck in failure. So I booked another session with my healer, to look into any past life connection I might have to this broken boy, in case the energy from them was still impacting this life.

While I waited for that, and with my eyes more fully open, I realized my golden man had also been one of those men that hadn't been available. It didn't deter me from continuing to believe there had been, and still was, more to our connection than that pattern, but I knew it was imperative I be honest and heal whatever was unhealthy between us. With a clear mind, I could see the patterns we'd triggered in each other, but it didn't worry me because I knew we were both changing and once healed would be able to have something even more glorious than before.

Starting with him, I saw how similar I'd been to the wife who fed their finances and paid for his life. He wasn't a user, as the devil had suggested, but was a man who'd become used to someone else taking care of him, which made his desire to learn how to stand on his own so vital. Knowing I'd never had any desire to control him, I could still see that the gifts I'd given were a slippery slope and another form of the support she'd lent. If he'd replaced his wife's presence with mine, then we would have fallen into their same pattern, which would have eventually broken us just like it did them.

Turning to myself, I reflected on how once my confidence had started to shake, my fear that I didn't matter had risen to the surface. It began to show through the afternoon I'd stepped forward to stake my claim on him shortly before his wife had returned. Not with her, but with a woman that had flowers woven into her hair, which he'd commented on while standing near her at a coffee shop counter. Stood two steps back, my reflexes had instantly moved me to stand by his side, so she would know he belonged to someone and wasn't open for the taking.

Revolted by the memory, I could see how my unworthiness had driven those actions that had been unnecessary. Even if she'd held a brief hope of what that innocent encounter might lead to, my faith in us should have stayed secure. Instead, the fear that I wasn't as good as someone who wore a crown of petals had gotten the better of me.

Then there was a similar experience soon after his wife had returned, when he'd told me of a brief conversation with a stranger, held on the subway. Scared of this new woman that meant nothing, but had been able to see him when I couldn't, I'd made a joke that wasn't funny – "Didn't I tell you to wear a bag over your head?" In hindsight, I could see what I hadn't then. I didn't believe I was good enough for someone as golden as him.

Then came the one that completely shocked me. Positive I'd wanted us to be together once he'd moved out of their married home, I hadn't realized that I was scared of that much commitment. Having him in my life without the safety of a wife in the wings had made the relationship too difficult to envision. Unconscious to that fear then, I could see the truth now in the way I'd balked inside when he'd suggested he pay for the inking of the owl upon his return. Wanting to give me something in return for what he'd received, I hadn't been able to fathom tying him to something that would last a lifetime. Thinking at the time that I was being logical, I hadn't understood I didn't have faith that our love would last as long as that image.

Moving on to the pattern we shared, I reflected on how

I'd felt, even at the time, how unhealthy it was that we'd spent every hour, when his son wasn't with him, with each other. My pondering reminded me of the co-dependency that had littered my life before him, and I realized his need had triggered mine. His burning desire to be together constantly had given me the comfort that came with never having to stand alone, which was similar to how I'd lived with the broken boy, as well as a few close friends that had come both before and after. Each relationship had crushed me when one person after another had abandoned what hadn't been healthy.

Having stood alone for a few years before I'd met my golden man, part of me had unconsciously rebelled against that pattern repeating itself with him. Resistance to it had sprung up when he'd suggested that someday we'd frequent the same gym together. This had instantly triggered a memory of my time with the broken boy; when every hour, including the one we'd worked out in, had been spent together. I hadn't wanted to live that way again, but since the wounds behind that pattern were yet to be healed, my voice hadn't raised any issues with his suggestion. Instead of learning from my past, I'd gone ahead and grown dependent on the presence of his golden light in my life, until he'd removed it. Without any sign that it would come back once we were both healed, I trusted he was doing his work and kept focusing on everything I needed to break free from to deem myself healthy.

Despite making these connections that would lead to more healing, and wanting to know more, I still hadn't asked my healer to look into any past lives had with this man I shared a profound connection to. I trusted her, but not enough to entrust her with that. I could tell by her tone, whenever he was mentioned, that she neither understood nor approved of him. The night of the cord-cutting incident, she'd sounded slightly disgusted as she informed me that he was full of fear. This news hadn't surprised me, all it'd brought up was my compassion for him since I knew the struggles he was enduring. I hadn't taken her feelings personal but had decided to avoid talking to her about him.

With no intention of asking her for any help regarding

him, I was shown by those above that I was the only one who could help us. It came through in a vivid dream that was more like a journey to another time and place. Sure that it was occurring in real time somewhere, I saw two angelic women, invisible to a cafeteria full of people in front of them, as they watched a scene play out between a younger version of *us*. Sat on opposite sides of the room, *I*, at least the *I* who existed there, stood and walked over closer to where *he* was sitting. *I* was hoping to attract *his* attention, but *he* refused to look up. Disappointed, *I* sidestepped *his* table at the last minute and threw away the tray *I* was holding.

Saddened, one of the two watching, questioned – "Can't we help them?" Responding, I overheard the other say – "They have to do this themselves." Trying to cheer the mood, she added – "She's awake in another life." Then followed it up with the twist I was already aware of – "…but he's still in a coma." Not understanding it entirely, I felt grateful for this glimpse into this other reality, as I pondered the meaning of what I'd seen the next morning. Taking it as confirmation that I was on the right track, I continued to move forward with my healing and hold on to the belief that there were greater forces at play in this relationship.

Then, at our pre-appointed hour, I sat down with my healer for our next session, excited to clear my past life connection to the broken boy I'd shared a portion of this one with. Now that I understood the energy that bound people together, I wanted any with him that was keeping me from making a commitment to be cleared. My healer pre-empted by promising he was paying for what he'd done to me in the life she'd found, throughout this one. With my knowledge of his tortured childhood, I understood how but had no desire for him to suffer. Still, I kept my feelings quiet. Having seen there were no cords from this life still in place, she talked me through the trauma from a past life that she'd cleared out of my system, as well as a portal she'd closed that had been keeping my energy tied to a parallel life we were still sharing.

Married to each other five lives ago, I'd been a vocal woman in a society that didn't approve of that from what was considered the weaker sex. Undeterred, I'd kept speaking my thoughts loudly and publicly. Shamed by me, he'd shunned me and taken sides with the leaders of our community to have me excommunicated from our village. Cast out, I'd been left to wander – abandoned and isolated – in a time when a woman left on her own had no option except to give up on life.

Having told me what I needed to know, she didn't go into details on the death that had been brought down upon me, but from the sound of her voice, I knew it hadn't been pleasant. Connecting the dots, I understood why our relationship in this life had been filled with so many attempts on his part to silence me. With the trauma of that existence cleared, she promised the fear from it, which had kept me from speaking out in this life, would no longer affect me.

Content that he was out of this life and that the one she'd cleared was no longer holding me back, I was saddened when she went on to detail the life where *I* was still living with *him*. A parallel one, which existed one life over, was occurring simultaneously and resembled this life more closely than the others that fanned further out into the universe. In that one, *I* had made a different decision that had branched the life *I* was living off in a difficult direction. Choosing to stay with *him*, *I* was raising two children that weren't mine. Trapped, *I* had completely given up on *my* dreams.

Shocked, it all made sense. Calling to mind the time I'd tried to convince him that we should raise his younger brother, who'd come to stay for the summer, I already knew the identity of one of those two children. This boy's home life had been difficult, and I'd wanted to change the course of his future, but hadn't considered that doing so would change mine drastically. My broken boyfriend had said no but had obviously buckled in this other timeline. Unable to help the "me" that was living over there, my healer closed the portal connecting me to that disappointment. I felt a tremendous sorrow at the knowledge that there was a version of me anywhere still living that broken life with him, but I wanted nothing more to do with it.

With the weight of so much sadness lifted off me and with the days heating, the joy I felt was increasing. I started to sense a shift in my golden man, as well. On a day I played hooky from writing, to feel the sun beating down on a nearby beach, I spontaneously felt him regain his footing. Standing on the cusp of the ocean, while looking out into the endless expanse of blue in front of and above me, I was told he finally felt like he was on solid ground again. It came as a heightened awareness of the sand below my feet, which felt unbelievably solid. Despite only lasting a moment, the strength of it shot its meaning straight into my mind.

Closely followed by a vision, I saw him on another day, as clearly as if he was in front of me. It came on in the middle of an afternoon and revealed he'd regained his balance. He was sitting straight up, back firm, but with a flexible ease, as his legs straddled a bike that wasn't moving. I knew the meaning it held for his life, and my joy for him was beyond measure. With the first year mark fast approaching, I was also overjoyed for myself because of what I'd been told would happen.

Feeling lighter, I went on to ponder what to do with the book I thought was finished and decided the best course of action was to self-publish the words I'd written. Not wanting anyone to tell me to change what I'd written to make it more marketable, I was afraid I'd buckle under their pressure and wanted to protect the newfound voice that was still finding its power. Plus, it would be faster. Wanting to let go of the past, I believed this release was a step that had to be taken before my future could start, so I rushed it.

My guides tried to warn me against it. Across one week, everywhere I went, one woman after another ran straight by me at full speed, only to trip and fall flat on her face. It didn't matter where I was; they appeared and fell, repeatedly. My mind kept telling them to slow down, and I finally got the message that their falls were screaming at me.

I knew I needed to stop rushing it, but my heart, which hadn't stopped yearning for his presence, didn't want to be patient for one minute longer. My mind, positive that for him to return, I had to overcome my fear of being seen, decided to put this book, which declared loudly that I wasn't perfect, out into the world. So I tried to force what I wanted him to do and published it before I was done with the work. I wouldn't see, until months later, all the typos and grammatical errors I'd missed that still had to be cleaned up. Eyes averted to them, I was filled with hope, and I expected success for it to come at the same time as he did.

I didn't sit back quietly and wait for it to happen. Creating a plan to market it, I tied its promotion to my healing. All efforts were geared towards helping me face my fear of being seen and heard by strangers. Walking across the paved pathways of two public squares, on two different days, I approached one person after another and handed them cards that quoted the words I'd written. Not expecting any sales to come of that activity, I did it to break out of the fear that had always driven me to hide in others' shadows.

It took a month to ramp up to the next fear-facing activity, but I finally worked up the nerve to post a link, on Facebook, to the page where my book was being sold. I'd always worn the face of perfection and worked hard to hide the things about myself that I didn't think were a match for the lifestyle I wanted to inhabit, so to come out in the open with all my insecurities was pure torture. Friends, ex-colleagues and previous bosses, as well as near and distant acquaintances, would all see it and that petrified me. But I reasoned I had to be willing to do it if I wanted him to voice his feelings about me to the world. I did it and then stood back, with eyes covered, waiting for the fallout. None came, and neither did he.

While it was valued as having a unique voice by a few I knew and a few that had never met me, my book was quickly lost amongst the millions of titles that surrounded it. Leading me to lose some faith and slip backward. With my savings running out, I was forced to make a tough decision. Could I continue to believe everything would work out and wait for what I believed was coming? Or did I take a job I knew I'd hate? Having turned down plenty in the months preceding the one I'd been told he would return in, I couldn't see around the next corner and despite knowing faith meant believing in what couldn't be seen, fear took over, and I accepted a position I didn't value.

It was a job with a company that many would think meant I'd succeeded at life, but I knew the truth. I was working for an acclaimed publication that I'd once enjoyed reading, but I was sitting on the wrong side of the fence internally. Those that wrote for it strode its halls with the same passion and purpose that I felt for my writing, but those that sold their words, which was the team I was a part of, were sidelined and cut off from them. I wandered the halls aimlessly, daily, trying to kill the hours that I was trapped there. The boss who was over me had tightened her grip on those below me upon seeing my duties eating into hers and with a fear for her job pressing down from above, had pushed me into an empty corner to do nothing. This lack of purpose, along with the heaviness in the air, generated by almost every member of my team voicing their dissatisfaction and desire to get out of there, was suffocating.

Daily, and nightly, I felt the depression of a soul that wanted to move forward but was stuck. The happiness I'd gained slowly drained out of me across the eight hours a day I spent there. The only way I could fall asleep, on the nights that led to another day of death, was to hold my bound words close to my heart and repeat – "I'm doing this for my book." The thought of leaving behind the money it was sending my account, or the connections I might make while walking its halls, kept me there, trapped in fear.

REBORN

REBORN

YEAR TWO

REBORN

CHAPTER 7
THE WEIGHT OF FEAR
MONTHS 1-5 OF YEAR 2

No call came to break through my despair, but I felt him try to make it, repeatedly. On a morning I was rushing through the streets, coming home from a random location, I was overcome with the desire to reach out to a woman I hadn't thought of enough to speak to in the 10 years since we'd been friends while living in a different city. The urge was irresistible, so I wrote and let her know I was ecstatic to see how happy she looked in all the photos she was posting on Facebook. Within minutes of hitting send the feeling faded, and it was replaced by shock, mingled with slight embarrassment, that I'd sent such an emphatic message to someone who was basically a stranger. Then I understood, almost immediately, that this was his feeling I'd picked up and acted on. The next would bring the first sign of action I'd sensed from him in a year.

After a few weeks of the agonizing pressure brought on by a job my soul wanted me out of and within a couple months of my book's release, I realized he'd read it. Glancing at the page that showed the few sales I was managing to garner, I wasn't thinking about him when a spike on the chart, symbolizing one sale, resonated and my gut shouted his name, telling me he'd purchased it. The following week was filled with emotional spikes that came out of nowhere. One occurred in the middle of another walk from one random spot to another. His sadness over my past experiences filled him, and me, with his desire to give me everything I deserved that I'd never received. Not sure why he didn't show up and do it, I could only assume he wasn't finished with what he was doing for his family but knew that by going to this daily death of a job I was killing my joy and making it harder to attract the happiness I wanted with him.

With my knowledge of the laws of attraction filling my brain, I let my soul lead the way and chose the life I wanted by quitting the job I hated. Giving plenty of notice so my savings could be replenished slightly, I knew they were nowhere close to the level needed to warrant such a risky move. So it was no surprise when, on one of my last days there, fear set in and pushed me to reach out to an old boss, whose company I'd left two years earlier because of the overwhelming exhaustion the work had brought on.

Telling him I was available to freelance seemed logical at the moment, but what I felt compelled to add was nowhere close to professional. The voice that was linked to my golden man was speaking again, and if I hadn't known it was his, I would have added – "I'm sorry I left the way I did. I wasn't healthy then, but I am now!" Resisting sending a second round of emphatic words to someone they weren't intended for, I laughed at myself and silently told any part of him that could hear me that I understood.

After the last day of that job ended, I went back to my real work and started ridding myself of more layers of what needed releasing. It came naturally. The fear that still had to go wouldn't show its face in the hours that were lit, but it started to wake me nightly. Terror pulled my mind out of sleep as it cycled through different areas of my body, and I knew, for no reason other than I knew myself too well to be fooled any longer – that this was a combination of all the fear both of us felt.

We were mirroring each other and what I was picking up of his was triggering what already existed inside of me. I felt and dealt with all of it each time it woke me, and I knew I would continue to do it for however long it took to rid us of its damning influence. Resurrecting the practice of sitting back and observing everything, I felt every painful ache that jerked through my body until the fear dissipated enough to allow me a few more hours of exhausted sleep. Nearly every night of the next two months was spent sweating it out in agony, and while I still didn't know why, I knew I was the one who had to do it for the both of us.

His wasn't the only man's fear I was picking up on. While sitting at my parent's kitchen table, one quiet morning during a weekend visit, the calmness I felt was attacked by the fear-fueled thought – "What's going to become of me?" The sudden onset of what I hadn't been thinking or feeling swept over me quickly, but by then, I knew enough to say to myself – "This isn't mine." That dispelled the hold it had over me quickly, and I looked over at my father sitting to my right and knew I'd just felt the fear he had for my future.

Not wanting to scare him, there was nothing I could do to stop it since there was no way for me to explain why I was making choices that completely broke with the norms of society and made me look like I'd lost my sanity. Smiling inside, I knew if I told him the truth, then he would really question my mental soundness. I doubted my own sanity plenty but reasoned this doubt proved I hadn't gone off the deep end since someone who had would never even raise the question.

It wasn't just feelings that kept me going. The messages my guides sent provided hope whenever I faltered. On yet another walk – this time, one in which sadness surrounded me and whispered how much easier it would be to give up entirely – I was startled to hear his name spoken out loud. It came from the mouth of a passing stranger, who for a split second as she was beside me, voiced – "You just have to hang out with Eric!" Said to her friend, I knew it was meant to give me something to hold on to. That along with the name of his son, which I was hearing five times a day, seven days a week, told me to hold on because his little boy was still the primary focus of his existence.

Hoping to amplify my healing, while my man did what needed to be done by his child, I decided to call on a different healer. One I thought might be more powerful because she held the title of a shaman. It was the woman the devil had told me to stay away from, but having discounted everything else he'd said, this warning wasn't heeded. After talking myself into her hourly rate, which wouldn't have been spare change even if my work status had been different, we had an initial introduction, which was held via Skype since she was spending some time on the other side of the country. I told her during this exchange that my desire was to uncover the root cause of the fear that riddled my life.

She saw it instantly. Not the cause, but the fear that was trapped in my eyes. She said I looked like I was still in shock from something terrible I'd just witnessed. Adding that there was an energetic "kick me" sign pasted on my back, which I'd placed there myself, she promised to uncover the past life causing both. She would do her work while I slept, later in her day and during my night, so we scheduled a time to regroup the next day, to go over the results.

Waiting patiently at the appointed hour, with my computer sat on my lap, her call never came. The message I sent, asking if something had come up that required us to reschedule went unanswered. Initially annoyed, my sixth sense told me not to push it. I didn't understand what had happened but felt a newfound aversion towards this woman I'd paid to help me. Despite the money she'd taken, that I felt should rightfully have brought me a report, I set what was due me aside and went back to working on myself while my man's thoughts periodically broke through.

Even though he wasn't speaking to me, I could hear him thinking whether or not he wanted to. I felt it all rattle off distinctly when I left the gym after one of my daily workouts. Going from the joy of an endorphin rush to the anxious fear of uncertainty, in an instant, my mind cried – "What would I even write?" With no intention of breaking through the boundaries of his cocoon, I knew this was his thought, not mine, coming up.

After pushing away my fear of him writing, which took me by surprise when I noticed it mingled in with his, pure happiness set in at the thought of what he was contemplating, and I continued on to run some errands. Then, while in the middle of getting my eyebrows sculpted, a painful experience that normally leaves no room for one's mind to wander, I was guided into the beauty of our memories and heard the decisive statement – "No one can take those away from us!" Since no one in my life was currently trying to, I knew he'd just regained some of his joy for what had been heavily attacked after the discovery of our texting history.

Leaving the salon, my feet bounced on the pavement lightly, before I was hit by a wave of resentment, as my mind voiced – "I can have whatever I want!" For me, in that moment, it connected itself to the desire for a slice of pizza, which made me laugh since I had one of those at least once a week and no one, including myself, was telling me I couldn't. Then, arriving home, panic took over, and a fear of the career I'd once performed at a senior level rose to the surface, and I questioned – "Am I even capable of doing it again?" That's all I needed to hear. I didn't know when it would happen, but in that moment a sliver of faith returned, and I knew once the fear of being in a committed relationship again disintegrated, my golden man would find his way back into my life.

Knowing I could only help him by removing all the energetic blocks standing in our way, I still didn't know how big a fight lay ahead. I was given fair warning though, through a question posed by a stranger. I heard it on a night I went out, on a spur, to enjoy a show with a new friend I'd made at the energy center. We went to watch her man sing the songs he'd written, at a dive bar in Brooklyn. Walking in, a woman smoking outside glanced down at the camo print on my pants, then looked up and stared directly into my eyes while asking with a serious tone – "Are you ready to fight?" Knowing what she meant, even though she didn't, I stared back with determination and said – "I am."

While I continued to fight my battles against our fears, and periodically heard his doubts, there were signs that tried to warn me I had to leave the home I was doing it all in. The home I didn't know was still filled with more than human thoughts and feelings. The warnings pressed me with an urgency I picked up on, but not wanting to let go of it, I ignored them, and with a fresh signature made the wrong move. I committed myself to another year of living beside the spirit who I hadn't felt since my healer had said she'd gotten rid of him, but who was still inhabiting the space he considered his home.

A month into my new lease and with my options limited by a severe financial penalty, his silent presence reached out again. The gust of his entrance flowed in as I was standing in the bathroom, staring into the wells of my eyes as they mirrored my thoughts back to me, and I silently acknowledged to myself that someone had come in through the other room's open window. Brushing the feeling aside, as I brushed through my hair, I moved forward on the path I wouldn't walk away from.

The signs kept screaming at me to move away from the death living there and those from above, who were trying to guide me, did their best to get me to listen at every turn. Daily exits from my home sent me straight into trucks stationed on the street, working to move someone else out. One word – MOVERS – taped to every pole, kept drawing my attention and repeatedly shouted that someone out there wanted to help me get out of there. Spoken from the lips of the lone stranger, who turned to look directly at me while walking by one day, I heard it clearly – "She has to move." Followed quickly by another statement that meant nothing to anyone else on the street, including her, but everything to me – "And he's still in prison." It was clear this woman, who looked mentally unstable, had been sent to deliver the words she was an open receiver for, and the repetitive call broke through. But without understanding the full extent of it, my love for the home I felt a deep connection to won out over common sense and kept me stuck in a place anyone would have run from.

My acceptance of this spirit grew as his strength and desire to help me became visible the night I forced myself to face my fear of speaking. An old pain resurfaced while I found the courage needed to get up on a stage and tell of the time my voice had been choked quiet by the broken boy I'd once known. Tears ran as I opened up and prepared myself to read the section of my book that turned the pain inflicted by him into a piece of beauty. Distracted by what lay ahead, I forgot to pick up the bag of trash I'd placed by the door, waiting to be taken down on my way out. Remembering as I hit the street, I decided to leave it for later.

Returning, elated from the reading that had elicited strangers' emotions, joy turned to shock when I reached for what was gone. Searching everywhere, I questioned my sanity. The certainty that I hadn't taken it down earlier, led to an obvious question – "Had someone else done it for me?" Setting that thought aside, I laughed at myself and chose to believe I'd done it and then forgotten my movements.

That wasn't the only thing I was forgetting. Despite the messages I was receiving, and its nightly purging, fear was overrunning all memories of my love. With the days taking me months out from when I'd expected his return, I was losing sight of the little faith I had left to hold on to. When my eyes were shut, his face, whose beauty I'd once seen so clearly, twisted itself into the mask of a red-faced devil. Not sure what to believe anymore, I couldn't understand what was taking him so long. There was only one thing, which my mind continually whispered could be the case, and the fear of another woman having replaced me let my doubt in our love root itself in even deeper.

The evil face I'd never seen while with him, that kept trying to scare me into losing sight of the man I knew he was, repeatedly appeared during a restorative yoga/chakra cleansing class that was created to be relaxing. Each session focused every move on clearing out one of the chakras, working on all of them across seven months. This one, in particular, was linked to the third eye and was yet another attempt by me to clear my vision.

What I ended up seeing, throughout the entire two hours spent in the most comfortable poses I'd ever been in, filled me with terror. Despite my relaxing muscles, tension rose as my man's face appeared and shifted into the hideous mask I feared was a sign that he was as manipulative as the devil-man had once suggested. With the moves working their magic, it eventually faded, never to return. What came next, in quick succession, was a phrase and vision that led me to believe I was destined to die young. Starting with a line that confused me, I heard – "You didn't need it anyway." – when the retirement fund I'd just cashed out to live on popped to mind. Then I saw a pile of my own ashes.

Jolted and numbed with shock at this information, I rose at the end of those two hours, one of 30 faces in a crowd, and turned with everyone to thank the teacher who'd led us through our movements. That's when she caught my eye, and I heard – "That had to come up so it could leave you." Realizing I had a deep fear of my golden man, I hoped I would never see the devil in him again and left the session resigned to my personal fate. Walking home, I reasoned that if I was meant to die, then so be it; I'd lived a life I could be proud of and had done everything with the best of intentions. I was just sorry I wouldn't get to see my nieces and nephews grow up.

After an hour of this type of resigned thinking, the true meaning behind the message broke through. It wasn't a physical death I was going to face, at least not yet. The work I was doing was changing the person I'd been and was going to change my life even more than it already had. Until the one I'd been living was dead and buried behind me. Elated that I was going to live and feeling that what was coming was better than what was dying, relief flooded my being.

Then my past came forward to try to trick me into trapping myself in an old pattern, but I resisted. Making plans to meet up with another man whose exit had once hurt me, the devil tried to tempt me through him. Meeting five years after the broken boy had exited and five years before the golden man had entered my life, we'd dated briefly and then become friends when it was clear he wasn't meant to be my love. From then on we'd met for drinks once or twice a year. He was someone I felt a connection to and wanted to be friends with, even though during those early drinks I'd still had deeper feelings for him.

The day of this meet-up brought in a surprise blizzard that led me to suggest we cancel. Pressing me to still meet, he agreed to walk over the snow-packed streets from where he lived across town, to one of the few bars still open two blocks away from where I lived. I went despite not having any desire, since the only thing I truly wanted was to be with the man I still loved, especially on that day, which was his 40th birthday.

Keeping that to myself, I ended up enjoying the time I spent with this man, whom at 10 years my senior had called himself an old man since the moment I'd met him. Acutely aware of age, he warned me to start dating again before it was too late for me. Feeling no fear of that, since to me age was only mental, and I didn't have a biological clock ticking, I knew I would ignore his advice.

Despite the words I didn't agree with, I agreed to head back to my place after, so we could share a smoke. Facing each other, while sitting on opposite ends of the couch I'd once snuggled in on with my golden man, we spoke about his woman; the one he lived with that was away for the weekend. She was someone he loved, even though he didn't understand her belief that it would make them a stronger couple if they were both free to do what they wanted with other people, as long as the other never found out about it. Understanding the implication for the moment, I pretended to believe him when he said it wasn't an arrangement he wanted.

Not having read my first book yet, which detailed our brief time as a couple, he asked me to read him a few sections from it. I did and enjoyed every minute of this poetic moment. Then I felt a pull that shocked me. Something was energetically drawing him towards me. Intense, it felt like it came from outside of both of us, but aware of it, I had enough warning to ponder the situation while I watched his leg reach out and rest itself on mine. Seeing his vision become clouded by the fog that surrounded us, I voiced what I felt – "Nothing can happen. I won't do that to your woman. And more importantly, I won't do it to myself. I deserve better."

Knowing this man truly cared for me as a person, I wasn't surprised when he looked pleased that I finally had an idea of what I was worth. Having fought off whatever this spell was that had been trying to lead me down a path that wouldn't have led anywhere good, we continued to chat for a little while longer. Then he stood to leave, and I rose to hug him goodbye. With arms briefly wrapped around each other, he pressed – "Would one kiss be so terrible?" Answering yes, I wished him a good night and sensed it would be the last one we saw each other in since it felt like the right resolution to this relationship.

Soon after I heard a new directive from someone sat next to me in a woman's full moon circle. I'd joined these in the hopes of finding a new community of like-minded individuals and to feel the support of being surrounded by others who were striving to connect to their souls. At the beginning of each everyone always briefly voiced the current challenge they were facing and each time I marveled at how synchronistic every woman's experience was to mine, which we were told was what always happened. The universe drew people together based on their similarities.

While one woman repeated advice she'd recently heard concerning herself, I knew to take it on when, while inadvertently looking straight at me, she said – "Go on a date." Not sure why I was being guided in that direction since up until then every message had been geared towards focusing on myself while supporting a reunion with my golden man, I decided to follow the advice and see what I was supposed to learn from this experience. So I started swiping again.

One name each, two shared interests and five pictures apiece. Our matching energy led us to both swipe in the right direction, and after a few messages that bounced the right kind of words between us, we met and guided each other through the eighteen hours that would give me the first touch of intimacy I'd had in eighteen months. Both of us knowing, before even meeting, that his flight out limited the amount of time we could share. Before the profound awareness, that came by the end, of time shared in another life. For this one, we both only had this to give.

For him, because he'd built his life to be lived wild and protected the freedom he worshiped. Sustaining it by living in two vans that were moved to every corner of the countries in which they were stationed. Then, when not in them, he crossed continents to reconnect with souls he'd met along the way. Traveling through every type of wilderness the world offered; he photographed all of it, including the strangers across it that spilled their life stories to him. While they spoke, he led by example, showing how one lived free of the binds that he thought limited life's experiences.

For me because I still knew, despite my faltering faith, that I'd already connected with the one man who ran deeper than even a soul mate. The one I couldn't see because of the blocks separating us, but could always feel as close to me as I was to myself. For now, while he took the time needed to heal his soul, I chose to take a break, from battling the blocks inside of me, and let this wild soul into my life.

He came with a promise, from me, to act as his guide, so he could capture the beauty of NYC's east side as seen through the eyes of someone who called it home. Walking up, as I sat outside the coffee shop I'd typed out the story of my life at, he carried the equipment he used to photograph his. Standing a full foot taller and bristling with a long beard, I didn't find him as attractive as my love, but the kindness of his soul quickly shined from his light blue eyes, as he held out his hand to say hello. The hand that would later show me what my hard work, clearing out what was weighing me down, had led me to become.

I planned to show him the small park a few blocks over. The one whose wild nature spoke to me every morning, as I reveled in the beauty of its trees while contemplating the flow of my life. Before starting our joint wander, we sat down, and I opened up. Comfortable sharing the depth of my thoughts with him within minutes, neither knowing what we would share in the hours ahead. It started with a mention of my reminiscing, while I'd been waiting, over the writing I'd done in the spot we were sitting. That led to me reading, and him listening intently, to some of those words that had flowed from my soul.

After his private reading, we stood to walk, passing through the community garden that he lamented looked like one losing its life. Surprised by what he saw; I'd intended he see the heart of the locals who cultivated it. Those who were celebrating the life of one of their own, at that moment, across its dusty surface. He couldn't see that but took a few shots inside and then one from the out directed up at the fading masks, created out of life's recyclables, which lined the top of the fence circling it. His wildness spoke up against the way my city strangled the life out of its nature, and he couldn't understand how anyone could live near so little. My heart railed against that, and I spoke about what bounces between all the people, that are its biggest source of energy, and how that's what drew those here that chose this life.

Walking into the park, we were drawn to the sound of people composing a spontaneous rhythm, as they instinctively beat their hands on top of drums they had brought there. We sat in an open seat, and while squeezed between its iron arms, felt the energy being drummed into the air, and I let the goodness of his envelope me. That's when I decided I'd let him through the barrier I'd constructed and would touch my lips to ones that didn't belong to those of the one man I still wanted mine to touch. I knew this wouldn't feel the same, but I wanted to feel it, so I opened myself up to wherever my time with this man guided me.

We rose so he could take a few shots as we weaved through the blocks neighboring my park; their walls colored over to bring towering scenes to life, and make one stop in wonder at the beauty free flowing out of people into the world. His camera memorized the pieces nature would wash away, and then the chilling air drove us inside to share a few small plates while a glass of wine each warmed us.

The conversation from early on came back and led us both into our authenticity. He shared stories of the parents that had raised him to wander. The childhood started next to the sea's cliffs in England, before crossing over so he could grow to cherish the raw landscape of Canada, and then instilled a love for the natural beauty living in Africa. He spoke of his profound connection to the mother whose death, in his 20s, killed his nine-to-five life and drove him back to Africa, where he lived a year in solitude, surrounded by everything else that was happier living wild.

He explained his unrestrained ways but also spoke of the three women he'd been connected to, at each of their own times, across his life. His lasting love for them shined through and led me to describe mine to him. The unconditional love for the one my heart told me to hold out for until he could grow free enough to feel it again, but that would preserve its place even if he never chose to show his for me again. Halting in the telling, I made sure he knew this wasn't stopping me from seeing him as a man. He understood, and we accepted each other's truth.

Having grown closer sharing our lives and our food, I invited him back to the quiet comfort of my apartment, so we could continue our conversation over cups of tea. On the walk over, I stopped to explain my intentions more clearly. I let him know that no decision had been made, one way or the other, on what would happen once we were alone, and that going in wasn't a signal. I went on to add that I would choose in the moment, but if he wanted more, then he should get some protection with the chocolate he was about to pick up. Admiring the bluntness, he let me know he would respect whatever I decided.

We drank our tea, as our voices spoke thoughts we agreed on, and I felt the energy between us heating. The kiss he leaned over to give me, the first I'd wanted in over a year, felt like I'd expected, but I'd already decided I wasn't ready for anything requiring protection. I didn't want to go that far with him, but I wanted to get closer and connect with the part of myself lying dormant.

We went far enough for the sound that came out of him to match his look, as he roared like any wild bear would. Far enough that it shifted the block of fear inside that was keeping me from getting close to any man, including my own. The shift in energy shook my heart; picking up on it, he switched his tone while wrapping me up in gentleness. The fear that I could be hurt tried to come up and overwhelm me, but I refused to let it take over; running it out instead through the tears that fell. Holding me in the safe space we'd created, he told me what he was feeling. Freely, he said – "I love you."

I felt his truth, and while I knew it was only going to last for a moment, I appreciated it. Then later, I tapped into what his eyes saw while looking at me. The beauty I'd started to transform into, by stretching and twisting out all the painful energy that had been trapped inside of me, was shining through in every move I was making while with him. I told him he was helping me see myself, so he started tracing all of my lines while voicing what each of the moves I'd held with growing power, during my yoga practice, had sculpted. We shared in this intimacy until we grew tired and then agreed that he would sleep over, so we could wake up next to each other.

With no pressure from either at night, the morning was free of regret, since what we shared hadn't gone further than where I intended. Tented in a moment of brightness that he constructed by pulling the whiteness of the sheet up high over and above us, I was taken back into a feeling. I couldn't remember where, but I felt a glimmer of the two of us together in the exact same way in a completely different place. The moment which I realized was from another life, came on and then passed by quickly. I told him and, for reasons of his own, he believed the same. I understood our more profound truth then. We were two souls that had agreed to meet again briefly, at a time when it would give us each something we needed. What I gave him is his truth to know. Mine is that the gentle soul of this wild man helped me see my power to create beauty and free myself from some of the fear blocking my love.

After the interlude of this man's short stay ended, the

other one, who wasn't my love either, returned. He came when a drop in my mood gave him a clear path to connect and ignite the feelings he thought were helping me. He turned my anger into a rage that got me screaming to the universe that I expected more from this life I'd worked so hard to heal. Having given up the career that was crushing me, to pursue the dream that fed my soul, I was exhausted by the fear of running out of money while I worked on making it happen. Having held on, without a word from my golden man, while willingly facing all of our pain that struck me, I was tired of shouldering the weight of this life alone, without his shoulder to rest on.

Ranting, I refused to continue down this path and promised to turn back if everything didn't get easier. The anger, rising with every word, turned me against my love, and swearing, I screamed – "I hope you're enjoying the woman you're fucking!" Thinking these feelings were only mine, the joy I felt just below the anger was frightening. Leaving the confines of my home, I moved myself away from the rage I didn't recognize. Going about my day, it dissipated. Then, returning to sleep that night, I was awakened by the spirit who was once again lying in the spot he considered his. The message he sent came through clearly, and my mind heard the words – "You're not alone. I'm here for you."

This wasn't the kind of help I wanted, in this life I was trying to fill with peace and positivity, and my fear screamed that this being was blocking what I wanted because he wanted to keep me close to him. The next morning I hurriedly sent a message to the healer who'd helped me with him before, to see if she could clear out what I hadn't invited in. Never thinking to tell her of the anger that had overwhelmed me, we spoke later that same day, and she echoed the message that had already been pounded into my head. The only thing to do was to move.

With thousands of souls trapped on my home's land by their deaths' tragedies, this wasn't a place where my sensitive soul could rest. She was shocked I'd been able to stay as long as I had. Able to clear many, but not all, she couldn't rid me of the spirit who'd decided he liked me. All she could see was that his unknown grief, over a loss suffered in a past life, had drawn him to me in my suffering. My fear surfaced when told that he loved my anger, and his connection couldn't be cut because a part of me liked having him there with me.

Feeling I was to blame for his presence brought on the knowledge that this home I loved was no longer a safe haven for me and may never have been. I felt utterly betrayed by myself. With no funds to break the contract obligating me to stay and nowhere to crash in the city I loved too much to leave, I tried to block this being that was blocking the happiness I'd worked so hard to find.

A frantic journey across town brought back enough stones for every corner of every room, door, and window; creating a grid that I was told would bar him. A quick stop at the corner store brought back enough salt for every door, window, grate, and hole; drawing a line across each, including across the inside ledge of the one my golden man had once pointed out was missing a cover, with the firm intention of keeping him from crossing over. This third attempt at protection, which made my home feel like a private prison, provided no sense of security, false or otherwise. The idea that the only move to make was to move out had been firmly planted.

Sweeping up all of the salt, but leaving the stones, I decided within a couple of weeks that my next course of action should be to let tourists book my home to stay in, during their visits to my city. I would book my own short stays in other people's homes across the city I refused to leave. But for the first one, I decided to go back and stay with my family in the town of my birth. That's when I started to learn the truth about the past lives I'd shared with the man whom, despite my doubts, my heart knew I was meant to share a future with.

CHAPTER 8
FINDING REASON
MONTHS 6-7 OF YEAR 2

With my hope for a peaceful life under attack, I soon found new hope thanks to a couple that helped people understand the ancient forces at play in their current lives. Their decades of knowledge had grown out of their extensive research into how the world's cultures had historically dealt with the universe's forces. Our call, set for a few days after the hurried exit from my home, had been scheduled a month prior.

They first reached me through a post sent out on Facebook, two months before I made that booking. It'd instantly stood out amongst the clutter. Drawn to it, I'd felt compelled to read more about the term they identified themselves as – twin flames. Its checklist of attributes struck more than one chord of similarity to my situation.

I learned in my reading that twin flames, despite the misleading name, are a romantic couple that when they first meet, enter into a bubble of pure bliss together, only to then be torn apart quickly and dramatically. Their meeting triggers the two, and they're both instantly catapulted into a major life change, which is always underscored by intense healing. While one takes on the role of the runner, the other chases, but both are energetically bound together through an emotional connection that can't be broken by anyone, not even either of them.

Their origin has differing explanations. Some say this couple has one soul that chose, eons ago, to split into two people. Each with a higher self that links them back to their one shared soul. Others believe they each have their own distinct soul, but that the two had once split off from the same original one. Either way, the two mirror each other's traits, as well as their wounding, and share one body of energy. Meeting in person, on this plane, brings them each the sense of coming home to the place they truly belong and hadn't realized they'd been longing to return to.

It's said that if either had been born into the other's circumstances, then identical decisions would have been made and the exact same life would have been lived. While a person can have many soul mates, ranging anywhere from a romantic relationship to a family member, each twin is only part of the one set of two. With this deeper connection linking them at a soul level, the one who runs remains encamped in the heart, mind, and body of the one who's already awakened to their soul's truth.

Twins choose their roles together, before incarnating, and rotate them repeatedly across the centuries. With each new life, the two take on the challenges needed to trigger and heal their wounds by re-living the lessons they hadn't managed to learn previously. But one thing remains the same across every incarnation – while the life of each is full of difficulties, the runner always takes on the harder path and becomes overwhelmed by the deep emotions that exist between them, while the chaser is freer to take on the task of doing the healing for both of them.

The reason for choosing this path, time after time, is out of a deep, soul-driven desire to help the world. Through their own personal healing, twins — the first wave of which numbers

144,000 — clear the negative energy impacting the collective. Unknown to the mainstream, but widely accepted in the spiritual community, it's known that everyone is energetically connected and recycling the same antiquated patterns through morphic fields of energy. Twins have the power to transmute those patterns for everyone by clearing them out of themselves.

Having lived this before I'd read it, every word resonated, even though I hated the name the relationship had been given. Sounding like it'd been born out of a pop song I would never listen to, its nod to siblings felt wrong, but it was the first thing I'd found that gave me a valid explanation for everything I'd been experiencing. But the doubt I felt over something, which sounded fantastical, was too strong to get past easily, so I set it aside initially. Only, those guiding from above wouldn't let me get off that easy. One article after another showed up in my feed, begging for attention, and the number of twins I started seeing daily became astronomical.

Part of me gave in to the possibility that we were one of these couples on the day I sat myself down on a bench and looked up to see, sat directly across from me, a set of teenage twins – one boy and one girl, both with red hair. I wasn't able to turn a blind eye any longer, especially not when it propelled me back into the memory of when, as a child, I'd been convinced, for no rational reason, that I had a twin out there somewhere. Trying to understand how what I'd felt to be my truth could be a fact, I'd questioned if I belonged to my parents. My childhood mind had pondered if I could have been separated from my other half by adoption, before age squelched the truth my intuition had felt.

Then this twin couple, that had mastered the healing these types of relationships needed, had been delivered to my doorstep, and despite my doubt underscoring everything they said, I was hooked from the first video I viewed. Full of both explanation and healing, I resonated with the former and felt the surge of power from the latter. Experiencing this across a few videos, one ignited something new in me. Waking in the middle of the night, which by then had become my routine, I sensed a golden light emanating out of my being spontaneously. With eyes shut, I felt no fear and knew this light streaming out of me was headed, like a beacon, straight to the man I'd once sent light to voluntarily. I felt its radiance and knew I was healing him with it.

From that moment on, I'd started doing their powerful healing daily, for both of us. It went deeper than anything else had before it. For the second time in my life, I felt myself lighten up more than I'd ever imagined possible, only matched by when I'd felt lighter because my golden man was beside me. With the weight of pain lifting, I started to connect to the parts of me I'd never been able to stay aligned to prior. Listening to everything, which was a lot, since they'd gathered plenty of material and gave it out across group calls held live weekly, I started to learn what my soul needed me to know.

Besides the healing, these calls gave information that provided answers as to why those I'd turned to, before that point, hadn't understood this connection. Anyone who wasn't a twin operated on a different frequency and couldn't see our truth, only the patterns our souls had incarnated into to heal. They also warned us away from psychic predictions related to timing, since free will was still in play, so anything other than someone's energy in the moment was near impossible to perceive. Not to mention all that was being flung at twins to delay and distract them. Along with this, they warned to never give our power away to anyone, not even them, and to only trust in what we felt was true.

Their sincerity and desire to help others shined through and was evident from the first of their words that I'd heard, and I knew I'd found my new healers. I would still tap into the help of the first one periodically, but these would be the ones I turned to in my battle to free the love I knew still existed. After a few weeks of getting caught up on all of their recordings, I'd booked the private session to obtain an analysis and deep healing of our personal situation. The night of my appointment finally arrived, and I sequestered myself upstairs in my parent's house, where I was hiding from the spirit that had scared me.

Having escaped his presence for the moment, my excitement

equally matched my fear of the information this call might bring to light. Timidly accepting the twin flame moniker, I worried they might tell me I'd been mistaken, or worse yet that I was correct in my thinking, but that he'd since met and entered into a relationship with another woman. I knew it was a possibility, both on a logical level and because their calls had explained that a response by a lot of runners, who were typically male, was to hide behind a woman they didn't feel the same depth of feeling for, and who therefore couldn't make them feel vulnerable.

That fear didn't come to light, but I heard a lot about us and where our fears had originated. They started with what I already knew about myself and confirmed I was sensitive and empathic to the degree that went well beyond a level even the oldest of souls attained. With a snort, I laughed and said – "No surprise there."

Taking it a step further, I finally heard that what I'd been feeling deeply and hadn't been able to shake no matter how much I'd healed was in fact real. With a steady influx of his feelings coming into me, which was matched by mine that were reaching him, we were both being constantly overwhelmed by the other's emotions. Relieved, the small part of me that still questioned my sanity was quieted for a few moments.

Moving on to the spirit in my home, they said he thought he was protecting me, and he was someone I'd known in a positive light in previous lives. Not seeing the depth of that connection, they knew he was a good soul being manipulated by a negative force trying to block the light from emanating out of me. Afraid of how low he would sink if I let go of him, I was doing what I'd learned to do so well before and letting myself drown to save him. Working the words that would clear him of negativity, they intended to help him rise up and move on to the path of his higher purpose. Regardless of this, my resolve was still set that I had to move, but that was a matter to be handled later. At that moment I was more concerned with the man I wanted to show up in whatever home I lived in.

The female half of this master couple, who spoke with a balanced and candid sensitivity, took it up a notch and explained the place our soul(s) called home. She saw clearly that he and I had come from a plane where those angelic in nature existed. Wanting to help the world heal, we'd been born programmed to do that, no matter the cost to us across each of our incarnations. Taking it a step further, she explained that we wanted to help so badly that we'd bypassed the process set in place before incarnating, to get here quicker. By doing that we came without the protection that others had in place around them. Having heard about a few tragic lives already and feeling the innate drive to heal that had taken over my current one, all the pieces came together. The only thing I still couldn't understand was why this man, whom I knew had felt our love while we'd been together, hadn't made it back already. They shed more light on that by explaining some of what lay behind our current separation.

Before doing that they answered a concern I'd raised by reassuring me I wasn't invading his privacy since his soul would only let them see and heal what was in his highest good. All else would be deflected. Then, turning to this life, I heard that the pain inflicted on him by his wife was the result of an attack that had been aimed at her, staged to load negativity onto him. The pain and jealousy that had been felt when she'd read our history had dropped her energy and left her wide open to it.

Wanting to stop the two of us from coming together, the darker forces in the universe, which this couple talked of openly, had magnified those feelings to the point of breaking her, so she'd turn and crush him. The result was the shaming and energetic tainting of every one of our memories, which had held nothing but the purest innocence when we'd lived them.

Clearing the three of us of some of the trauma and karma our triangle had created, they went on by going further back. Multiple lives surfaced, both as Amazon and Native American warriors, and wherever they occurred, in whichever time, the outcome had always been the same. Incarnating, again and again, into civilizations that were on the cusp of annihilation, we, but mostly he had tried to stop it. Then, when our efforts hadn't changed their fates, we'd shouldered the blame of being responsible for the destruction of everyone we'd loved.

Not realizing we hadn't been sent to save them, but to hold a safe space for their transition over to a new existence, we'd gone on to suck in all the pain and horror every person had felt. Over and again, we'd made the same mistake and had carried out the wrong mission. Our true reason for incarnating into so much death and destruction had been to act as beacons that drew others into the light, but forgetting that upon birth, instead, we'd tried to help by weighing ourselves down with all the darkness and negativity that had been spewing around us.

Born into this life still carrying that weight, I was pleased to hear my efforts at healing had done much to help me but saddened to know he was still struggling under the shame of those failures, which were suffocating him. Adding to that, he didn't believe he deserved anything good in life because it was his perception that he'd destroyed his wife and child and was staying away from me out of fear of what he might do that would hurt me further. They cleared what they could, but the male half of the couple, who had a sarcastic edge to his speech, told me I had plenty more homework to do on that one.

Accepting that duty without question, the next thing they relayed that I would have to do for him took the air out of me. He needed me to reach out to him. Sucking in a fresh breath, I remained silent. Sensing my hesitation, they felt my fear, and the woman kindly shared the story of how she'd been the one guided to tell her man of their twin flame connection and how it'd left her shaking. I wasn't shaking, not yet, but the thought of the pain that would come if he didn't respond, or worse yet, sent a cold message in return, petrified me.

Trying to help, they asked me to tune into my other half and sense what he was doing, at that exact moment, in relation to me. Not knowing if I could, I did, and saw what this master man told me, a split second before he voiced the vision we'd both had – "He's stuck in the mud and reaching his hand out to you for help." I didn't respond since the visual had already shocked my senses.

They advised I sit with it and let myself be guided to act

when it felt right. Coming as no surprise, they went on to reassure me that my man's spirit was already incredibly close to mine and that his personality had the capacity to hear about this connection, far more than what most twin men could handle. I felt and knew both. They then left me with the woman proclaiming how lovely a soul I'd been to connect to, and with her man laughing because a subconscious part of me didn't believe her.

Grateful for them and their insight, I pondered what I'd heard and kept seeing his hand reaching out to me, so I worked up my courage and sent him a message a couple days later. Asking for nothing, I kept out the truth I'd discovered, which I was scared to share, and declared how much he'd done for my life. I intended to reassure him he hadn't destroyed me, and that I was a better person for having met him. I told him his strength had inspired me to find my own, and I knew I would never falter again, no matter what came along to hit my life. Not wanting to put any pressure on him to respond, but wanting him to know what I still wanted, I ended by saying that if he was ever open to it, I believed what we could have together was pure beauty.

No response came, but I felt every one of his emotions, acutely, for a week after. It started immediately in the form of choking. Right after I hit send my throat started to repeatedly squeeze itself shut. Seeing it as a sign of his inability to speak to me, I suffered through it in silence. Even when I woke in the middle of the night, convinced I wouldn't be able to pull another breath down the tube that felt like it had completely collapsed in on itself. The physicality of it grew, and if I'd looked in a mirror, I would have seen the skin in the middle of my neck convulsing with quick, sharp intakes as if someone was pinching and pulling it from the inside. Recalling the curses placed on twins to stop them from reuniting, mentioned in many of the calls I'd listened to, I realized I must have pushed the boundaries of a heavy one, and this was the result of doing that.

The next morning was spent painfully rasping, but almost as quickly as it'd set in, it lifted, and by the afternoon I was back to normal. My new normal, which included hearing him say on repeat – "I can't! I love you, but I can't!" Followed the next day by the feeling of him pulling away and closing himself off. Only to be compounded the day after, when he thought, and I heard that any man would be lucky to have me. I didn't want any man! Despite my doubts about us, which came and went almost daily, and even though our memories had all but faded – I still only wanted him. It was ingrained in me, in a spot deeper than I could ever possibly reach to excavate.

Returning to life in the city I loved, hoping he no longer carried the blame of having hurt me, I moved forward in the one way I could. It was time to move. Despite knowing this spirit that was haunting my home would never hurt me, I didn't want to continue being dragged down by either his feelings or whatever was working through him. So I booked someone to take my place, as well as a spot for me to stay in across the river, and waited for the day of my second departure to arrive.

The spirit's attempts to keep me close, which had grown in frenzy, no longer scared me. Not when the light that I'd just changed turned itself off out of nowhere. Smiling to myself, I put in a new, brighter bulb. Not when the bed that had once lifted easily wouldn't budge under a weight that kept my suitcase trapped underneath it. Letting him know nothing would keep me there, I pulled up harder. Not when the door, stuck on nothing, wouldn't open more than a quarter of the way. Squeezing myself out, I locked it closed behind me.

Away from the space that I could no longer call my home, I felt a deep happiness that had been given a clear channel to rise up from inside of me. Lasting only for my short stay away, my short stay back, in-between bookings, confirmed his presence. Deep grief, over a comment that hadn't bothered me when made days earlier, overcame me. Pushing it away during the day, I then moved my hand away when his reached for mine in the dark later that night. Only to have him reach for it again in the new spot I laid it down to rest. Resolve reset, I was driven to leave quickly and took a last minute booking for my home and moved myself over to sleep in a hostel while looking to find a new spot I could stay in for a longer period. It was clear I had to remove any need to ever sleep there again.

A solution presented itself the same day I returned from living amongst tourists, and I quickly accepted a spot to share space with a woman who lived how I wanted to, surrounding herself with people who were alive and vibrant. After signing a check for my new life, I packed what I needed and prepared everything for back-to-back guests, with the first one arriving the next morning. Happy with thoughts of what my new life would bring, I didn't know what waited for me as I laid my head down in the bed I'd shared for far too long with this sad soul.

His grief struck me so hard that despite my knowledge, I couldn't see through it. With no way to get out of this pain, that was intensifying by the second, my rage returned, and I screamed as I sobbed. The only thought that seemed right was I didn't want the pain that came with this life any longer. The tears fell as a thought rose to the surface and escaped from a mouth that had been smiling only a few hours earlier – "Kill me. Please. I don't care how painful the death is that you choose for me. Anything will be better than living with this torture." That thought was quickly taken over by another. "Why ask for what I could do myself?" The realization was delivered to me that my determination would see me through the pull of a trigger once placed in my hand. The feeling that I could do it filled me despite the deeper knowledge lying underneath it that this wasn't my desire. Scrambling to regain my senses, I grabbed the phone lying beside me and with buds planted firmly in my ears, threw on one of the master couple's healings. I listened on repeat as they spoke the words that would clear away any dark force trying to take over my mind.

In the morning's light, I pondered the night's thoughts and decided this soul must have been trying to get me to stay with him in any form possible. Quickly picking up what I'd packed to carry away, I left the spot I no longer considered a safe haven. The first few blocks wrenched my heart with his grief and tears welled in my eyes. His feelings brought the knowledge that I'd broken the heart of someone who felt like he was being abandoned. Driven across an invisible line, his pain lifted, and my happiness settled in, as the connection to this soul, whom I still didn't know my deeper tie to, was blocked by distance.

With a steady two months of nights secured in this other woman's space, I now only needed to return to this other one for a quick hour or two at a time, to clean it between bookings. Having tried everything to cut the legal obligation I had to it, I'd given up on those efforts and resigned myself to having this light link to him for the remainder of my contract. Each trip back brought on another attempt by him to persuade me to stay. On one, one of his short statements broke through while I was wiping the mirror I'd once looked into daily, and I heard him tell me – "I never stopped loving you." Despite hearing the recrimination in his words, which were intended to turn my heart against the golden man I'd once enjoyed time with there, I refused to let his anger take me over.

Finishing up as quickly as I could, I picked up my pace as I stepped outside, only to hear repeatedly, with growing intensity – "Help Me!" Rushing away, I reached an underground platform and sat impatiently, waiting for the train that would move me away even faster. His pleas continued to drill into me and looking up at a passing officer, I had to resist the urge to make this plea out loud to him. Entering the train, relief hit, but as it screeched forward his repetitive cry replaced itself, and my mind heard the scream of my name – "C R I S T I N A!" – repeatedly, until I was too far away for him to reach me.

Exhausted, I knew this spirit had no chance of succeeding in keeping me with him, and I slowly released all fear of him, as an awareness of my strength grew daily. With a pipeline to this power, I made a new move. It'd been six weeks since I'd sent a message to the man I wanted to have reach out to me. Remembering the master couple had said he could handle the truth about us and that it would trigger a knowing in him, I decided to follow the signs I saw, both written and verbal, telling me the timing was right. The sticker with the words Fool's Gold, which I knew was another name for Pyranite and carried the energy of – You can do it! – was suddenly plastered everywhere my eyes turned. This message was underscored by the woman I walked by, who stated clearly – "He's ready to hear it."

I found my courage spontaneously, in the middle of an afternoon workout, and picked up my phone to send him a link to the healing session that laid out everything. But I made the fatal mistake of expecting the worst and trying to protect myself, caveated – "I hope this resonates, but even if it doesn't, I won't stop believing. I will move forward with my life, though, wishing you the best of luck and happiness in yours." In truth, my belief of this twin flame theory was shaky, and I'd needed to defend it against his disbelief before it was uttered.

Despite feeling him listen to it repeatedly and sensing he liked hearing the sound of my voice, he never responded. The only words I heard that were related came from another passing stranger, who told me the night after I sent it – "He's overwhelmed. It brought up a lot that he has to heal." I understood and empathized, but the pain of this new rejection hit harder than I'd expected. I couldn't believe this man, whom I'd thought would never willingly hurt me, could hear the pain in my voice and still not send any response.

I didn't know the extent of the negative weight woven into our energy bodies, which was filling the space in-between us with more blocks than could easily be traversed. Still, in the dark, my mind started reeling, and my anger rose, while my faith in us plummeted. Trying to escape that pain, I decided to ignore what I'd heard from the master couple – which was that it was impossible to forget a twin for longer than a short while – and instead I tried to follow the path of the words I'd written. I attempted to move on without him.

CHAPTER 9
TIME SPENT TELLING THE TRUTH
MONTH 8 OF YEAR 2

With the weather warming, I turned to the world around me and away from the one I'd been envisioning. I wasn't open to just anyone's energy coming into my life, so with 10 times as many flicks to the left as to the right, I kept looking for one who sparked an interest. Liking the look of one well enough, his words drew me in further – Life Less Ordinary. Having lived a life that had proven itself to be far from ordinary, I thought it sounded like we might understand one another.

My swipe led to a quick connection, and I set my truth loose even before we voiced our first words in person. Leaving the heavier reason unspoken, I was faced with my first dilemma when he asked an innocent question about where I lived. Unable to lie, I didn't know if the uncertainty of my life, and that I was no longer living to the standards set for those my age, would be a turnoff. I went ahead and told him what I wasn't sure an established man could take – that I was starting a new life following my heart's desire, one that wasn't supported by a paycheck. My truth brought back one word from him – Respect.

With interest growing, we turned the topic around to speak about him. After reading that his production, which was what had brought him to my city, was only there filming for a few short weeks, I typed back that I was up for a drink if he was open to hearing about a creative project showcasing my passion; one I was in the middle of scripting. With an open mind, he replied he would gladly listen and advise on how to get my footing in his industry. We agreed to this exchange that we thought would be small, but that would end up bringing each of us more than either expected. We set a time to meet on a Saturday night, not knowing we were starting our few short weeks together as a couple.

Immediately upon meeting, I assessed the energy between us and quickly made the mistaken determination that this wouldn't be going any further than a conversation, so I felt clear to launch into the heart of the matter moments after my first drink was set down. Since I was talking about my passion, there was no way around it, and even if there had been, my inability to be anything but honest would have led us straight into it. While sipping wine, I spoke of the story I'd been inspired to start outlining a few months earlier, that I hoped to get filmed someday, which began with the loss of the man who was still encamped in the corners of my heart. The one who, despite my recent decision to move forward without, I knew I still wanted to have come back and stand tall in the spot he'd left empty.

Each act described went deeper into those first few months when the loss of him had triggered all of my hidden pain to come to the surface so it could be cleared away. Without getting into our deeper connection, I explained that it had all happened to get me back to the purest form of myself. Sharing my truth with this stranger created a cord of positive energy between us and set him free to speak his truth in return.

His words spoke of sacrifice as he explained his decision to exclude a woman from his life that his heart was full of love for because she lived in a place foreign to the one he was from. He would have loved to live where she was, but couldn't because it wasn't where the little girl, who had a direct line to his heart etched in blood, could be taken. The first few years of this little one's life had firmly rooted him in a city close to a mother who was no longer his life's partner.

Not able to be split from the one who was made up of half of him, he was choosing to stay away from this foreign woman, even though they had both wanted a shot at a whole life together. Without knowing what might happen in a few years, he'd let go of them to be fair to her, so she could find someone free to love her in the moment, even though he hated thinking about her with anyone other than him. His story hit close to home, and I instantly knew he'd been brought into my life to remind me of how difficult a situation my golden man was in.

I could see clearly that his dedication to this little one, who had the right to his focus, was making it difficult for him to see anything except the complications that came with this woman, that wrongfully told him she couldn't fit into his life. As he explained his decision to me, I made one of my own quickly. I decided without a second thought that I would help this unknown woman fight for the love that was similar to mine. I'd speak on her behalf since I knew she had to stay silent, so any decision he made would be done free of her influence.

Not wanting to tread on his truth too heavily, I tried to keep my words as light as I could. I told him that teaching his daughter to believe in the power of a love that could feed your soul, in a world that no longer fought for what should be cherished, would set the best of examples for her life. He had the opportunity to embed in her heart, for the entirety of her life, the freedom to follow the path of pure passion.

I left it there for the moment, unaware of how much more I would come to say on the matter in the weeks to come. The truth flowing between us brought a new kind of energy to the situation, and a bond of mutual respect now existed between us. With neither able to enjoy time with the one we cherished, a shared glance affirmed we both wanted to enjoy what we could have in the moment with each other. Then his hands reached out to hold my face, as his lips leaned in to touch mine.

I enjoyed the way he kissed me more than I'd expected and decided I wanted to go where no one's eyes were looking over at us. I wasn't sure, but I thought maybe this kiss was a sign that I would enjoy opening myself up and connecting on the most intimate of levels again. Something I was starting to want in general, even though I still couldn't have it with the one man I wanted it with. Before leaving the spot we were in, to go where he was temporarily staying, he chose to tell me another story; one triggered by our shared kissed.

Bringing up another woman he'd once gone out with in a different city, he reflected on a time when they'd shared a similar moment. This woman, who'd passed through his life briefly, had been someone else who enjoyed his kisses. Into it initially, she'd quickly stopped them and told him that while he was a good kisser, there was an ex in her heart that couldn't be forgotten. My mind smiled with the knowledge that the universe had nudged him to tell me this story, right at that moment, to remind me I had a man that shouldn't be forgotten either.

Maybe it was spurred on by that story, but the moment we sat down behind the driver that was taking us where no one could see us, I started to feel my heart's rebellion. What was I getting myself into with this man I didn't know and no longer wanted to even kiss? Telling myself this was something I had to push past so I could live in the present, I stuck to what I'd put into motion. He didn't pick up on my newfound hesitation and continued pecking me with kisses all the way from that seat to the one on the couch in his suite.

Determined to go through with what my mind was telling my heart I needed, I found what joy I could in the moment and let his kisses lead me to the room he slept in. Taking off the physical barriers between us, I couldn't let down the one my soul wanted to keep up. My body tried to fight my spirit and showed him it was enjoying his touch, but my soul was stronger. Everything was rubbed to a raw discomfort, and all I could feel was a deep pain surfacing.

I considered continuing, intent on moving my life forward, but without consciously sensing the change in my energy, he recited another story that led my choice by example. With an ironic timing we would come to laugh about later, he talked about the time after he and an ex had parted, when she'd had one quick night with a mutual friend of theirs that had led to a lifetime of them being tied to each other through a child. Their story wasn't a happy one since they ended up disliking each other. Hearing it helped my soul's desire break through to my mind, and I led us away from any physical contact, instead, driving us down the path of more story-telling until I chose to get up and take myself back to the other person's home I was living in.

Our time together could have ended there. I would have let it, but he drove it to be more, into something I would grow to temporarily cherish. It started with his nightly check-ins that gave me the sense of what it was like to have a partner who was able to support me; a feeling I hadn't felt much across this life. I found myself starting to enjoy these brief moments spent typing out my day's activities with a man who was becoming less than a stranger, even though our connection would only be punctuated by two more nights spent in each other's physical presence. Each exchange was deepened by my heightening words, the ones I believed would change his perspective and shorten the time it took him to move to the destination his heart had already selected for him.

Our second night together came right before he was taken a few hours away, to a different location for filming, and it changed everything between us for me. Over dinner, I went deeper into my truth and told him the story I'd held back earlier. I spoke of the spirit that I'd left my home to get away from. The one I hadn't been able to clear, who thought he was protecting me by fueling my anger. His unquestioning acceptance of this, despite his disbelief in what I believed in, made me feel supported. Walking out into the night's drizzle, we pressed one of each of our arms against the other's back and walked over to the home I was residing in. When we got there, we sat down at the big white table, in the kitchen fashioned like it belonged on a farm, and shared more of ourselves with each other.

Not intending to gain sympathy, I read a portion of the story that I'd written about my life, in the sole hope that he would hear the beauty I'd carefully crafted when I'd strung its words together. It was my truth about the broken boy I'd let control me in my twenties, who was still controlling me one life over. Not sure if he heard what I wanted him to, I empathically picked up on his sorrow for me.

Flipping the mood, we turned the conversation over to one of his stories, and he told me about a woman that had been special to him, whom he'd practically lived with, in another country, a different time he was filming. The loveliness of those details, along with his reminiscing of having escaped the entrapment of a long relationship he'd had in his twenties, with a woman from his country, shouted that this man had no desire to live where he was from. It'd become obvious that he was only living there in-between the temporary lives he was building around the world, and I could see how he was restricting himself from building any real, permanent happiness. So I led the conversation back to his love.

I chose my words carefully and promised they were only intended to widen his perspective, so he could then make his own decision after having seen it from every angle. Being honest to both of us, I also admitted I hoped there was someone out there speaking similar words, on my behalf, to the one who had once been mine. With all that out in the open, I started the second round of my fight for love.

I brought up the fact that had been seeping to the surface in all of his stories. It didn't seem like he wanted to live in the country he'd been born in, where his daughter was now being brought up. The unconventional life he'd chosen was already taking him away more than he was staying. Admitting he'd wanted to leave Germany for over a decade, I asked what made him think his daughter would be any different than him? Instead of thinking of it as making her life harder, there was the possibility that he'd be opening her life up sooner than she could open it up for herself, by giving her the opportunity of living in two countries.

I went on to add that, from my experience of having been one, a child learns by example, and when one teaches how to be controlled by circumstances, then that's how one is raised to believe life should be lived. Instead of those limitations, he could teach her to grow unrestrained by the conventions she'd been born into. He took in my words, saying they were helping him see things in a way he hadn't of previously and would take them away to think on later.

Our conversation then turned to the man I wanted to speak to who wouldn't, that my heart said couldn't speak to me. I didn't know for sure either way, but in answer to when I'd last spoken to him, I told of how I'd laid out everything to him by sending over the recording that detailed what I'd uncovered. I explained that the risk had been taken since I didn't want to hide who I was in this life any longer and wanted him to know the whole truth about us. The man sitting across from me, who had already accepted my truth, told me this other man would respond. I took in his words and hoped he'd been guided to say them, but left it at that and moved on to us.

Leaving the past behind and turning our gaze away from what the future might hold, his hands held my face once again, and we went back to enjoying the touch of each other's lips. Still knowing this wasn't meant to last for long, this was when my feelings for him started to grow slightly. With no plans to go any further that night, my mind questioned if we should go where I hadn't been able to the other night, on another night before he went back to his homeland. He was leaving the next day for another location but would be back for the weekend, and I knew that if we were alone together, then the chances were that we would.

After he laid his final kiss of the night on me, I checked my messages and saw one that told me nothing more than another kiss was meant to happen. The brother, who never wrote first, was asking me to travel home the following weekend, to celebrate one of the nephews I loved who was turning six.

Unsure if it was my own internal blocks at work, or higher wisdom guiding me, it didn't matter, this was a call I couldn't refuse.

With this deeper knowledge of each other tapped into, the next week of nightly messages brought even more comfort, even though it was clear that we weren't two people who could ever deeply understand one another. He could accept me, but could never really believe the truth etched in my bones. This didn't stop me from enjoying what we were sharing, and I was grateful for this short time we had where I could feel this man's authentic interest in my life.

We grew even closer on the day my trip home kept us physically apart. He wrote in the late afternoon to ask if my nephew had beamed when he'd opened the gift of a small guitar I'd searched for because he'd asked for a real one. My desire to see him open something that might turn into his heart's desire had driven me to wake up at five a.m. for the five-hour drive home.

Only to miss the opening of all his gifts because of the frantic calls that had come in from the guest who'd booked a stay in my apartment, who had been kept from turning its lock open by the spirit that was trying to stop her entrance and force my return. I told him about this but hid how the darkness had momentarily turned me away from my true self. Blocking any sympathy for this guest I was hosting, I'd snapped at her while she cried in my ear. Then, I'd gone off on the representative from the company she'd booked through, who'd called me to help her resolve the situation. Fighting to get back to myself, I called and calmed her down enough to try the key one more time. It'd finally turned despite the 10 times it'd been stuck in place before.

Skipping over those details, too deeply upset with myself to admit them to anyone else, I also kept quiet about how I'd reacted when I'd walked straight into the moment right after all the gifts had been opened. Quickly jumping to the conclusion that no one had even noticed my absence, my anger spiked back up and I'd snapped at everyone. Taking myself back upstairs and away from the happiness, I'd felt the darkness overwhelm me, trying to push me to turn around immediately and head those five hours back to someone who wanted me.

A path that would have led to us spending a night together and taken me where everything trying to guide me had already led me away from. I hadn't headed back; instead, I'd wrestled back control over myself and made my way back to the family who I'd come to find out had come up to call me down earlier but had left me alone when they'd seen I was fighting something triggering my anger. I told him the light version of what had happened when he asked for details about the moment that should have been happy, and he responded with sympathy. Adding his concern, he told me I really had to let go of that apartment. I agreed.

With an even deeper attachment to his supportive nature growing, I let myself enjoy the feeling of having someone out there that cared about what was happening to me. I knew then that I wanted this. Not with him, but this temporary passing of someone like him in my life was confirmation that I wanted it to come in a more permanent nature. Despite this feeling, I ignored his message later that night. The one that said he wished I was there with him. I knew enough to keep my boundaries up and myself from growing too attached to the wrong person. Instead, I replied the next day with a message that was completely unrelated and written to keep a safe distance between us.

Our third week together was a repeat of the second, and our nightly messages brought us even closer, despite our geographic distance. We'd become a routine that was more than just friendly, but not much more, that I'd grown to depend on. But my words started to completely shift us away from any flirting. I did it in the form of reminders.

First, of the little girl I assumed, and he confirmed, he was excited to see once his filming wrapped. Then, of the woman he wouldn't let himself see but admitted he could still feel. His admission of the cord that still connected them came over one night after I'd explained the vivid dreams I'd had about the man I always felt. Telling him what I knew he'd understand, I wrote of the dream that showed he'd secreted himself off to live in isolation on a farm, to protect his little one, and wouldn't allow himself to even look in my direction. Following it up with the second, I went on to tell of the dream that had come later that same night. In that one, I'd taken his child by the hand and gently guided him into a spare room, and then with my love arching his neck at a steep angle, to keep from looking down at me, I'd taken his face in my hands and forced him to look into my eyes. That's when he'd screamed – "I love you, but I can't!"

Fully understanding my missing love's motives, the man I was speaking to recounted what he didn't love. Two things that had made his day less than joyful had both come from his homeland: the man who was directing their project with anger and the restaurant's German cuisine where he'd gotten stuck eating a late dinner. He hated eating that food more than anything and couldn't stand this man's snapping control over everything he did.

He couldn't see how much he talked about his dislike of all things, except the one, that were from there. Giving him my support, instead of my opinion, we ended the night with his comment that it was too bad we had such a short time in this life to talk to one another. We left it that we would talk more on Friday – when he would be back in my city for a few hours before a flight would take him back to the place he didn't want to call home.

The last day of the three weeks our lives were intertwined arrived with a downpour. Despite the lack of shine from above, I could feel the joy inside as I trudged through it to meet him at the same spot we'd met in on the first night of our three together. The feelings inside surprised me, and I forced them to settle down. I'd no desire to see this go any further than the next few hours of conversation we had ahead of us.

The happiness I felt inside, that spiked when I saw him, turned to tears later when his words, intended to help, had brought up some of the jealousy still buried inside. Those words from him, which laid down the hard truth that I had to think about my love in love with a new woman he may have since brought into his life, were followed later by words from me that were intended to make him see that his sacrifice may turn out to have a negative impact on his daughter. We each said what we thought would help the other, and while we both knew there was a possibility the other was right, it was still hard to hear.

His reasons for what he said were unclear, and once again I wasn't sure where his guidance was coming from, but I understood I was meant to hear it, so I could accept it and remove the control it held over me. If my golden man was to come back, I couldn't let the jealous fear of other loves experienced stop me from letting his into my life again. Letting go of the few tears his words had brought on, we quickly went back to the place we'd created for us. His hands reached out for my face while his lips touched mine, and we let the eyes around us watch as we enjoyed the comfort of each other.

Ready for that to be done, I turned us back to the topic of his life. I spoke to him for the little one who couldn't speak for herself. I came from the position of having been raised like her, a child whose parents had chosen to sacrifice where they wanted to be because they thought it would provide a better life for their children. The weight of that sacrifice had pressed down on me from the time I was little and kept a heavy pressure of guilt on my entire life, up until I'd recently done the hard work needed to release it.

I told him what I knew to be true bluntly. No matter how much it was kept hidden, a parent's dissatisfaction with their own life couldn't help but be emitted and would only lead a child to feel guilty for a decision that was made on their behalf. I went on to add that I knew only too well how this feeling could affect the choices she would come to make for her own life. Ending by stating a truth I'd heard, lived through, and believed in, I told him – "The worst legacy a parent can leave their child is their own un-lived life."

Those were the last of the words we spoke about the love we had in common, and we shared a final kiss to send him off. Then, right before his flight flew him out, he wrote to me about us, and we ended our time with messages that spoke of what we'd shared. He thanked me for letting him into my world and showing him a new perspective on his. I thanked him for the attention he gave my life and showing me what it was like to have a supportive partner.

We'd been temporary though, and I signed off with our truth. I'd been sad to walk away from him, but our nightly words of support were over and couldn't continue now that there would be an ocean in-between us. I'd been aware all along that he fit my pattern of unavailable men, but having kept a close eye on it, I wasn't going to let it extend out further than was healthy. He already knew what I'd known all along. Our time together was never meant to last long. We'd brought each other the comfort we needed for a short time, while we couldn't get it from the ones our hearts truly wanted. Now it was time to go back to our separate lives, where I planned on returning to the fight I'd been waging for my love.

CHAPTER 10
LIFELINES
MONTH 9 OF YEAR 2

Only, fear kept creeping in to make me doubt everything, and confusion reigned. Running, one day, from my home to the gym, at the gym, and then a quick run to get groceries after, I reprimanded myself incessantly. Why did I still want a man who wasn't making a single move in my direction? Was it time to give up on him?

My mind pinging with doubt, as I entered the lanes that lined everyone up to pay, I mumbled – "What am I supposed to do?" Looking up, just as the question was uttered, I saw my answer. All six of the screens above each lane screamed loudly in bold, bright strips of color – PLEASE WAIT. PLEASE WAIT. PLEASE WAIT. PLEASE WAIT. PLEASE WAIT. PLEASE WAIT.

A smile took over my face, as I shook my head at the madness of this life I was living, and I thanked those guiding me while agreeing to continue holding space for him. With that decision made, I made another. I was set on avoiding the pain of returning, even for the briefest of hours, to the home I'd once loved. Determined to find one person to rent that space out to for the few months it remained in my name, I wanted to remove any need to enter it. A solution appeared in the form of a student looking for a summer rental, and I made one last trip over to prepare it for her.

The silence that hung in the air didn't fool me, and I knew it was a trick to make it seem safe to stay. Leaving, I ran into a group gathered outside, standing directly below my old bedroom window. Remembering all the times I'd been above and heard this guided tour stationed below, I asked myself the silent question – "What happened here that warrants so much interest?"

Checking online, the answer turned up quickly. The worst tragedy the city had experienced in its entire history, up until the most recent one had struck, was directly connected to the block my home resided on. Considering the age of this renovated old tenement, I imagined it was the same structure that had stood 100 years back when the people who'd lived in it then had taken a boat to get to an afternoon picnic in Long Island. During that ride, a thousand people had been forced to make a devastating decision when everything caught on fire beneath and around them. Weighed down by their garments, these German immigrants, made up of mostly women and children, had no real choice ahead of them. They could either remain on board to burn or jump over into the cold water they hadn't the skill to swim through.

With more understanding, but still no idea of my connection to them, my heart ached itself wide open. I felt an immediate and deep compulsion to help those souls that, instead of moving on into the light, must have returned home, in shock, and become trapped on the land they'd once lived on. With a call booked for two days later, that I'd scheduled months prior, I knew the two that had the ancient knowledge could help me understand this situation more clearly. When the hour of revelation arrived, I presented the story to them, and they confirmed what I already knew and then colored in the scene with the details I was missing.

Their knowledge ignited mine, and as they spoke, I felt the truth in their words. Living at that time and connected to those people, I'd been waiting on Long Island to receive them, as they'd been faced with what death to choose. Unable to do anything, I'd been helpless, as I'd watched the boat burn from a short distance that was too long to traverse. Tears welled in the present, as they went further into the past, and explained how there were those I'd loved that I'd blamed myself for having put on there. An overwhelming feeling rose from somewhere ancient and tried to confirm I didn't deserve those I loved in this life to stay with me. Letting them know, they did what they could to clear the karmic debt that wasn't real but was keeping me in its pattern through my misperception.

Turning to the soul that had made himself known to me in this lifetime, they explained he'd no desire to see me end up like him. The feelings that had overwhelmed me on our last night together had come through him from a darker entity but had in no way been where he wanted to lead me to go. They went on to add that he'd been there on that boat back then and had stayed here since because of others, who were stuck, that he felt a sense of responsibility towards. They did what they could to clear those souls who were ready but said I could do more since when I was open, I could hear spirits who needed to convey a message.

Feeling no surprise, since I'd felt a few others since the first, I asked if they could help clear the fear that petrified me when my senses picked up on them. Looking into that more closely, they cleared the trauma from when I'd taken my own life, intent on escaping the pleas of those the world had no longer been able to see, that I hadn't known how to help. With that done, they talked through a few phrases I could say daily to clear and protect the field surrounding myself and the people I loved.

But before I went off with that knowledge, they went further back into the story we'd only just begun to unravel. Without knowing all the details, they felt that my man's son had been one of the ones I'd loved that had been on that boat because of me. His death had weighed me down with my personal guilt and his father's pointed blame. Feeling deserving of both, I still carried them to this day and was unconsciously convinced I didn't deserve anything good to enter my life because of it. Clearing that weight instantly lifted me higher, and then they went deeper.

A repeating pattern, there'd been other deaths on other boats across other lives. The one consistency was that the four of us – me, my man, his son, and his son's mother – had been recurring players in every scenario. Which one died changed with the differing decisions made in each life, but the outcome had always been the same. Whether he'd been able to save his son, or because of the impossible nature of that, had chosen to save me instead – more shame, guilt, and blame had been added to the burden we'd left each life carrying.

Then came the lives that had ended while we were on dry land. Repeating our story, but with a different ending, there'd been some lives where my man had left his wife and son for me, and one too many when his son had died after that act, a few times while he'd been on my watch. Not as skilled as a mother, his death had never been my fault necessarily, but a misplaced look was all it'd taken for him to take the quick step that had ended it and placed everyone's blame squarely on my shoulders. The woman reciting our history tried to reassure me by insisting – "It really feels like it wasn't your fault." Setting blame aside, all I could think of was that this explained everything.

We'd both known, while we'd been together, that his son had to be done right by. He'd believed his burning need for that was based in biology, and I'd thought my innate desire to protect children was what guided me. But it had run deeper for both, and these deaths explained why our separation had had to occur, as well as why seeing a child wandering too many feet behind an oblivious parent had always made me want to scream and scoop them up to safety. Not to mention the repetitive sight and sound of his son's name that was still popping out at me daily. Clearing the space between all of us, of all that pain, brought a deep sense of relief. Not just for the clearing, but for the explanation that finally made sense of this situation.

But what didn't make complete sense was when they told me that my golden man was afraid of my power. Not feeling like I had any, I couldn't see what there could be about me that scared him. The only thought I could think of was that when we'd been together, he'd been so consumed by me that he might be afraid I would take his focus off his son if he were to see me. I'd known, from the beginning, that while in each other's presence, it was impossible to resist the love that existed between us. Which helped explain why he'd cut me out so completely.

Unable to see what had propelled these cycles of death that included his son, the masters saw another cycle of death embedded in our systems. We'd repeatedly sacrificed our love and our lives to save the masses. With either his hand or mine held high, we'd volunteered to be the one, on countless occasions, that had taken the bullet so others would live. Using a scene from a recent movie, they equated it to when the captain of a ship had gone into a radiated chamber to flip a switch and stop a catastrophe from occurring. Done again and again, each time we'd died carrying the blame of having only saved 500 out of 501.

Turning from the pile of bodies she was seeing, the female master softened as she saw the soul of a little girl spring up to join us in the energetic device our souls had entered into for this healing. Known as a Merkaba, it consisted of two pyramid-like shapes, inverted, which created a chamber. This little one had zoomed up out of nowhere to nestle in with us. Never having seen this before, she questioned who this was, and I answered with what I'd already come to believe.

Having seen signs of it for months, I told her there was the soul of a little girl that wanted to be born to us once we came back together. She'd made herself known to me through my nieces. The littlest one, who didn't ever speak to anyone except her mother, had twice turned and called me mommy when I went to see them, before shock at her mistake had driven her away. On yet another visit to see my family, the older one, who was still little at the age of six, had repeatedly insisted on cradling her doll in my arms like a baby.

Noticing the coincidence, I'd realized it was a sign of something and had reached out to my old teacher, the one who'd taught me to trust my intuition. I'd asked her if it was possible that a baby soul could choose its mother. Not wanting to give me the answer, her reply had been to feel into whether it was the soul of some future baby or my inner-child trying to send me a message. Doing what she'd instructed, the vast openness that permeated my body when I'd thought of the former, versus the tight pain that had negated the latter told me it was indeed the soul of our child.

Reminding me that nothing could be predicted, this master woman tried to give reassurance that even if this soul didn't manage to be born, she would always be with us, helping with our healing. With no desire to have a baby and having already heard I wasn't meant to, I cut her words off and said I wasn't bothered one way or the other. With a heart that barely twitched over the thought of this child, I shrugged off the miracle of her as if it didn't matter.

With the truth I needed filling in the blanks I'd been living with, I re-set my determination to what I really wanted – to reunite us. Unsure if I'd already ruined my chances, I was comforted by their reassurance that I hadn't, and couldn't, destroy him by reaching out. Being one herself, the female master explained that while twin women are powerful in nature and many had on heavy boots that at times, in their pain, they used to stomp on their men, I'd come nowhere close to doing that. If anything, the way I was built made me behave in the exact opposite manner.

Picking up on an intense self-hatred, which we both carried all the way up to the soul level, they cleared the guides I had that were infused with it and had repeatedly instructed me to not push myself on him. Which explained why I'd latched on so tightly to the cocoon effect and had gone over a year without contacting him, despite having thought of him daily. Believing what they said, regarding contact, I decided to let this healing, which had been heavy, process before committing any action that brought me closer to him in the physical world we shared.

In the meantime, I had to focus on the life I was trying to rebuild. I continued to live in a stranger's home while searching for my own clear space to occupy but was set to return to the one I'd left behind when I could, to do the job I'd assigned myself. The next two months passed by quietly and even though there were a few times I sensed someone in the room I was renting, I now knew how to protect my energy and send what I was feeling away with the words – "You're not welcome here. Please leave."

With my nights full of restful sleep and a healed, higher vibration, I chose to accept a contract position that brought in more than enough income to help me set myself back up. While it wasn't linked to the dream I had of weaving truth and beauty together in my writing, it was a good spot with a small company that was trying to start up a new, health-driven business. With that in place, I was able to find my own space to live in. One that had a clean environment with nothing stuck between its walls that could scare me.

Waiting for my new space to be ready, I enjoyed the more mainstream existence I'd returned to and continued to heal my love and myself, while finding the courage to send him more messages. With no expectation of a response, I did it to overcome his fear of me. My expectations were met, and I started to equate it to talking to a man in a coma, one I wouldn't let go quietly into the death of sacrifice without a struggle. The first I sent was kept simple. Almost three months after the one that proclaimed I would move my life forward, away from him, I countered it with the words that let him know – "I tried, but it's not possible. I'm still here, and I'm still open. I hope someday you are too." I left it with that for the moment.

Waking the next morning, in the wee hours, I heard the faltering sound of a piano being played by someone that was obviously practicing. It seemed a strange hour for a lesson, but I understood immediately that it might not even be occurring in the time I physically existed in and was intended to tell me that while faltering, my love was trying to feed his soul. Then I heard his anger through the lips of another. A girl, stationed directly below my window, was screaming at whoever was on the other end of the line she was connected to. Laughing, I heard her annoyance, but knew it was filled with guilt, as she shouted – "I told you I have to work. I can't talk to you right now. AND I'M NOT SORRY!" Her sorrow, as well as the reason for hearing this message, came through loud and clear.

Not knowing what work he was doing, but guessing it had to do with his family, I was intent on following my soul's guidance. So I kept my promise and went back to the home I'd left behind, right before it was time to hand it over to its owners. After clearing out all my belongings and scrubbing down everything left between its walls, I sat myself down on its bare wooden floor. I braced my back against a brick wall and did what was needed. Tuning in, I asked the question that had never come up before – "What do you need me to know?"

What I already knew came through clearly, and I was struck by the knowledge. The spirit who believed he belonged in my bed had lived there with me, and our two children, in the time when we'd been a married couple. The girl, who was older, and the boy, who was younger, had been two of those I loved that I'd watched die from a distance. My guilt over their deaths had been compounded by the fact that when they'd lived there'd been a part of me that had felt trapped by them. I saw the truth that fit all of our other scenarios. I'd wanted to be free, so I could be with the man I truly loved, who had a son by his own wife. Upon the deaths of all our children, I'd placed the blame of being an unworthy mother squarely on my shoulders.

Finally feeling the full goodness that this spirit had once embodied, I knew he was repeatedly crossing over to return to the home these children had once known because he wouldn't leave without them. Sadness overwhelmed me, but I worked through it and used the new precision I'd learned to clear them. Begging for forgiveness, I sent them into the light, while professing my love for them. Feeling the new lightness in the air that surrounded me, I heard his next message, intended to help me, clearly – "Leave."

I spent the night grieving that life's loss and connecting this life's feelings to it. I'd always been fearful, sure for no apparent reason that I couldn't handle the responsibility that came with having another living being dependent on me. I finally knew this perception wasn't a reality I had to continue recycling. I chose to let go of my guilt and forgive the person I'd been then and the one I'd been born to become now.

With his charges released, the spirit, who'd only wanted to protect us, could end his self-inflicted entrapment on the spot we'd once lived in. I felt his final goodbye one morning while on the way to my new position. It came with a rush of love that enveloped me, filling my heart with his hope that the rest of my days would contain nothing but happiness. Grateful for what I was receiving, I sat on the train speeding forward and hoped for the fulfillment of that desire.

… REBORN

CHAPTER 11
SHIFTING TO TRUST
MONTH 10 OF YEAR 2

With the shift to a happier, easier life started, shifts occurred at the place I was working. The first came with the woman who arrived in the form of an introduction, sent in an email by the man I reported to who managed everything I did closely. With no words spoken about her, I silently questioned if this woman was hired to lead my role or replace me entirely.

It was hard to see her clearly in the profile photo that shrouded her in a warm light that glowed brightly all around her. Two weeks into a contract meant to last another eight, I prepared myself that it might end sooner. The uncertainty of my footing was the only certainty I felt, and the inability to know where I stood would continue to shadow me for the rest of the time this position lasted.

Needing every week of the funds this temporary job was providing, I answered the introduction with deference. Her response didn't clarify a thing, but it set a tone that matched the pleasing light around her. Even before her first day, the ensuing messages exchanged and meetings she came to, told me that whoever she was to me it was certain I would enjoy however short my time with her lasted.

Reasoning that I didn't want the role to last much longer anyway, since the only long-term commitment I was willing to make was to my writing, which I believed needed independence to foster, I decided I wouldn't care if this permanent hire became my replacement. This decision, which stood on the shaky ground my chair was sat on, would eventually lead me to repeat one of the patterns I thought had been successfully broken. I was going to let her glow eclipse mine and step myself back into the shadow it created.

Her first full day was a welcome one, and I was immediately engulfed by what she emanated, which created a spark of motherly warmth in the masculine dominated atmosphere the seven of us that already worked together inhabited daily. With a quickness that was both shocking and pleasing, we soon became partners that depended on each other. Told we would work in tandem on all the projects that were more than enough for two to handle, all uncertainty seemed to vanish, and I dove into this new partnership that brought me instant joy.

Without hesitation, I opened up to her during a trip we took to visit a vendor, telling her all about the supernatural experiences I'd had with the spirit in my apartment. Nonplussed, none of it surprised her since she'd heard of similar encounters, and she accepted my truth unequivocally. From one day to the next, we grew closer, and I had my first bouts of genuine laughter in ages.

I soon filled her in on everything, including my twin connection, over the drinks we routinely had after our work ended and before her weekly date night with her man started. After a couple weeks of that, I was pleased to hear our partnership would continue when one of the company's partners asked if I would agree to make my contract open-ended. With everything in this arrangement beaming with a soft glow, I happily accepted an extended, temporary stint in this existence I was enjoying.

Then another shift hit. One that tried to lead me away from what I believed in and pull me back into another one of my patterns. I noticed it at the end of the week that brought our team its first round of after work drinks. Seven out of the eight of us attended. Two of which, one being my friend, arrived early and waited for the rest with two untapped pitchers. At the start of our journey over, the four that trailed behind stood in a circle and spoke about nothing in particular while a train moved us away from the building we worked in with all the other entrepreneurs trying to start something new.

With no shift in vision, I felt the focus of one turn to me and knew this man, one of the two partners in this company, that had only spoken to me from nine to five up to then, had just seen me as a woman he found attractive. This pang my senses had picked up shocked me. Our interaction eight hours a day, four days a week, for the previous five weeks had been filled with nothing but our talk about my work on his business; punctuated by my annoyance with how he'd managed me without any trust for my motivation. Looking over, I saw his gaze pointed down at the shoes I was wearing, the one pair I had that were pointed as sharply as all the points he wore daily. Not knowing where this path I'd just stepped on was going to lead, I let this feeling slide off quickly, believing it was as temporary as my short-term contract.

After walking up to ground level, and while walking over to our drinks, we fell into stride with one another, and he asked me what I wanted. I knew he meant for my career, but knowing my life's purpose ran deeper, I answered from my heart and said I wanted to create works of beauty that inspired people. Hearing I could create anything I wanted out of this position I had with them, my heart fluttered, but then fear shuttered it. My mind instantly backed away from something I might grow to want that could then be taken from me. Without giving a reason, I let him know I wasn't ready for any kind of long-term commitment. Uncomfortable in his presence, since I'd seen the sharp way he managed the world, relief flooded when we reached our destination, and our conversation ended.

Then the drinks started pouring, without stopping, and

this man, who stood taller than any man I knew, but was still shorter than the best man I'd ever known, showed me who he was. After a few drinks, almost everyone left, and I was alone with my friend and the man whose sharpness had softened. Without any provocation and with rapid-fire, he handed me what everyone else was already benefitting from in their permanent positions with his company.

It started with a fair offer to pick up the tab for the phone I'd been using for their business and a computer to work on since the memory on my personal one was nearly exhausted. I accepted what felt fair without blinking. Then he asked me to come on a trip to Iceland, which is where the company was rooted, that was intended to bring their team closer. Pretending I didn't know he'd been promoting this invitation internally, I felt grateful and gave a small smile with my acceptance. Thinking his kindness was tapped, shock overcame me for the second time that night when he told me to protect myself medically and charge the majority of my insurance back to the business. I nodded a yes to this offer, which felt in no way like anything they owed me. Saying nothing, I was uncomfortable getting something I didn't feel I deserved.

After my friend closed out and went home to her family, the two of us, who couldn't reach those we wanted to be with, stayed and continued talking. Going into the next round, he started to advise me. He pointed out what he'd picked up on, which I already knew about myself, considering there was little I hadn't pulled to the surface over the last two years of heavy introspection. I needed to negotiate better on my own behalf. He admitted that when I was hired, he would have given me more, and would still give even more than he'd already handed over earlier, as he pressed me to ask him for a month's notice.

I fought back against what was in my best interest; I had a hard enough time taking something I didn't think was owed me, much less asking for it. He eventually backed me down by telling me to trust in how much others needed what I was giving, and I agreed to take two weeks notice when they eventually chose to end my contract. We ended the night having met in the middle, but only because I knew if I didn't agree to what he was giving, then I'd lose the respect I'd gained.

Later, in the cab he put me in as the night's final act of generosity, I messaged my new friend, in disbelief, about all that I'd received. Filled with the hope that life's benefits were finally coming my way, the fear of it all disappearing crept up from down low and I sent out a plaintive cry, for her eyes only, directed straight at him. The seeds of trust had started growing, and I begged him to not take back what had been given, which was so much more than he'd known. My need to trust struggled against the overwhelming terror of counting on someone who might drop me. I set both my hope and fear aside, and I told myself not to expect anything one way or the other.

On the first day of the next week, I bulleted out our conversation, asking if I was ok to move forward with everything. He immediately sent back a bold 'YES' next to each line and with newfound faith, tinged with an ancient discomfort, I took my first steps down this new path. Putting in the receipts to be reimbursed for my equipment came easy, but I had to push myself to purchase the trip's plane ticket. With lingering doubt, I couldn't help but feel this reward could still disintegrate since the trip was further than two weeks out.

The following week was a replica of the previous ones, and we ran through it without any extra attention or offers. Then the next Friday night came and raised a question on what had driven this sharp man's kindness. The messages I read that came a little later than was appropriate didn't say anything inappropriate, but my replies were still carefully selected to keep our exchange as vanilla as possible.

My fear came from my past. From the man who owned the business I'd once worked for, who had gone from being a trusted friend I'd laughed with, to someone who had used his power to force me to accept his words and actions that had crossed every line, despite the discomfort it caused me. I pushed my past back and reasoned this man was not that one, and being a foreigner in this land, he was only looking for a friend while he waited for his wife to move herself and their newborn over so they could live here together.

He confirmed this over the next few weeks by filling them with nothing but exchanges about our work, held during working hours, and leaving my off hours free of any questions. Regardless, the trust seeded stopped its growth as the sharpness of his management style returned and caused me to shut down towards him. That along with an old phenomenon, which was reoccurring, shifted us back to where we'd started.

The tension built with every piece of praise, some for my hard work but a lot for her pleasing personality that he and his partner gushed over my partner while treating me as if I wasn't her equal. All the work I'd done to change the life I'd been living in others' shadows drove me to rail against a pattern I didn't want to see repeated. Only, I knew I was the one who'd instigated it. I'd watched myself do it in every meeting where I pushed her forward and stepped myself back. Feeling trapped by my own actions, I accepted the injustice I felt in silence since my footing with them was still unsteady, and the recent investment into my new home had exhausted all of my capital.

Then came the week that took the team on its trip, where we would spend every hour of the day and night together, in a country where at that time of year it stayed light well into the night. In all of this never-ending brightness, this man lightened up and completely changed how I perceived him once and for all. Away from the strain of our work, he became someone else entirely, and his wit came out to entertain us.

Even before my laughter started, the feeling that came with the protection he offered softened my defenses. It happened spontaneously when I told him the story of what had happened the week before our trip, while he was home visiting his missing family. I walked him through the drama that had put me through the wringer by driving me to think I'd lost all the material comfort I'd regained over the previous few months.

Not trusting the word of the management company that had gone bust the week after I'd handed them all my money and a few days before they were scheduled to hand over the keys to my new apartment, my faith had faltered and led to three days of torture. Reading an article that informed me the state was opening an investigation of fraud against them chilled my heart and sent my mind spinning. With their office boarded up and without a key in my hand or a lease in my inbox, I had nothing to guarantee what I'd paid for and my paranoia skyrocketed.

I walked him through my hounding of the leasing agent and added the twist of an unreliable source of hearsay. While at the dentist to check out an infection, and after relaying the nightmare that had started the night before, I'd heard from his receptionist that her friend had been scammed and left homeless by the same leasing company. Only to then hear from the dentist that because of an aggressive infection, a front tooth would have to be pulled after I returned from my trip, which would cost me thousands. That was inevitable, but in the end, I hadn't been scammed out of every penny and left without a home, so I could put a comic spin on everything.

Only wanting to entertain with an insane story, he looked at me with care while his voice responded that what had been piled on me was a lot. He closed the conversation down by opening up my eyes to his kindness when he told me to hold back in submitting the bill for the insurance, that even the dentist called a scam in its lack of coverage. To instead, expense the full bill back to the company, so I could be reimbursed 80% of what it would cost to pull out a piece of me. Shocked, yet again, I was doubtful this would come to pass but grateful for the chance it might.

His kindness the first day of our trip didn't stop me from laying into him that first night. The question he'd thrown my partner's way earlier that morning, minutes after we'd arrived, which had been prompted by my question concerning work I'd sweated over while she'd been on vacation, made me feel deeply that my opinion didn't matter. Swallowing it in the moment, the injustice simmered until it rose back up later that night after too many drinks, poured by other people's hands, had been picked up by mine to be drunk down.

The glass that never went empty no matter how many times it was lifted, and the sun that never went down no matter how late it got, skewed all perception. A casual comment triggered my anger over the earlier question. With everyone asleep except for the nervous young guy sitting across from us, who watched as our witness, my feelings came out to tell the sharp man bluntly that I didn't like being treated like I wasn't equal to my partner.

Confused by me, he said it was simple. I hadn't committed to them as she had; therefore, they treated her different. Toe-to-toe, we debated our sides while his voice stayed steady, not reacting to mine as it shook with emotion. He kept going back to the same point. This was my choice since I was the one who didn't want more. Telling him my heart was pouring itself into every moment I gave to their work, even if I wasn't saying I would do it forever, I let him know that in my opinion, they didn't value me.

Blaming the glass in front of me for the tears that were welling, my voice kept repeating the fact that this place wasn't a healthy one for me to stay in. Well past the hour when everyone else had put themselves to bed, and believing all respect had been trampled, I stepped myself away to sleep off the last few hours of the night whose light had only dimmed for the hour this conversation had lasted.

Waking weary and bleak, wrung out by the truth I'd let loose, I was unsure how to continue on this trip that had just started. Turning to my friend who was just waking, I gave her the highlights and even in the shadows, the shock on her face was evident as she said 'oh dear' to what I'd done. Giving a few words of support, they would turn out to be only a handful we would share on the trip ahead. We both had our own souls to search, and she needed distance from mine to connect to hers. Alone, I braced myself for the day ahead. Unsure how this man would treat me now that I'd acted out, he stuck to his pattern and shocked me. Kindly wishing me a good morning, he then spent the day acting as if nothing had happened.

I spent the day suffering, unable to forgive myself for what I'd done that I didn't believe was right by him. I finally drew on my courage to approach him later that afternoon while he was alone, standing off to the side of a glacier that had been left darkened by a volcanic eruption, which we'd driven up to glance over. Walking by his side, I spoke a softly voiced apology that came from the heart, and he asked – "What are you apologizing for?"

Intent on not backing down from my truth, I let him know that while I stood by everything I'd said, both my timing and emotion were inappropriate, and for those, I was genuinely sorry. In his way, which had evolved from sharp edges to steady support, he replied that neither was a bother. Making a point of turning to look directly into my eyes, he confirmed he did, in fact, value me. Having seen me raw with emotion, he hadn't flinched. Without intending for it to be, my trust was secured.

While my friend's boundaries were set firmly in place, keeping a perimeter around the partner I'd once counted on, the distance between this man and me steadily diminished. Feeling safe since, despite realizing he was attractive, I felt none for him, I lightened up and let our connection grow. Knowing I was coming from a place of innocent intention, I let myself enjoy him and the laughter that he drew out of me, which I'd never been able to resist before. Having no desire to do anything that would hurt anyone, including myself, I only wanted to laugh again. Even though I knew what laughter could initiate between two people, especially when one hadn't been fed by the joy that came from it for far too long.

His endless one-liners sliced through the air from up front to where I was seated in the back, and littered every turn of the changing scenes we sped by, driving all of us into fits of laughter. My nature started to play off his and brought to light the humor we had in common. Laughing, almost as hard as I had with the man who'd made me laugh the most, and like I hadn't laughed in the years since I'd heard his sarcasm, my boundaries slipped.

Despite the joy I was feeling, the patterns of my past hadn't been forgotten. Laughter had blinded me before, overshadowing the truth in situations, only to leave me crippled once the light shined brightly on them. My last fall had taken all blinders off permanently. This man, and what he could bring up in me, was a slim shadow of my golden man, even though I found myself forgetting him briefly, for the first time, in these moments. But I still knew better than to close my eyes to the disaster this could become.

So I watched what we were doing carefully and took note of every shift between us. My mind clocked how much we enjoyed standing next to each other by the rail of the ship that took us out to see nothing that either of us thought was so special, while we spoke about how much more special life was with laughter and music weaved throughout it. Enjoying it immensely, I carefully contemplated everything I heard. So his comment, handed over without any malice, about the wife who was the most charitable woman he knew, but didn't have a sense of humor or like to listen to music, raised the appropriate alarm.

Not knowing for sure and with no intention of asking, the chance that he might only feel kindness towards her cautioned me. So I hesitated when he threw out his next comment, the one that suggested we take a day trip to a beach together, once back from this cold trip, since we both preferred hot ones. Holding on to the hope that I was wrong and wanting the joy from this friendship to continue, I agreed to an outing I knew I wouldn't allow us to take.

Watching as he chose to get up out of one seat to move over and sit down next to me at that night's dinner brought up a deep annoyance from within. My instincts warned me to see the danger approaching, but I only touched on what was happening briefly and then let myself go back to enjoying the moment. We laughed through that dinner, the drinks that came after and then the entire next day of touring. My loneliness and his spoke to each other, and a bond was created that I could feel we both craved. I knew my soul would be crushed if I crossed the line between us, but I didn't want to give up the connection, so I pledged to keep us in the light, that way I wouldn't have to.

The next shift happened the last night, after the sun's light had dimmed and before it started to shine down brightly again. But before that hour could arrive, he solidified our connection by doing what he did better than anyone had in recent memory – bringing out my laughter and handing me his protection. It started over our last meal, when the laughter bubbled up between us, in the summer cottage our Chairman and his wife had invited us into. It continued over a few more rounds of drinking, coupled with a few rounds of the most brutal card game ever, where everyone's hidden desire to beat each other rose to the surface.

The card game where the two quiet ones that had always been kind went in for the kill repeatedly. Where the friend I'd recently counted on, called a sister a world away, to ask for confirmation on a rule that turned a hand against me. The same rule that earlier on had been left unstated when it would have hurt one of the company's partners. Where later, this partner turned on me and shot – "You're not a winner." – straight into my face with a serious look on his.

The card game where the protective man, sat across from me, slid a few of his cards over when I only had a couple left in my pile. With gratitude, I pushed them back over. Undeserving, since I hadn't won them, I didn't want them. The card game where, a few hands later, my dice rolled and won the largest pile of cards. Feeling more uncomfortable with the win than I had with the previous losses, I reasoned to myself that it didn't count since it had come from a roll of dice based on nothing but luck. Ending with a large pile next to me, I was more than happy to walk away from that game, without realizing I had a major block to receiving any kind of abundance.

The game's influence quickly lifted, and the team's good nature settled back in, helped along by playing rounds of each person's favorite music. Everyone chose three songs at a time, to be played on the system the sharply protective man created with an app that connected two phones together, successfully creating a surround sound system. There were a few of mine that most didn't like, then the one I had to cut short when it brought up the tears linked to the memories that were still the best, but almost every song was one the man I was connecting with nodded his head to. My awareness watched while he saw we had more than humor in common, and my ego enjoyed his appreciation of my taste. I let myself have this moment while keeping my eyes open to the situation. Then I chose to shine a light on it at the last hour; after everyone else had slowly slipped off to sleep.

I knew I had to say something when he said my hands, which seemed normal to me, looked beautiful to him. Choosing my words carefully, I pointed out this slope we were on was slippery, even though our only interest lay in friendship. The fact remained that he was a man, and I was a woman, and we enjoyed each other's company, which meant the lines could become blurry. Pretending I didn't think he had any interest in anything other than friendship, I threw some of the blame on other's perceptions and told him that even if we did everything right, we would still be noticed, and I would be the one hurt from that kind of attention. Then I lightly touched on the time when my previous boss's friendship had hurt me.

Giving him more credit than that, which he'd earned, my speech took a turn and explained that even though everything between us was innocent, I'd felt uncomfortable when his message had arrived slightly too late that one night back in the beginning. I was trying to relay that I could never feel like an equal to him since my responses would always have to be tempered by the fact that he was above me at work and therefore had power over me.

Not seeing my point since his position had recently shifted, so it didn't manage mine any longer, he turned the conversation on its head by choosing to be honest. I hadn't been wrong with what I'd intuited on that night. His interest had been there then, and if he weren't married, he'd want more with me. Opening up slightly, he touched on how long it'd been since he'd stayed up late into the night having a conversation he enjoyed this much with someone. I could see we were both savoring this intimacy that would become corrupted, for me, if it grew into something that hurt someone.

My awareness kept me from letting go and enjoying what I knew would culminate in pain. Having worked hard to become my best self, I didn't want to turn away from the woman I was born to become, not again. But he couldn't understand the depth of my reasons for resisting, so he asked an innocent question a few minutes later – "At this point, what's the harm if we kiss?" Patient, knowing that no one was responsible for understanding what this would do to my soul except me, I explained it would kill the innocence. Accepting the words he didn't understand, he said he would continue to respect me, with or without one.

Proud of my words, I was soon shocked by a shift I hadn't seen coming. My body struggled against the overwhelming desire to get up, go over, and kiss him. Then a deeper knowledge rose, and I knew this action wasn't my desire. I resisted his feelings for a little while longer, as we continued our conversation, then stood tall as I chose to say goodnight and walk myself away from this temptation.

Happy with my action, my thoughts tossed themselves around as I turned over restlessly, still fighting the desire I knew had come from him. It urged me to go back out and up to where he was sleeping and crawl in next to him. Understanding the danger that would come with that momentary satisfaction, I continued to resist doing something I knew would pile on more pain. With this came wisdom – only by facing real temptation, and resisting what wasn't in one's best interest, could one truly trust oneself. Gratitude for this lesson filled me as the desire disintegrated, and I closed my eyes for the two hours of sleep left before everyone woke.

With a hand pressed against my heart, the next day was spent with eyes averted, a cloud separating me from the group. Not sure if the pain I was pressing against was rising from inside or emanating out from the man I'd connected to more intimately, my gratitude for where our conversation had ended was amplified. Any action other than the one I'd taken would have led to this new coldness between us knifing my heart even deeper. Instead, I felt the softer wounding of having a connection that was being kept hidden, even though I knew his only intention was to protect both of us.

Still, that last day of travel spent driving from where we'd been staying in the country, to the city where we'd take a short wander before returning to where we belonged, passed with excruciating slowness. Eventually ending with a grateful sprint away from the discomfort I'd felt standing so close to him and my distant friend, both of whom I knew had their own paths to follow, at their own pace. Already knowing where my path was headed, I didn't know how much longer it was going to take to get to the man I belonged with, but my hope was that it would come sooner rather than later.

CHAPTER 12
CONTINUING TO PERSIST
MONTHS 11-12 OF YEAR 2

Leaving the new apartment I'd returned to, that now felt lonely in its emptiness, I entered the office the next day, curious to see how the recent shift would impact my daily life. Seeing me, the sharp man instantly softened and smiled. I made sure the width of mine given in return wasn't too wide and said hello to him and the only other person there that day. The morning flowed with routine, and at noon, his request to run out for lunch felt normal since that's what the team always did together. The only difference being it was only the two of us going.

    Then a change happened that would guide our mid-day meal from that day forward. He suggested we eat before returning to the office. Sensing he wanted to be alone with me, I thought to resist, but wanting his companionship, guided us to a park a few blocks over. While sitting on a bench surrounded by trees, I praised their calming virtues, hoping to help him learn how to take the edge off his life. Keeping a decent amount of space between us, while speaking about them, I reassured myself that we could have the friendship I wanted. But then his desire for more overwhelmed me.

Filled with his need to have my hands reach out and touch him, I resisted. Surprised at how quickly it'd enveloped me, I knew his ache had triggered mine, which came from my new genuine attraction towards him as a person, as well as the length of time since I'd experienced this intimacy with anyone. But I knew the driving force behind it was his feelings, which were unintentionally working to persuade my empathic sensitivities, so I voiced silently – "This isn't mine." That led the feeling to instantly lift entirely, leaving me to wonder if this friendship could continue.

Assuming it wouldn't, it did and completely blurred the lines of one. It started with a few innocent messages sent during our off hours. Ones that pinged a volley of words between us, until he slipped in a line questionable in its suggestive nature, driving me to end the conversation saying this couldn't continue if it went where we shouldn't. But he was only put on pause for a moment. With a new day, a fresh exchange would start and continue until another line, which more than a small part of me enjoyed reading, pushed against my boundaries and drove me to push him away again. But instead of stopping everything altogether, I continued on in this manner, daily.

I took in every message with eyes peeled, struggling to not slip back into the pattern I'd already sighted – that this man, who wasn't available, was a safe one to spend my time with. Not because I didn't want a commitment. I just didn't want one with anyone other than the one man I couldn't have yet. I knew this man, no matter how soft he acted, could never truly come into my life and become a real barrier to my golden man returning, since he had a wife and child in the wings that would arrive to pull him back into the life he was supposed to be living.

Not wanting to give up this connection, while I worked on energetically clearing the other one, I tried a new tack. I told him everything. From the spirits I saw to the past life experiences I'd had, to the man I refused to give up on, I laid it all down. It came out a week after our trip, on a night after work, while we spontaneously walked to a park I'd once lived near. Sitting on a bench once we got there, he listened intently, as I heard a stranger in the background singing – "You pretend he's your friend." I knew it was a warning, and I took it in, but still continued.

He took it all in and accepted my truth without question. Knowing he didn't believe in what I did, I felt how that didn't get in the way of his belief in me. Moving away from the singer whose words I'd believed but was ignoring, we went to have dinner a few blocks over. On the way there, we spoke of his life. He shared a story from when he was a child, and tragedy had struck with the loss of an eye to a pair of scissors his brother had been holding. With no periphery vision, all sports were taken out of his life instantly, and he stopped going to parks to avoid the temptation they held within their boundaries.

Then came another tale of temptation from when he was older. Walking through a mall, he'd approached a woman he found attractive and after a shared coffee, had been led to drive them back to her apartment. She was more sexual then he'd expected and had started to tease him before even arriving. Once there, she'd fully undressed in front of him, and they'd done a little before, his curiosity satisfied, he'd taken himself out of there. Smiling, I understood the warning he hadn't intended to give. I was something new he was exploring, something he'd be able to quickly remove from his life if he deemed it best to avoid the temptation or once his curiosity was satiated. Thinking I had enough wisdom to protect myself, I continued.

We never exceeded one outing weekly, and despite knowing I wasn't technically doing anything wrong, I resisted telling my partner at work about us. She'd gone back to being a friend, and I didn't want the judgment, which she wouldn't have given, that I was already laying on myself. I kept on pretending everything between us was innocent, which was somewhat easy to do since some of it was. He listened, as a friend who wanted the best for me, to what I was doing to break down the walls my golden man had put up to keep me out.

Over one lunch in particular, he pressed – "Why not call

him?" Responding that calling felt like an invasion of his space, I couldn't admit I didn't have the courage to do it, considering he might answer and then I'd have to face my fear of our first conversation. It was easier to pound against his barriers in writing. Revealing the contents of the last of the messages I'd sent, the man sitting in front of me said nothing while I shared the lines that had made me vulnerable.

Listing out everything I was afraid of in regards to him, the hope had been that it would make us equals, and remove some of the fear I'd been told he had of me. Each fear was juxtaposed next to another. Amongst the litany, I unveiled my fear that I'd never feel the way I had with him again. Next to it was the fear of being made vulnerable again by those feelings. Fearing I would never see him again, I countered that one with the fear of seeing him for the first time after so much time had passed. I ended the list with the fear that he would never respond, as well as the fear that he would. Having felt him read it two hours after I'd hit send, his sadness had engulfed my heart, but no reply had followed.

Despite sharing this with the man who was staring at me softly, and enjoying the feelings he was bringing up in me, I knew what we shared could never reach the same depth. Saying he'd like to have a conversation with my man, he said nothing more about the message and quickly switched topics. Turning to his annoyance with the woman in our office who handled sales, he vented that her light touch drove him crazy. In telling me what he wanted out of her, I knew I was getting advice for my situation – "Persistence beats resistance." I laughed and said I was sure he'd been guided to give me that message. He added to it by stating firmly – "Call him." I couldn't do that since it was too scary, but I would continue to write.

I would also continue to see this man weekly. Our connection felt lovely, and I enjoyed every minute of the time spent together, including the after dinner walks that tended to land us on a bench that extended our time together. Neither voiced what we both knew while we sat on those benches we found. The desire to kiss, which was a feeling that now belonged to both of us, was growing stronger, even though I was resisting its pull and he clearly wouldn't act on it unless I initiated.

Then came the moment that fooled me into thinking I could easily stay on the right side of this line that had become blurry. Following our routine, we ended up on a bench one night, and while there, the beauty of the surrounding trees brought out what felt natural, and I started to speak of my golden man. Not hearing a word, or possibly choosing to ignore all of them, he spontaneously made an awkward, sharp lunge towards me. Startled, I jumped away without thinking and put my arms up to bar him from moving any closer. Proud of my instincts, I decided this was proof I could keep this relationship innocent, so I continued and soon crossed the line that was steadily disappearing.

Inviting him over, he came by in the late afternoon on one Sunday to fix my computer by clearing its memory. After that was done, we sat on my deck to drink a few beers and eat slices of pizza, like friends do. Moving inside, we sat on the couch to watch a movie, like people dating do. Switching back to the deck after, we sat opposite one another and talked under a dark sky too clouded over to make out more than a few of the stars that were watching us. That's when our friendship crossed my imaginary line of innocence. His hand touched mine, and my leg brushed his. Not sure who'd initiated, neither act was one I'd intended to happen. We sat there like that for a few seconds, then the sky cracked opened, saving me with the rain it poured down on us.

Heading inside for a minute, we hugged a lingering goodbye that was too intimate to be mistaken by anyone as friendly. Sickened by myself, I tossed and turned all night, while my mind repeatedly told me I wasn't a good person. I headed in to work that morning railing against what I'd done, and when it was time for lunch, I accepted his invitation, ready to say this couldn't continue. Asking how I was doing, the truth came out, and I said rotten. Hearing that I'd had a sleepless night, he shut me down quickly and said he didn't want to discuss it. I reminded him that he'd asked, but then let it go since I knew this wasn't a depth we were able to reach together.

Knowing it was up to me, not him, to protect myself

from this, I vowed to myself that I'd end it, and I let him shift us over to discussing the German movie we'd watched, which was the type he appreciated. Mentioning another one he might like, I went on to add an off-hand comment – "I was German once." He paused for a second, then remembering said – "Oh, on the boat?" Laughing, while shaking his bowed head, he stated slightly amazed – "You say it with such certainty." I laughed and shrugged my shoulders, knowing it sounded crazy, but that I wasn't.

I also knew something else was happening that went well beyond my pattern of choosing unavailable men. It felt as if I was infected. Other than that one touch we'd shared, the thought of touching him was easy enough to resist while together. I could see through the momentary satisfaction it would bring and knew the desire would disintegrate the second either of us gave in to it. The difficulty, which I'd never experienced before, came when he wasn't in my physical presence.

Lying in the dark, night after night, I was consumed by a desire that felt devilish in nature, which drew my mind to imagine him lying there next to me. The need was insatiable, and when the spell took over, it pushed out everything I knew that was right. I didn't understand it, nor did I like it, but I couldn't resist it. It was as if a fog, sent by a demon, was shrouding my senses. Overcome with a lust that felt dark and twisted, it persistently pulled my energy towards this man that I knew I didn't really want. Despite discontinuing our dinners, this lust continued across the month that would be the last of the six I worked there.

Thinking this lust was coming from inside of me, I turned to the ones helping me rid myself of all negative energy. I voiced what was happening on one of the master couple's live calls, which I'd joined weekly for almost a year by that point, hoping to heal myself and the relationship I knew was golden in nature. Piping up at the point when they asked for volunteers to share their current struggles, I told them, along with everyone listening, about this man who was bad for me, but good to me. Too embarrassed to tell the whole truth, I skipped the part where I felt spellbound. Working quickly, with half the information, they only saw the vague shadow of a life we'd shared, which they said had been minor, as well as one of my repeating patterns.

Trying to clear the pattern, they confirmed I was settling for the little I thought I deserved and hungrily scooping up what I hadn't received in ages. They did what they could to clear what was caused by my energy of unworthiness, but I wasn't fooled into thinking they'd done anything other than remove another layer of this wound that was still sabotaging my life. Setting my story aside, I then tuned in to the one that was spoken directly after mine by another twin woman, and her words sent fear rippling through my body. Her twin, whom she'd been in friendly contact with, had told her that out of respect for his girlfriend she had to stop emailing him. Since everything said on each of these calls had been consistently synchronistic, I worried this was foreshadowing that I would get the same message.

Setting the fear aside so I wouldn't manifest this outcome, I focused my attention on something else that struck a chord. Not knowing its relevance to my situation with the once sharp man I was connected to, I didn't pursue it deeper but memorized the names of the high beings that could remove a spell of delusion that was placed on a twin pair to interfere with their reunion. Doing a broad sweep clearing for it on the call, they left it at that, and I didn't make the connection to the demonic desire that was deluding my senses. Regardless, their help made things easier, and the burning need to touch him was lightened. This energetic easing of what was drawing us to each other, along with a short trip to visit his family, gave me the space I needed to resist seeing him outside of work again.

Deciding to add to my protection, I told my partner at work a few details about this newfound friendship. Without any judgment, she said she'd already sensed it and gave her advice – "He's a good guy, but you can't trust him." We could both see his truth. He was lacking something in his life and was trying to fill that hole with what we were doing. If I gave in, then I would be the one to suffer since it was inevitable that my feelings would deepen if we became physical, and even though they couldn't compare to what I felt for my golden man, I would be hurt by how it would end.

Soon after these measures had been taken, I had a touch of the real intimacy I craved. While sitting on my deck and sipping a coffee, on a Sunday I was spending alone, the spirit of my golden man chose to join me. Taking me by surprise, I hadn't expected it but instantly felt his presence profoundly. He sat himself down in the chair to my left, and his deep desire to be there in person crossed the space between us. Settling in for a second, his anticipation for the time when he could be there enveloped me. I felt the same and was satisfied knowing, at least in spirit, we were on the same page.

Inspired by it, I shortened the time in-between the next few messages I sent him. The first told of something I believed, but was mistaken on, as I declared – I'm not afraid of you anymore. That was followed up with news about a new love I'd acquired. Sending a picture of a pup I'd recently adopted, I proclaimed him a beauty, both inside and out. I shared his name – Bo – but left out that in ancient Swedish it stood for what I wanted for the both of us – To Live. What I did mention was that never having believed I could handle this responsibility before, the joy I received while watching him play was beyond anything I'd ever thought possible. I ended with the line – I imagine the joy your son brings you is well beyond this, and that makes me happy.

Continuing to write periodically, while wrapping up my contract, which was ending with the arrival of a new leader intent on moving the company away from all things creative, I considered my next move. With the lack of success my first book had garnered, I had too much fear to rely on my creativity to support me financially. Turning to energy healing, I thought over how much it had done for me and decided I would train to be a professional healer. I liked the idea of helping others and loved imagining the relaxed, Bohemian look I could create for myself in that life scenario.

While that was being decided, I was faced with another tough call to make. My tooth, which had been examined before our trip to Iceland, still needed to be pulled out. Since that diagnosis had been handed over, I had thought to look into the energetic root of the problem. Calling on my first healer for help, she cleared the lifetimes that were re-creating this pattern of loss – from a boxing ring knock out, to a direct kick by a horse, and a disease that made them all fall out – I had lost many, many times over.

With the energy of those traumas lifted, she turned to an incident from this life that was a direct cause of the infection behind this extraction. A program, which had been installed to block me from starting down this path I was on, had been implanted by a jealous street psychic who'd given me a tarot card reading seven years earlier. I'd pushed past it and continued on, but that persistence had caused the bone, which held my tooth in place, to wear down completely. To the point where the two dentists I was seeing were in complete shock of the infection's rapid movement.

Holding this new knowledge that they didn't have, I questioned if the tooth still needed to go or if the new bone could be grafted in without that extreme measure taken. My instincts drove me to cancel the first surgery, sure that I was right and they were wrong. Rescheduling, I asked for another evaluation. The one who was a specialist and had multiple degrees hung on his walls, validating his superior knowledge, persisted and told me adamantly – "You know that tooth has to go."

I knew nothing of the sort, but couldn't hold on to what I believed in, not in the face of his certainty, so I relented and let him do what he thought was best. Only to find out after that his insistence was driven by a belief, which proved to be wrong, that the infection had been caused by gum cancer. He'd won, and it was out, so I took in what my loss of faith had caused and continued on my path to becoming the type of healer I believed in while missing what could have been saved if my confidence in what I knew to be true had been stronger.

Signing up in advance for a six-week training with the master twin couple, I also pre-paid for a weekend workshop taught by my first healer. Before either arrived, I closed out the mainstream life I'd been living. My last day, two days before my first training, arrived. With half the office, including my partner-friend, away for a trade show, there were only a few of us in the office that day. The sharp-soft man happened to be one of the three, and we all went out for farewell drinks once the day was over.

Two drinks in and the two who weren't us wished me well before heading off to their loved ones. Left alone, desire instantly overwhelmed me. Drawn to him, I gave in to it. We kissed. Leaving, he reached out and took the hand he'd once admired, and we walked over to the subway. Standing at the top of the stairwell, which led to the train that would take me to the pup I had to get home to, we kissed again. Walking away, he turned and waved while smiling. Rushing to the platform, I paused once there, and all desire evaporated, instantly replacing itself with regret. Typing furiously, I messaged him seconds before the train sped up to say I couldn't see him again, not now that I could no longer resist him.

Disgusted, I lay in bed awake all night and shot one venomous accusation after another at myself. "Who was I if I still wasn't the woman I wanted to be? How could I ever face my golden man now that there was proof I wasn't a good person? What had all my healing been for if I still couldn't resist doing something so terrible?"

Escaping my thoughts, I finally slept for a few hours. Then woke to a new one. While it was true I'd done something that wasn't good, it didn't mean I was a bad person. Worn down by loneliness, my wounds had gotten the better of me. It was time to direct my compassion inward and send forgiveness to the one person I'd never offered it to before. That was the gift the universe handed with this lesson. By committing an act I deemed horrible, I'd been given the opportunity to forgive myself. I took it and moved on to becoming a healer.

REBORN

YEAR THREE

REBORN

CHAPTER 13
AN ISOLATED PROGRAM
MONTHS 1-3 OF YEAR 3

Starting a new regime, I slipped out of the material world almost as quickly as I'd slipped back into it six months earlier. Returning to the time when my days were filled with healing, I started to split my time between learning how to do it, practicing what I was learning, and having it done on me by the master couple. Determined, I'd had enough and wanted to eradicate everything left that was holding me down and keeping us apart.

My first training taught me how to connect to the angels so I could channel their healing light into another person, while my hands pulled out what had been stuck in their auras for centuries. Every minute felt like hard labor and made me question why I would ever want to do this kind of work for a living. With each pull, I forced my arm through someone else's energetic sludge to help release it. At times it felt like I was hitting a wall of brick, which required a pull of strength that left my arm sore from the effort. I didn't enjoy it in the slightest but decided to see if it would get easier with more practice.

I did a few trials on friends, which felt better, even though I counted down the minutes of each, anxious for the session to end. Then the pain brought on by one multiplied the doubt I had about my original decision. Hearing that the sharp man I'd left behind didn't seem well, from my ex-partner that was still a friend, I reached out to ask if he needed help. Pleased to hear from me, he admitted he did, and although he wasn't one to call on a healer, agreed to let me clear his aura. Saying I would do it from a distance, to not entice either of us with the temptation that would come from physical contact, we set a time for the next night.

Once it arrived, I instructed him to lay in a comfortable position in his home while I sat in mine and spent an excruciating 60 minutes tuning in to his energy. Every point on his body where I focused my attention, each of which I'd learned connects to a different negative emotion, made my arm ache with pulls that struggled to get through the densest energy I'd yet to encounter with this practice. The physical struggle was worsened by the vision that appeared when I turned my inner-eye to his throat. Blood streamed out of a gash that had been sliced across it in a past life. The sight arrived with intense pain and the knowledge that it had been caused by a friend who was his closest companion.

Once through his full body, I took some time to intuitively dig for more information, then called so I could talk him through what I'd discovered. With a bite of sarcasm, I let him know how much he'd exhausted me, and then went on to explain what I'd felt, seen, and heard. The only thing I left out, purposely, were the words I'd heard and refused to attribute to me – "I love you." But I listed everything else out bluntly.

While working on his liver, which was connected to the energy of anger, my mind had heard the sound of an unknown woman yelling, and I'd felt his fear that he would never be happy. He took it in, and his silence confirmed I'd picked up on what he worried over. Moving away from that, I explained the blood, as well as the cause of it that had come to me after the healing, which the pendulum I was learning to use had confirmed with multiple hard, sharp affirmative swings from left to right.

I was the best friend that had killed him. He didn't sound convinced by my words, as he scoffed at my story, but I knew his rejection of it came from disappointment. A joke he'd once made had revealed his true desire when he'd asked me what position I thought we preferred in the lifetime when we'd been romantically connected. Having removed the chance of us being that type of couple in any life, I pointed out his tendency to reply to everything I said with the line – "It's karma." – and went on to explain how our connection was just that.

We'd been two teenage boys, who were the best of friends, driving in a car together on a night that it was pouring. As the one behind the wheel, I'd placed the blame squarely on my own shoulders, and he'd sent more my way with his last dying thought after a crash had sent him through the windshield that cut his neck wide open. Carrying the guilt of his death for the rest of that life and through all the ones that came after, our connection in this life had always been meant to lead to my forgiveness. Explaining it all, he remained doubtful of the details, but after a pause of silence replied with thoughtful force – "I forgive you." With that, I knew our connection had reached its conclusion.

Shortly after seeing this scenario, I heard about a connection my real man was experiencing. Continuing to send messages that went unanswered, I deemed the reply I continually heard in my head to be a fear that had to be cleared, and I refused to believe the words – "I have a girlfriend." Even though they came twisted with a doubt that I could feel went beyond my own. As if enticed by what he was reading, my man was trying to convince himself to ignore his feelings because he'd already committed himself to a new woman. Regardless of the repetitive phrase and feeling, I couldn't even begin to comprehend what I was too scared to face, so I set it aside without looking at it too closely.

Having started a regime that gave me enough new information to focus on, ignoring what I wasn't ready to process was easy. I was a couple of weeks in to the master couple's six-week training and completely enthralled by what I was learning. Deepening what, by that point, I knew came natural, I was practicing how to tune in to the depths of my being and pinpoint the wounds that needed healing. Once located, I would draw on the list of high beings given, that the male half of the master couple had spent decades researching, and call on them to clear whatever had come up to be worked on.

There was no trick to it. The only thing I had to do was call on the right one for what needed to be done, and then wait to receive the clearing I could feel work its way through my system. Ask, and you shall receive, which was a line familiar from the Bible, the only difference being that we were calling on those that were revered across every ancient culture and religion. These teachings didn't hold a bias towards anyone in particular and taught us how to reach out to those who were pure in each, with precision. They were all waiting, listening, and ready to help at a moment's notice.

Despite this empowering information that was helping me go deeper into what needed to be wrung out of me so I could raise my vibration higher, I was growing tired of hearing things in my head and had begun to lose faith that I would hear my golden man's voice again. So I decided to break my moratorium on dating other men. I accepted there was a link between us that would never cease to exist, but wanted someone in my life that I could both see and touch. Ecstatic with what felt like a smart move, I started swiping and enjoyed every second of it, for the 24 hours that that feeling lasted.

Then his spirit and mine joined together to crush my heart under the weight of their combined sadness. Its crippling effect dropped down on me out of the blue while I was on my deck the next afternoon, and I went from enjoying the rays of the sun that were beaming down on me, as I happily glanced over my new prospects, to being buried under their joint disappointment. Feeling their utter devastation at my decision to give up on him, I knew I couldn't stray from the path I'd been programmed to follow. Deleting the app, I promised I would stick to the healing that was my charge, and a soul-fueled elation filled my being.

Re-committed, I vowed to not let the fear of his continued absence bounce me back to the idea of dating anyone else again. I'd found the one I knew I was meant for, and my soul had wisely given me enough determined persistence to see this through, so we wouldn't have to repeat another round of this painful cycle in our next life. Continuing forward, I soon found the courage to send him the dream I was afraid to share; the creative project that brought our story to life, which I was hoping to someday work on together.

It must have jarred him since it led to a reply, the first in the nine months that had carried 10 messages spread across them. He started by confirming that he'd read and listened to everything I'd sent, all of which he found both humbling and inspiring. Then he went on to voice the exact words I'd once feared hearing. Out of respect for the woman he loved, he wanted me to stop contacting him. Confused, my eyes glazed over, and my gut piped up with what my instincts felt – but I'm the woman he loves. Which directly countered his next line. It claimed he was in a happy, long-term relationship. Reeling with shock, my mind went blank, and I stared into the empty space that lay in front of me, so I was able to clearly hear the words that came into my head next. With a scoff, one of my guides declared adamantly – "No, he's not!"

The rest of that afternoon passed by in slow agony, and I knew to fear the night that was coming. With darkness came the thought of him in bed with someone he was lovingly holding, and I screamed the pain of it out to those above that were listening. They heard every word and responded by tearing the sky open and weeping right alongside me. The loud cracks of thunder and sharp slices of lightning that were ceaseless in their efforts to shatter the sky, along with the torrential downpour that pelted my window with its full fury, were the only suitable companions for the pain tearing through me. My anger rose alongside nature's screams, which equaled my rage and was the only force that could match what was pouring out of me.

Swearing at him, I shouted that he didn't deserve me, and he definitely didn't deserve the kindness I'd shown him or effort I'd gone through to heal him. After listing out a litany of what he didn't deserve, I called up the words he'd once used and wailed them out, wanting to know what had happened to coming back when it was all over. Spent, I eventually began to murmur, questioning what terrible deed I'd done that I deserved to be shut out of his life so coldly, while another woman was allowed in so easily. The only thing I refused to do was curse him. The words rose and tried to break through, but I wouldn't release them since I knew there were enough of those already on us, and I didn't want to add to the pile.

The next day brought the slightest amount of relief, and I reasoned with the part of me that had been shattered that this was what he needed. It wasn't up to my ego to decide what should happen on his journey. Using this logic that came from a higher source, I managed to get through the day without any more wailing. Then, I received a deeper sense of relief that night, while on a support call the twin couple held routinely for our class. It came after they brought in a load of universal light and love that was intended to nourish us. As they recited the messages pouring in from everyone who said it'd felt amazing, I grew despondent, since I wasn't feeling anything. I piped up to tell them, and they turned their focus my way.

Seeing my charred energy body, they were astonished by a vision of a life when I'd been slowly scorched to death by fire across a three-day period. With lifetimes littered with trauma, we'd all burned to death at one point or another, but this particular one had been extraordinarily excruciating and was blocking me from receiving anything out of a terror of the pain that might come if I let down my defenses.

Asking the group to join their energy together, they circled me with it and sent a balm of love to gently soothe the burns that were hindering me from receiving what I deserved to feel. The influx of their energy enveloped me in its warmth and positivity, healing the wounds I'd received then, as well as softening the hit that had recently sent me reeling. Content with this world I was in, which was full of positive energy given unconditionally, I went to bed smiling and slept straight through the night.

The next morning I was inspired to respond to his message, despite my initial plan to remain silent. I felt happy for him that he was happy, and that's what I told him. Keeping the belief that I was the one he loved to myself, an epiphany had made me realize that if I truly loved this man unconditionally, then I would never want to hear that he was sad or lonely. No saint, I didn't want him with someone else, but if that's what he needed to be happy, at this moment, then so be it. Beyond a desire for his happiness, and despite the pain his attempt to attain it caused me, I knew this experience was one that was necessary. It was both a test of my faith that our love couldn't be replaced, even if he temporarily found another one, and meant to show me that not even my worst fear come to life could destroy me.

Pleased that I'd been able to overcome my pain enough to reach this conclusion, I added something else to the message. I included a link to the second healing I'd had with the master couple, the one that explained the tragedies involving his son that were stuck between us. Wanting him to know the whole truth, my hope was he would finally wake up and realize outside forces were working against us. My effort didn't garner the result I'd hoped for. Feeling his annoyance as he listened, I knew I had no recourse but to leave him to live his life and learn the lessons his soul had intended.

Despite this logic, the side of me that felt wounded wanted to lay blame and scream that he'd abandoned our love while I put myself through the wringer to heal it. But two truths rose to the surface. I'd chosen this path voluntarily, believing it was something I, and most likely we, had avoided for centuries, but that didn't mean he had to ever choose to do the same. That was the first and the second would lead to my next round of healing. Everything that happened served both of us, so I had to use this experience to clear more of the jealousy it had brought up.

No matter how hard his relationship was to face, I knew we'd formed a contract with this woman's soul, asking her to be his girlfriend at this time to teach us the lessons we couldn't learn by being together. I knew mine centered on the insecurity of not being as important to him as another woman, but not knowing the whole story and with no intention of invading his privacy by tuning in to it, I could only assume there was karma between them, which needed balancing and had nothing to do with me. I could only hope he was learning whatever his soul required him to, and he'd be ready to move forward as soon as was humanly possible.

In the meantime, I resolved to respect his wishes regarding contact and decided to set aside the story I'd hoped to work on together since it was too painful to do alone. Only, no matter what he'd said, I couldn't bring myself to believe he was truly happy. Not when the feelings I wasn't trying to pick up on told me different. Or when I felt, a week later, his new sadness when he realized that he would miss reading the emails he'd banned. Setting all of his sadness aside, I tried to ignore the truth I felt deeply since it didn't change the situation. He was the one who would have to decide what he wanted for his life.

But, still believing deeply that I was meant to heal both of us, I continued to do that for him. If once healed, he chose to continue to be with this woman then so be it, but I was intent that he would be able to choose the life he wanted free from any karma, wounds, patterns or binds that were keeping him from believing he deserved real happiness. I would do that because I loved him, but also because the manner of our connection ensured that whatever was hindering him was holding me up as well. So, in truth, I was doing it for both of us.

Soon, he surprised me by appearing in a vision that told me I had more of a role in our continued separation than I'd realized. I watched the scene that looked like it'd been written into an action script unfold with curiosity. Lying wounded in a hospital bed, two large men were protecting me by blocking access to the room where I was healing. After a few moments, my man appeared, but couldn't get by them. Turned away, he left without a fight. Looking down, a piece of a brown paper bag, torn off and crinkled, appeared in my hand, and I saw the words he'd penned clearly – "I'm sorry! I can explain everything."

Shocked, I realized those bouncers were the energetic barriers I'd placed around me after our breakup. I was blocking him as much as his wounds were keeping him from facing his true feelings. I'd once heard that if a twin pair weren't reunited, then it was an indication that both parties still had wounds that needed healing, but this visual reminder of that was overwhelming. Taking it in, I did the only thing I could and continued healing.

But by that point in my training, I'd done enough to realize I really didn't want to become a professional healer. It brought little joy to perform it on others, and the time spent doing it didn't flow effortlessly like when I was writing. Still not sure how to make a living doing what I loved, and with my training over, I did the only thing I could do. I focused on using what I'd learned to keep healing us.

I didn't have to do all the work alone. Prior to learning of his relationship, I'd booked my third session with the master couple, which landed a month after his shocking news had. In it, I learned more about what was really blocking us. Having flip-flopped nearly every day since, regarding my life's direction, I'd become convinced I was channeling his confusion. A lot had changed in my life, but the one thing that was recent, and maddening, was that I couldn't stick to a decision to save my life. Sure that his blocks were the root cause of this; I decided to have them focus the session entirely on him.

We kicked off with my explanation of what had transpired since our last call. Telling them what he'd told me, I went on to explain what I'd felt from him since. Whenever I connected to our soul's love, the one they had taught me to draw down from where we were unified in the universe, I would inadvertently pick up on his gut-wrenching unhappiness. Sensing his sadness within seconds, they agreed it was wise to focus on him since they hadn't tuned in to anyone, in ages, that was so tormented.

What they discovered came as no surprise. Lifetimes of training had programmed him to sacrifice himself, and our love, for the greater good of everyone. The two of us had contracted this agreement in one life after another, when, depending on the period, we'd incarnated as samurai warriors or spiritual crusaders. Believing in honor and obligation over everything, we'd repeatedly kissed each other a final goodbye, so one or the other could go off and die for whatever cause we'd deemed deserved our lives. Then the other had become increasingly devastated, left to question the action that had been agreed upon. Even though our souls had intended for this life to be different, that programming was still active in him, and he was full of the training that had taught him how to cut off his emotions and sacrifice his life.

Trying to clear it, they were forced to pause so they could address another issue. He refused to be helped. Putting up blocks to stop the healing, he wouldn't go up to a higher vibration unless all the other souls hanging on to him received help as well. With every group that was cleared, he took on a new one, continuing to weigh himself down with their struggles. The vow he'd once made to sacrifice his life for others had to be upgraded so he could help them without drowning himself in the process.

Moving back to the heavy task of his healing, they uncovered curses that were keeping our love apart. Made by spiritual leaders that had once believed the path to enlightenment was a solo journey, we'd given our power away to them repeatedly, and they were still impacting us. They'd cursed us to never come together and programmed him to believe he could only do his duty without me there to distract him.

They, along with our samurai instructors, had added another program that needed removing. To them, there was no worse shame than being saved by a woman. Having me do that was torture beyond belief because he believed the man was meant to be the savior. I had some of this teaching still running in me as well, which had made my pursuit of him a difficult one to maintain. Despite having pushed past it repeatedly with each message I'd sent, more needed removing, so the master couple cleared it for both of us.

Feeling overwhelmed by all that lay between us, I faltered and questioned why I was continuing down such an arduous path. Especially when this man had told me he was happy and wanted nothing to do with me. Warning that I was becoming depleted, the kindness in the woman's voice reached out and told me to keep questioning what he'd said. Then she added – "He says he's happy, but I don't believe him." Her man piped up – "Neither do I!" The only part of him that felt happy to them was the one that wanted to sacrifice himself.

Needing to know, despite realizing that it didn't matter, I asked if he even remembered how happy we'd been. He did but also felt adamant that his actions were what was right for everyone. Speaking his thoughts out loud, the woman's voice kindly said – "I had to sacrifice you. Why can't you get with the program and sacrifice me?" Knowing we'd sacrificed ourselves, and our love, plenty, I would never do that again, no matter what he chose to do. Instead, I would keep following my intuition, and be guided by those that could see the bigger picture. In the meantime, I wanted to pull myself out of the isolation my recent round of healing had instigated.

REBORN

CHAPTER 14
CUTTING OLD CORDS
MONTH 4 OF YEAR 3

My exit from solitary healing began when a twin woman, who would soon bring two others my way to reunite our centuries-old tribe of four, popped into my life. She came off the page created to offer our group the support we could only provide each other. This social connection, made up of primarily the female half of splintered twin-soul couples, was formed at the end of the learning series the master twin couple had led us through.

Leaving us to it, we were all now both supporting and practicing what we'd learned on each other. Each asking for assistance when needed, the group would help pinpoint the wounds, karma, curses, vows, contracts and negative energies working to keep each of us separated from the men who were the other half of our same soul. Dedicated to our souls' purpose, we'd all been combatting the dark forces – present in the universe since its onset – for our own periods of time.

Each fully intent on beating whatever was keeping our unconditional love from stepping up and shining out.

A comment made by me, to a post written by another, drew this one to message me privately. Having already learned how to flip a switch and see back into the lives she'd lived, she offered to help me see back into the lives my man and I had shared since that skill was still a difficult one for me to access. In exchange, she asked for help with a situation she was experiencing in this one. Willing to do anything to beat back the forces pulling us in different directions and wanting to step into my power to heal without the help of the master couple, I was open to joining my efforts with hers.

My eyes didn't blink as my hands typed back the yes that invited her into my field. Without knowing that clearing that life's trauma would unravel a thread of tragedies, eventually leading to a few that the first women to take this class had shared across time. Starting off as strangers, this first woman I connected to, whom I came to call D, would push me to face the darkness, both inside and out, that I'd been hiding from, before a push from above would guide me to rescind the access that yes had given her to my energy.

Feeling discomfort with her from the first volley exchanged, her words spoke of the jealousy striking her from a few women who were her colleagues. Still not having fully risen above my own and not wanting to be dragged down further, I nudged her to look deeper, to see what the mirror they were holding up was telling her needed clearing within. Coupled with what I'd picked up on when I'd tuned in to it, which was that the energy coming from these women felt lovely, I was sure there was something bigger that needed to be dealt with. This led to a discussion about the country she was from, the one my parents had immigrated from, that I'd come to resent after a short stint living in one of its northern Italian cities in my late twenties.

Even before I'd been immersed there, I'd cringed at the jealousy rampant in its people when, as a child, I'd seen my parent's friends routinely compare each other's lives and possessions. Mentioning the jealousy circulating in its culture,

I told her she might be experiencing this situation as a nudge to heal the wider jealousy in the collective she'd been born into. She didn't disagree, but sidestepped that advice and called out the overall revulsion I felt for her country, which she'd sensed behind my words. Sending over her thoughts that went against those feelings, I read her list of everything about it that was beautiful, which was everything I'd once loved, and I was driven to check where my deep disgust for the country I'd grown up idolizing lay within me.

I already knew that most of it came from my fight against its governing grip, which used fear to control the people living within its borders. Feeling it tighten around me, while living under its regulations, I'd rebelled and rejected my roots, but had never healed this legacy of disempowerment. I cleared myself of the ancestral binds still pervading my energy system, and then the realization struck that some of my antipathy came from its northern rejection of my poor southern heritage. Making peace with that, I reconciled with the part of me that would always be from there.

Deciding to leave it and her behind, I was pulled back in a week or so later by a new message she sent over. It contained a recent shot of some ancient stones, pillared and arched to create a looming doorway that had once led into an old prison. Her words accompanying it asked me to feel into what had happened between us when we'd both lived there, in the place that still went by the name of Liguria.

It was a city in Italy that I had many connections to, but up until our conversation had no idea of this one. Immediately upon looking at what she'd sent, my stomach dropped, as a vision of what she'd already seen appeared. Born a woman in that lifetime, the man I'd always shared my energy with was dangling from the top of the arch, hung for being a witch. My ancient male eyes stared up in devastation, surrounded by the crowd of eyes looking at the spot where they routinely hung those like us.

Then, my understanding deepened. Out of jealousy, the one I was speaking to now had spoken out against him then, leading directly to the hanging that had separated us and left me alone, overwhelmed with the raising of our children without my love by my side. After clearing the terror from that life's trauma, stuck between us since then, the one who'd triggered it asked for my forgiveness. I gave it without question, knowing that all wounds inflicted stem from wounds triggered.

Still wanting to move myself away from her, I decided to dwindle my responses to her messages, but she wouldn't allow it. Her words called me out, shining a light on the negativity I was feeling that she was picking up on. Knowing any feeling that wasn't positive was one that needed to be expunged so I could put a stop to all self-poisoning, I replied that she was right. That's when another life we shared unraveled. Pushing me back for the second time, this time, she led me to a life over in England that had been lived while one of the two wars was being waged by the world.

Initially humored by the seeming insanity of the situation, the smile was wiped off my face when I instantly felt an umbilical connection. A familiar resentment overwhelmed me as I stated – "You were my mother." A mother that had killed herself out of sadness, over the loss of a father who had gone off to die and left her to live without him by her side. Choosing death, she'd left a daughter feeling abandoned, alone to take on the responsibility that came with an orphaned younger brother.

Confirming what had been felt deeply, D went on to apologize for this second wound that I connected to this life's fear of being rejected and abandoned. Taking longer to resolve than the first, I set to work clearing the visceral resentment I was feeling so I could replace the empty space it left behind with compassion and forgiveness. Thinking I'd fully freed myself from the past that had kept us connected through its negative karma, I decided to truly open up to the possibility of a positive friendship with this woman.

Then, the real purpose of our re-connection started to reveal itself a few weeks later. As I laid my mat down one day to practice yoga with a group of women, I stumbled across my fear of being sliced by the daggers of their jealousy, if any were to notice me shining brightly next to them. Watching myself hide in my own skin, to not risk a hit that wasn't coming, the fear shifted my focus. Instinct drew me back to the message I'd once seen, warning that someone hated me. That led straight to the memory of the strange experience with the shaman I'd once called on for help, back when I'd first started searching for healing in every corner of this life.

Why, after looking into my past lives, had she chosen to ignore me? Had she come across one that we shared where jealousy and hatred had lain between us? And why did I still feel repulsed at the thought of her? With more knowledge than I'd had at the time, and a tightening in my throat that came with these thoughts of her, I wondered if she'd cursed me. Asking the high beings who specialized in clearing those to help, I felt more squeezing and knew I was on to something. Having felt it repeatedly, almost daily, since I'd had my first session with the master couple a year earlier, I'd learned this feeling was brought on when one came across a curse that had been put on them.

Certain my request hadn't managed to clear all of it, I asked D if she could look into it, and she immediately saw what I'd sensed, but took it to a place I hadn't expected. This woman was weakening me by siphoning my power for her own use. Grateful for this clarity, as well as the moments she'd spent helping, I felt deeply that I deserved it as reparation for the wrongs she'd once perpetrated. Picking up on that emotion, she handed over a loaded comment – "You know you did things to me too." Having only seen myself as a victim of lifetimes of tragedies, I hadn't yet faced the life that had kicked off all the others.

Without saying what I would see, she prompted me to look back into ancient Egypt. Fear tried to stop me, but I pushed past it and went where I'd been blocking myself from going before. I was ready to see what I'd been hiding from myself, the deed that lay underneath the guilt that had led my soul to write hundreds of disaster-ridden storylines, which had played out repeatedly.

Lying down, I went up high and asked spirit to direct me back to that time. Shame immediately overwhelmed me. Sensing what I'd done, I couldn't see beyond it and thought I'd never be able to face myself again. I'd killed her. Not just her. There had been a child incubating inside of her, waiting to be born into that life. The killing hadn't been committed with my hands. Worse. I'd turned our ruler, who listened to me, against her.

After whispering enough words to him, he'd turned to his private guard, which my twin-soul had been the head of, and had them torture and kill her for me. Going against his nature, but unable to refuse an order by someone he'd vowed his loyalty to and the desires of the woman he'd loved in secret, he'd obeyed. Thinking I'd faced the worst of it, I told D how incredibly sorry I was for what I'd done, and she went on to add that two other twin women had been there and suffered because of me. Two I didn't know personally, but whose names I'd seen posting comments on the wall of support we all shared our thoughts on.

Spending the night reviewing what I'd been trying to make right through my own suffering, across every life since, I went searching for what else I was to blame for. I couldn't see what I'd done clearly, but I felt the blame and jealousy, and the rest filled itself in. Jealous over the close friend I'd had – called T now – who had been close to all of us then. Jealous of the woman in a marriage of obligation to my twin-soul at that time – called M now – who would soon bring her harmony into our new-old group. Jealous of the power D had that I hadn't believed she deserved. Feeling saddened by my darkness, I wrote one message to all four the next morning. The words came straight from my heart, and I begged them all for forgiveness.

D – whose words would always come over quickly – equally alleviated and added to my guilt. Saying what she believed to be true, she let us know she'd already forgiven me for all of her woes: having her child killed, her body dismembered and her twin-soul murdered. My modern mind couldn't wrap itself around these historic horrors, and despite feeling belief rise out of the depths of my being, I was having the hardest time not calling myself crazy for giving time to this conversation.

T – a sensitive soul that didn't want to look at the

darkness – took some time before responding that she didn't see me there for her torture, but the pain of her uterus being removed then was palpable now, so she needed more time to resolve what this was bringing up for her.

M – who had already cleared enough to raise her vibration high enough to not be triggered by this – didn't care about old stories of being burned back then and had nothing to forgive since she didn't see me as the culprit. She only wanted the healing to happen.

Turning towards that, she launched straight into what she'd already done to clear all of us so we could move forward, closer to a reunion with the men we would always feel the closest to. Having placed us in an energetic circle the night before, she'd put them behind us and then one step back were the women they were currently seeing, that they'd been deluded by the darkness into believing were the ones they should be with. Then she called in the high beings, the ones that would work through us across all the work that lay ahead.

There were three that were connected to Egypt across eternity. The one with the determination to journey the length of the world to find and heal her love – Isis, plus her twin who had been torn to pieces and strewn across the four corners, only to be found by her and reborn into himself – Osiris, and their son that had the vision to see everything more clearly and deeply than any other – Horus. Along with them, there was the one who had an infinite supply of both energy and power – Archangel Michael. He would be the one we called on the most across our work. Coupling him with the Lords of Karma – who oversaw the Akashic Records – together they could clear nearly every trauma across any life they were asked to heal.

Once this higher team had been assembled, M had the power to clear what was holding down the four of us, who had each been held up as high priestesses that were familiar with these universal powers back when we lived together in that time. Starting by drawing on Horus' vision, she was shown the cords intended to bind us to the negative energies that had turned us against each other. Calling on Archangel Michael's sword, he cut through them quickly. Free of our chains, she cleared the curses that were blocking us from standing in our power and next to the men who belonged by our sides.

Finally turning to all the darkness working through our men's current women, she freed them so they could follow their soul's true purpose and find their own highest paths forward. Once all was lifted, she brought down the nourishing energies of the universe to fill us with the unconditional love that was our guiding force. Filled with that love, she then placed protection around us. We received what she asked for. Two inches of rose-pink energy circled us, then the big bouncer high beings came in to surround that light, and Archangel Michael sealed it all with his blue dome of protection.

The eyes I'd been born with this round were new to all of this, so her words made my mind gasp in astonishment at what she'd done. Elated, I thought this meant it was over and my years of exile from the man whose emotions I felt deeply, but whose voice I hadn't heard in what seemed like forever, could come to its end. I had no indication of how much more there was to do before our path was clear of all the negative blocks that had been placed between us back when the world's pyramids were still being used. This first shared life, which was nearly healed, would look like a small blip compared to the second one the four of us would soon come to face together.

But, before that came up, another deed needed to be undone from this one. Directing me once again, D brought my discomfort to the surface when she insisted I had to release her power, which I'd taken back then. Speaking up to defend me, M reasoned that what I'd done was neither alone nor out of greed for what hadn't been mine. This is where our connection to the shaman, still stealing power, had started.

It seemed that back when my energy dropped to the lower levels of jealousy, she'd been able to manipulate me to help her gain the power that had fed her hunger. Unable to do anything about her, I could only reverse my own actions, so I called on the Lords of Karma and Archangel Michael to guide me in releasing what wasn't mine, which I'd never used out of the guilt that came with it. Feeling lighter, we all stood in our power and demanded that more of it be returned to us from the woman, shrouded in darkness, that was still trying to suck it out of us. Standing together, we then said good work and goodnight to each other, mistaken in believing that what we had to do together was over.

REBORN

CHAPTER 15
THE START OF OUR STORY
MONTH 5 OF YEAR 3

Waking the next morning to D's afternoon, messages that spoke of another life, where more darkness had infected us, were waiting to be read. Still in Egypt, but at a later date, she told us that we'd been part of a larger tribe of twin couples, born to teach people how to live guided by love, not fear. Having experienced this greater love in the current lifetime, the idea that we were meant to be an example to others resonated.

We'd all felt the immense power of this love. Sourced directly from the universe, it was boundless and could never wither. A love infinite in its goodness, that placed neither conditions nor judgments on anyone, including oneself. A love that existed free of all jealousy and flowed eternally between twin couples, and was attainable by anyone who pushed past their fears to allow it in. We'd each been born to love in this way.

Despite all the lessons learned and healing done, in the time since I'd had this love physically present daily, I was only just beginning to understand the underlying cause of my separation from the man I shared it with. I'd taken in from early on that each couple was made to exist within the stereotypes of the society our love was meant to thrive in, and hence was bombarded by the same negative energies and self-inflicted challenges as those around us. I got that our minds forgot, immediately upon birth, the challenges our souls had laid out for our love to overcome. I could see that this amnesia ensured we lived like everyone around us and experienced the same terrors they did while we worked to lift everyone's energy higher. I understood that we incarnated to overcome the pits of shame, guilt, hatred, jealousy, betrayal, and pride that ensnared many through the world's fear-based desires. But, had never considered the dark forces that were behind what we were fighting to clear.

Having heard of this darkness, which resided in the universe and created those pitfalls, from the first of the master couple's videos, I hadn't seen it for myself so hadn't put much thought into it. They'd told us, in one of the calls organized to support our individual work, that it had encroached on the original intentions for the planet by embedding codes that carried the slightest bit more darkness than light, which threw yin off-balance from yang and tipped the scales in its favor. But those had just been words that I hadn't considered thoughtfully. I was now seeing the early indications that this was where the real battle lay. Our love was up against the dark force that fueled the fear underneath every ounce of negativity felt and dealt across the world. The one we were meant to beat out of our personal energy systems, as well as the wider collective consciousness.

The jealousy and power struggle we'd already cleared for in Egypt was an example of a time this darkness had won out over my goodness. It was a lifetime I'd entered laden with the losses of the lives lived before it, then exited with more weight laid on me and between us. I was sure our four souls had engineered our meeting in this current life, despite the miles that divided us, so we could work together to clear the root of what was keeping love from winning out over fear.

Only, what had begun then was still actively working to stop us now, springing up to try to keep us from fighting it.

Waking the morning after we'd agreed to work through this second life together, I was slapped with T's fear as I read her words that screamed across the line to D, pleading – "Don't go down there!" With no idea what she was talking about, her anxiety overwhelmed and infused my system with her fear, and I seriously questioned if I could continue working with these women. But my resolve had already been set, and I wouldn't turn away from this path I knew was going to be lined with a lot more fear that needed facing.

Only, not yet. First we had to discover the story linked to these fears. D, who was working through her afternoon, reassured us she hadn't gone anywhere and already knew not to. She was to act as our seer and guide us with the knowledge she picked up on along the way, but the danger to her, if she entered the darkness, was too great a risk for her to take. Not sure why that was, we moved on, and she began to recount what she'd already seen that had happened back then.

In this second Egyptian life, those of us who'd incarnated together had intended on bringing in a greater amount of light and love, to aid in waging a bigger battle against the darkness. Our souls had banded together to work in solidarity so the love, which existed inside and between each of us and our partners, wouldn't get pummeled to death once again. With uncertainty in my abilities blurring my vision, I took in what was said as M confirmed D's story.

The first battle that had been sprung on our group, with the intent of separating us, was between our men and the men we'd come to help. Afraid of the love that would loosen their grip on power, these men had cried out for war. Letting fear in, our men worried over what a war would do to the women and children they loved if it reached the land we lived on. So the men had ridden out across the desert to meet, try to speak to, and if necessary fight them. We'd kissed our loves goodbye, full of our faith in their strength to return to us. None had known how hard that would be to hold on to as the days grew into months that multiplied and fear of what might come back instead of them set in.

The women were left waiting, with nothing to hold on to except faith in their love, which is what bound us together as one tribe. Fifty of whom we were connected to in our current life and whose energy we felt in that pyramid. The four of us, who had recently banded together to right the wrongs done in Egypt, 45 who would only appear as shadows in our visions of that time and names on the wall in this one, and the shaman who knew how to work our fears against us, both then and now.

She stayed quiet initially, watching without our knowing, as we each unearthed what had happened to us back while we were left waiting, fortified behind the walls of a pyramid that had slowly turned itself into a prison of our worst fears. Mirrored in this life, we four fought our fears as we forged ahead to piece it all together, while our men continued to stay away. Intent on understanding the broader meaning, we knew we needed to figure out how to tackle this healing that would help bring them a few steps closer to home.

Seeking answers, we spoke to the couple steeped in mastery that had taught us what we needed to know to do this. Having told them briefly of what we were engaged in, they told us to be careful. What we were taking on was powerful, way beyond the level they had taught us, and by putting our focus on it, we drew its attention our way.

Unsure of what drove the others on, I was sick of the fear that had been soaked into me, and had torn apart the man who emanated the most beautiful light I'd ever seen. Still pressing its wedge between us, fear could attack as much as it wanted, but I wasn't going to let it deter me. Especially not when what waited on the other side of this battle was the only man I could ever love with my entire soul.

Knowing our story from this life – the one that had started with a pure love that was naïve in its beautiful innocence, before it'd been riddled with the shame and jealousy placed on it by another – I shut out that reality to find out what our story had been back in this earlier time. Turning to the Lords of Karma, I probed for the memories that had been forgotten by me and recorded by them.

Tuned in, I saw it clearly – fear had overcome our faith. Gone for what we'd thought was forever, we'd given up on our men and lost our belief that they were strong enough to make it back. With all hope disintegrating from our hearts, fear had taken hold of our minds, and the darkness had worked its magic through the words of the shaman, who'd expected to reap her reward upon our deaths. A discussion was waged, and then a decision made.

The majority of the women had chosen to die by their own hands, instead of enduring the savage invasion of their home and bodies by the opposing force of men. Most of the mothers had wanted to gently lay their children down to meet their deaths, instead of watching their eyes fill with terror as swords flung their spirits out of this world. Under the spell of fear's manipulation, they'd believed this was the only path forward; one paved with a false peace that would lead them out from underneath the stones that had turned into a living entombment.

Sharing what I'd seen, it was confirmed. Resonating with T, M had seen the same. Adding to my vision, D explained our death of choice had been poison, baked into the bread our hands had been kneading to sustain our lives. She'd been the initial instigator but had turned away from doing what she'd advocated. Fighting fear, D and I had dispelled its whispers and chosen to not eat what would choke out the last of our breath and suffocate the babies sleeping inside each of us.

Instead, screaming out pleas, we'd banded together, begging the others to stop and not swallow it either. We failed to convince them. They'd already succumbed to fear, whose whisper had turned into a bellow, and the breaded poison had been eaten and welcomed by what was already entrenched inside of them. The darkness that had birthed this fear rejoiced while it watched the deadening of the innocence inside the children who had been fed first.

This darkness, which had grown larger with the fear we'd fed it in return, had been tracking the men's imminent arrival and knew it had won this battle. Fear had been wedged in-between love by destroying what the two had created together, at the hands of the one who had given birth to the embodiment of that love. Thinking they were making the only choice available, the women, who had chosen death, had unwittingly placed this poisonous energy between themselves and their eternal mates. Terror and blame had remained stuck between each pair well past this death. Left to seep itself into all of their future incarnations, until it was found in this one by us four.

There was no doubt that this was one of the deeds to be dealt with, but we went on to hear more before deciding on our first action. M shared the story she'd unearthed. As one of the men who had gone out to fight in that life, she wasn't there with us, but her twin was one of the women who had been. Tasked with protecting the children, she'd deserted them before their last meal had been handed over. Fear of losing her love had sent her out in search of him. In the desert, lost and wandering, she'd been found by a small group of men. Her body had been raped and destroyed by those who'd broken through the protection our men had left us to provide.

T, still hurting from the wounds once inflicted on her womb, wasn't sure what had happened to her, but knew the poison hadn't killed her either. That's when the pieces started to come together and handed over the answer of why, out of all the women, we'd come together to work on this healing. None of us had died by our own hands.

Her death hidden from her, T could feel the immense weight of stones covering her body. Keeping her trapped deep, somewhere her vision couldn't see into, she could feel men laying alongside her. Her role had made itself known. For now, she was only meant to guide us to the ones stuck wherever her remains were lying, but there were more souls to free than that.

All the men who had eventually made their way back, only to face the death of their women's faith in them, had died and parts of their souls had become eternally disconnected from them and their other halves. We knew they needed to be found, and we each needed to find our love on our own. We didn't know their exact location but knew some of them were piled into another grave that had a mass of men buried together.

That's when more of my knowledge surfaced. M and D told us we needed to free the trapped fragments of their souls so they could rise up to the heavens, and I added in that we had to re-bury their energetic bodies with ours so our remains, that would always exist in that timeline, could lay together in union. T agreed but said to free one we would have to find and release all the ones that were entangled together.

Setting our group discussion aside for the evening, my thirst for this story had been awakened, and I went inward to find out more. I brought the truth I'd felt into forward to the other women the next morning. The men, who had returned to find us dead, either by our own or another's hands, had remained in the pyramid. Their senses heightened by our deaths, they'd felt the darkness in the ground underneath them, which we'd let loose through our fear.

Screaming that God had forsaken us, they'd sworn to honor our love by fighting this darkness to the death. Turning their backs on the torment our deadened bodies gave them, they'd turned their eyes down to face what had beckoned them into the tunnels that ran like a maze underneath their feet. Leaving the life that had already died behind, they'd gone down there, only to be struck by the same spells that had deluded us and would work to keep them trapped in the dark, running around in circles, for centuries.

Then D laid her understanding about the two of us out on the table. She believed she was the keeper of the light, and I was her polarity – the one who held darkness within. Speaking in her broken English, she made me sound worse than I believed I was, but I understood her meaning. My man and I were more deeply connected, than others, to the pain the collective had suffered for eons.

Her words resonated with the pain inside of me, which I'd felt deeply across my entire life, and it fell in line with what the master couple had told me. I knew it was time, in this incarnation, to fulfill my true purpose and instead of soaking up all of the pain of everyone who was suffering, I was to act as a beacon to draw those who were afraid up and into the light. In this work, my role was to go down deeper into the darkness I'd always run and hidden from, to retrieve the souls that were still stuck there.

As we messaged over these realizations about our joint mission, through a flurry of rapid-fire chatter, T and I took a moment to acknowledge the tension that still existed between us. Bottled for centuries, her pain, experienced in the time when I'd been a culprit, needed a release. Reaching out in a private message, we agreed to take some time to clear it together. It had to be done before we proceeded so that it couldn't be turned against us. We set a time to speak face-to-face, via Skype, the afternoon of the next day. The booking was made easier since, despite the miles between us, we both lived on the East Coast and shared the same zone in time. Thinking we were leaving the past behind for at least the next 24 hours, we would soon realize this job was going to run 24/7 until we could find our way through what had been done.

CHAPTER 16
FACING DARKNESS
MONTH 5 OF YEAR 3 CONT'D

My eyes opened early to meet the darkness the next morning. I glanced over at the small screen lying on the pillow next to me and saw lines of a hundred messages waiting to be read. Ignoring them, I looked at the numbers illuminating the time at four a.m. and turned inward to do my morning ritual of clearing and protecting the energy of my man, myself, and everyone we were connected to. Lying in bed as I finished, I sensed a presence inside of me and knew I wasn't alone.

Creeping up my leg, I could feel something sinister trying to take hold. Losing my sense of self, a feeling overwhelmed the belief I'd always held in my intrinsic goodness and tried to convince me it had all been a lie I'd been telling myself. Looking back over the past wrongs I'd committed and thinking over the times in this life I hadn't lived up to the image I held of a good person, the lie that I wasn't good made sense in the moment.

Feeling the creep of darkness rising up my body, I considered giving in and going where it was leading. Hearing I could have whatever I wanted and it would all come to me much easier, my exhaustion over this life, which had held plenty of struggles, weakened my resolve, while darkness slowly tried to draw me in further. Pausing, I considered everything I was feeling and then made my decision.

I accepted there was a darker side to my complex personality, a natural counter-weight to my light, but I was and would be the person my soul had intended – one who was good and did good deeds for those around me. Denying the dark energy invading me its yes, I went on to marry the two sides of myself and brought my dark side into harmonious union with my light. Complete, I opened my eyes to the first of the light streaming through the shades and felt how this union had strengthened my power.

Turning to the words I'd ignored earlier, I saw a steady stream of frenzied chatter from D, responded to by M's calming touch. At the bottom of the other side of the world from her, M's Australian evening would always be D's Italian morning, which would always be the middle of our American night, so while we aimed to work together, T and I woke every morning to endless messages. Laying in the darkness of my early morning, I caught up on the healing they'd kicked off.

Aided by their clear sight, they had both managed to find their other half's remains, and M described in detail what she'd done with hers. With a deep sense of ritual, she'd created a new, golden pyramid made out of pure energy. Its walls were lined with tombs that contained two caskets each, giving every couple a place for their remains. Placing the highest of blessings on it, her intentions encapsulated the entire thing in divine light and infused the energies of harmony, union, and universal balance throughout. Finding her twin out in the desert, she'd asked for their angels to come to her aid and a procession fueled by their love had carried him to their resting place.

Once done, she'd turned to the children and created a second, smaller pyramid that had Archangel Michael's blue dome of protection around it. With the help of her twin, she'd anointed each child with sacred oil, but there were a few that still had the poison running through them and needed saving. Fear was keeping these children, along with their mothers, trapped in the dark rubble, and I was told that I was the one who would have to free them.

Feeling more of my power after that morning's innerbattle, but still uncertain of how to use it, I kept silent as I listened. D, who hadn't gone into details on her re-burial, explained that her and her twin's spirits were positioned at the top of the original pyramid. Streaming light down into it, they were guiding those that could exit on their own over to the pyramids that M had created nearby.

Growing tired, she pushed me to hurry up and free them. Reminding myself of the call I'd always felt to save children, I swallowed my fear and turned my third eye to them. Asking for my energy to be guided back to Egypt, I saw D's white light shining down from above, and I entered the pyramid we'd all died in one way or another.

Walking through the main cavern, my vision picked up the shaman standing over to the left. Beckoning, she begged me to help her. Seeing this as a trick to manipulate and detour me, I let her know she would be helped after everyone else was if help was indeed what she was after. The demonic presence behind her took over, and her pleas transformed themselves into howling laughter. Passing her, I flicked off a few minor negative spirits hovering on my path and was then met by growling dogs that were scary in their fierceness, before they instantly turned sweet on me. Placed there to protect the children, they sensed who I was and walked by my side into the inner chamber housing them.

Met by the endless wails of a grieving mother, kneeled over her child since the moment of his death, I set to work clearing her of everything keeping her trapped there. Ridding her being of the delusion spell that had worked its magic on all the women who had taken in its poison, I then turned to her ensuing feelings of resentment and anger, directed straight at D for having set them on the path to suicide. Her blame, held deeply against herself, and a fear of the darkness were the last to go.

With her energy lightened, I cleared the blame and bitterness her child was directing towards her for his death. Asking that they be cleared of all the poison running through their veins, I saw their soul fragments rise up and then my man's spirit came to help me carry the residue of their energetic remains over to the caskets M had created for them to rest in.

I knew why I was the one that had to do this work. I was connected to them through the blame I held against myself. With her wails lifted, the other three mothers were clear of her influence, and the same healing for them and their children took less time. Once the angels took them to their new beds, I asked for the whitest of lights to come down and clear the chamber of all the negative energy their poison-fueled feelings, felt for ages, had filled it with.

With them released, along with some of my fear, I felt more of my power and chose to head over to the opening that led down into the tunnels. Still too afraid to go into that darkness alone, I called out to the men that were down there and let them know I was coming for them. Returning to my time, I told D and M what had transpired. Applauding my efforts, which I was aware had only been possible because of their push, the joy exchanged between the three of us, for this team effort, was authentic. T – too entangled in the current life she shared with a young son and a difficult ex – couldn't track the tirade of early morning messages, so she didn't respond, but the two of us were still set to speak later that day.

At our appointed hour we saw each other's faces, and the two of us who had once been close, before jealousy and pain separated us, said our first verbal hello in this life. T's lightness came through the line, and I felt my ancient desire to shine alongside her beam. But, in that moment, my guilt and her fear were still heavy and kept us from going into what we'd intended to clear. We acknowledged it, then quickly moved past the first and on to the second shared life we were working on. Discussing what had been found and done, while adding a few words bemoaning the multitude of words streaming in daily, we decided to go back together and see if we could find our missing men.

Closing our eyes, we both turned inward, only to be pulled out of it quickly. My puppy wouldn't stop jumping his paws up onto my shoulders, leaning over me to look into the screen that held T's face. This gentle giant had been with me for four months by then, and I was surprised by this new behavior. Jet-black in his outward appearance, he carried nothing but the brightest light inside of him and was obviously attracted to the one inside of her. T confirmed that this was how all animals behaved around her. Putting him out on the deck, while his barks continually whined to be let back in, we got to work.

Tuning in together, my senses picked out of the debris what we both felt was true. Neither of our men's bodies had been buried in the vicinity of that first pyramid. While mine had died there, leaving some of his energy behind, his remains had been carried away as a relic. Preserved and enshrined at a later date, as a symbol of that era across time, in a museum of history. Hers had lived, but returning to find death, had fled to Asia, to live out his life alone, without any love in it. We ended our delving more informed, but without healing anything that had once transpired between us. Having glossed over it while standing in the light we both wanted to stay firmly rooted in, we said goodbye for the moment.

With this new knowledge of where my love was lying, I immediately turned to the task at hand without delay. Sending my energy out to find the portion of his that was trapped on display in England, I got to work. I called on our personal team of healing angels to help me break through his glass prison; freeing and bringing him back to the land of that body's birth. Carrying him on their shoulders while I called out to the body that had once been mine, we proceeded to the tomb where we could lay down together. Immediately upon arriving, our energies jumped into one casket, refusing to be separated by the slabs of two individual ones, even if they were positioned next to each other.

Then the one that had been our unborn child came to cuddle in with us. Relief embalmed our energy bodies as I asked the high beings to place protection, in the form of crystals and Celtic crosses, around our tomb. The last touch, meant to bring joy to the ones we'd been, was to add the notes of our favorite music, which would never stop playing, as well as golden flowers that would never wilt. Thinking the others would enjoy these touches too, I asked for every tomb to be given the notes and flowers that each couple preferred, before departing.

Happy with my deeds of the day, I called it a night, with no indication of how many more challenges were waiting to be confronted. The next morning's messages chronicled a fresh discussion that had been held while I slept, but didn't list any new healing done. I jumped in to record my latest deed, and D immediately responded, leading the two of us to dive deeper into the story of what had happened back then, which was intrinsically connected to the soul-aching separation we were trying to rectify now. We flung our feelings into the air and tried to piece together all the confusing aspects we'd uncovered.

Had my man made it back, only to find me dead at the sword of another male twin? One who had been the friend that left him to die, wounded in the desert, out of a fear that he wouldn't make it back if he continued to carry him. Yes, that felt right. Had I lost faith in my other half's strength to make it back to me, a few moments before he managed to arrive? Yes, I was sure of that fact. Had my mouth opened up to insult the man who left him behind with a tirade of curses, leading to death for my child and me? Yes, that matched my vocal history.

Had D died from the bone-crushing fear of having to live without ever seeing her twin again? That mirrored her suicide in a later life, but dying from fear, as a natural cause, didn't make sense to me. Had D's twin, desolate at the loss of her life, taken his own? That's how she saw it. Or had my twin, upon his return, killed D for instigating the suicidal killings? Had her twin arrived too late to intervene, but in time to fling his sword at him? Is that how he'd met the death that had led his body to be carried away by others? My senses, stronger than when we'd begun, but still not able to see the death blow that had been dealt him, led me down this hole of confusion.

Reeling, I finally declared enough and decided I didn't need any more details. I had more than enough information to go on.

Starting to fray under this constant pull into the past, fear kept me from moving on to the healing I knew I had to handle on my own. Fueled by one of my biggest terrors in this life, I avoided the call to head underground, into the darkness of those tunnels. I doubted I would know what to do once I found them and feared going up against whatever was down there, alone. Feeling my smallness, I questioned if I was powerful enough to do what was being asked of me.

My fear was amplified by the message we received the next morning from the master couple, who we'd been periodically messaging our progress. They started off by warning us that we needed to clear the heavy curses that had been placed on D, which was why she had to stay at the top of the pyramid and not enter it. Reminding us we were up against a great force, they asked us to work with caution and advised we never go in to clear anything without each other's support. While we were all powerful souls, they didn't want us to breach the limits of our newly awakened abilities. My fear fed, I questioned the push to go down there alone. Had it been the work of the shaman? Was she trying to lead me somewhere that would leave me vulnerable? I didn't know, but I took their message seriously and let fear win the moment.

Arriving, later that day, at the few hours when we were all awake, the four of us started to discuss everything over our group thread. Mulling over the master message we'd received, we also pondered the words recently posted on the wider group wall by some of the other twin women, those not involved in this with us. There were more than a few that had asked for help clearing a sudden, intense anxiety that had overtaken them.

Within a few days of our past life probing, we'd each started to feel a high-strung anxiety, which we'd chalked up to the stress of the work at hand. Now we were hearing the same feeling had infected the other women. Tuning into it, we realized the heaviness we were all feeling was a fresh attack the shaman had instigated. Already knowing that she knew about us, we'd been unaware that setting our sights on the past would trigger her awareness of everyone we were connected to in the present.

That's when my eyes turned from the larger screen I was typing on to the small screen that was ringing with an incoming call from T. Too rushed to type a message since her phone was dying, she was frantic to tell us what she'd just sensed. The shaman's eyes were tracking us. Not sure how, but sure she was seeing everything we were doing, T's fear crossed the line and entered me.

Frantic, I wrote the other two to let them know about this new discovery and made a plea that we ask the couple, who'd taught us their mastery, to step in and help us fight this battle. Resolute in their answers, they both believed it was ok to tell them, but that the four of us had been brought together for a purpose and this was our challenge to overcome. It was what had to be done for each of us to step into our own power.

Leaving each other with the extra protection of outward facing mirrors embedded within Archangel Michael's blue dome of protection, I went off to write the message we'd all agreed on to the masters. It would summarize what had happened, so we could see what tips they could provide, but it wouldn't go as far as to ask for their intervention. Sending it that night, we received a reply the next morning. With too many details for their busy eyes to handle, their short response left me disenchanted.

Seeming to have missed the jeopardy I was sure the entire group was under, they thanked us for our service and asked we make our messages shorter. Writing their help off, my resentment spiked, but I reasoned it away. With them having stepped back, I realized the women were right, and this task was one we were meant to work through. Later that afternoon, I made the abrupt decision to face my fear and take action. Since there was no one else to do it, I knew it was time for me to get to it.

Tuning in, I asked my soul to guide me to the coordinates of the pyramid, in the area of Egypt D had since identified as Heliopolis. Placing the dome of protection around me, which Archangel Michael consistently provided, I filled my masculine side up to full with his strength and called on his twin, Faith, to match it in the feminine. With them fueling me, I marched myself down into the tunnels. The beam of their energy came down through my crown and emanated out from my heart to stream a ray of light ahead of me. Going as far as I could, their light went further into the darkness to find the men who were lost, to guide their way up. Their beacon was reaching deeper than it could have because of the steps I'd taken.

Feeling the men weeping, I called on Archangel Michael's light to clear the fear and torment that was weighing their energy down, which had been initiated by their love's death and then compounded by the sacrifice they'd made of themselves. Then my man's spirit arrived. Standing tall by my side, he joined his strength with mine, and we grew more powerful as we worked together. Feeling the beauty emanating from this union, I asked for the men to be healed of what was keeping them trapped, the same things keeping him away from me in our current time.

The feeling of having lost their masculinity, after the misperception had taken hold that they weren't strong enough to save those they loved, whom they had been resolved to protect. The belief that their only recourse had been to sacrifice their lives, so they could deem themselves worthy. The loss of their faith in themselves, which had been torn out of them after seeing that their women had lost theirs in them. Their anger, misdirected at God, for having forsaken them. The list went on, and I called it out while the pain of each clearing wrenched through my body that was breathing in the present. I worked through it all while intending for more light to reach them. Then I turned to their delusions and asked the high beings, tasked by the universe to dispel those, to clear them so they could stop stumbling in the dark, out of a deluded fear of the light.

The weight keeping them down lightened, but the darkness around us grew heavier, and I realized we had to get out of there in a hurry. Blocked by what our efforts were fighting, the Archangels' light had been cut off and was no longer reaching me. I quickly turned back to the tunnel's opening and fled with my man in step. Looking over my shoulder every few steps, I sent out the remaining light inside of me and directed it towards the men, determined to lead them out of this purgatory. I voiced what I'd learned as I stumbled forward, and my words told their trapped soul fragments to rise up and reconnect with the part of their souls that existed up high, watching and waiting for them.

Reaching the top, I stopped short, blocked in by the boulders that had been placed in front of the entrance I'd just entered. I directed what little light I had left towards the pile, but I couldn't move it. That's when my man stepped in and used his strength to sweep aside what would have trapped me had I been down there alone. Stepping across the line between darkness and light, we were instantly bowled over by the steady stream of lost souls escaping what had held them down for centuries. The men's energy, finally free, rushed to return home, to be greeted by the love that exists, no matter the distance or length of separation, across eternity.

Back in my time, where he hadn't yet come to stand by my side, I felt my man's spirit leave me and return to walk alongside the body whose ego was still blocking the both of us. I realized at that moment that this separation was leading me to my true power, which wouldn't have happened if he had come back already. This gave me a new appreciation for the journey we were on.

Replaying the events that had just occurred, to the women who stood with me at the moment, I cherished hearing M's acknowledgment of my bravery. Still needing that affirmation despite everything I'd just done, I realized, despite my growth, that I had yet to reach a place where I fully believed in my own power. Feeling a healthy dose of pride, mixed in with a touch of lingering doubt, there was still a voice in my head that wondered if we were just feeding each other's imagination. With my faith still tinged in doubt, I turned off the competing feelings so I could take in M's wisdom.

With more knowledge of rituals, she informed me that the work on these souls wasn't done. D's light had already led their energetic remains over to meet those of their women, but we still needed to breathe life back into them. At a complete loss on how to do that, I asked if I needed to do anything. Feeling like I'd done my part, I really wanted to rest and catch my breath in the world that surrounded me.

With D asleep and T distracted by her duties, M said she could handle the work but would appreciate it if I held some sacred, safe space for her while she did it. Not wanting to leave her to deal with it alone, I did as she instructed, and burned candles and sage while focusing my energy in on hers. Reading the words she was going to mouth, I was left baffled by the degree of her bewitching experience.

The ancient words she channeled cracked the men's mouths open and sacred air breathed life back into them. Calling on them to awaken, she asked for them to become alert, rejuvenated, and protected by the high beings watching over them. Then she brought in a holy key and set it to spin over each of them, bringing everyone's belief in their dreams and faith in the light back to them. I spent the better part of an hour staring at those candles, while M completed this elaborate ritual. The energy shifted around me with every word, and my hope grew with each breath. At the end, we shared gratitude for what we'd accomplished together.

With that day's heavy lifting done, I decided I'd take the next day off to focus on my life, which needed some attention. Having finished my contract position four months earlier, I had a lot of fear rising over when I was going to make more money. Anxious that what I'd saved was dwindling, I was conscious that this work, while important, wasn't going to pay my bills nor help me get by in the world pulsing around me. The fear of running out of cash tightened my heart, but I knew I was being tested by it and needed to hold on to my faith that the universe would bring what I needed at precisely the right moment. I knew that, as well as the fact that the all-consuming nature of this work was only possible because of this interlude I'd been given, but I still wanted to restart the life that had been put on pause.

REBORN

CHAPTER 17
STRUGGLING TO STAY THE COURSE
MONTH 6 OF YEAR 3

Heading out the next morning after a quick glance at and away from that day's early stream of messages, I tried to kick off what was meant to be a routine morning. But the past, ever present, refused to be silenced. A few hours in and it struck full force. On the walk back from a muddy trip to the park I took my dog to play at daily, I made the mistake of pulling out the phone that was tucked into a pocket. The frantic energy emanating up from the messages that inundated my screen quickly took over. Scanning the jumble, I got the gist.

M and D had gone back and found another pile of bodies in a pit outside the pyramid. I couldn't follow all of the healing they were doing, documented in half-formed sentences flung back and forth, while their energies were directed into ancient Egypt and their bodies sat breathing a world apart. What screamed out at me was my name, sat next to D's shout to hurry up and help. Typing that I was 10 minutes out while pulling my mud-caked pup along beside me, I rushed to get home and join the healing; the frenzied pace of which had already worn me out. Not sure why everything that happened so long ago had to be done with such urgency; my resentment, at being pulled back in by messages both bursting with hysteria and barely decipherable, boiled.

Arriving, I put my dog on the deck with his mud and laid myself down to focus. Shutting out the messages that were pinging every millisecond, I zoomed over the pit to see what needed to be done. With D and M standing on opposite ledges while directing light down into it, I knew I should join them, but it wasn't happening. Breaking back in through the door he'd learned how to open, I heard mud being slapped everywhere in the present.

I furiously typed that I had an emergency in real time to attend to, and rushed us into the shower to wash him off before any damage could be done. While the mud ran off him in rivulets, I swore angrily that another one of my days had been hijacked. Having rinsed him off, I then cleansed myself of the negative energy emanating off me and was able to overcome the angry feelings that I hated. After washing off the mud I'd picked up while bathing him, I returned to what the stream of messages had kicked off.

Going to the spot they'd just left, I knew what I had to do and did it without any questions to them or doubt in myself. Back at the pit, I jumped down into it without hesitation. They'd helped the men up who were able, but I had to do what I'd done before and go down to free the ones too entangled to rise. These men had died by fire, set on them by the opposing force while they'd still been alive. It'd kept them roasting and screaming in agony until their final moments, only to then have death turn around and trap them.

Asking for all the pain blinding them to be disintegrated, I then turned to their fear of the light. It came from the delusions placed on them, as well as the correlation they'd made between it and the flames that had delivered death. Clearing the former with the same team as before, I then turned to the latter and called on Kuan Yin – a goddess of compassion from China – to ride in on her dragon. Breathing a steady stream of light onto them, their burns were soothed and healed with the gentle beam emanating from his giant mouth.

Bringing down the golden sword wielded by Archangel Michael, I asked him to cut the chains they'd died wearing, that were still holding down their energy. That clearing done, I brought universal energy down to stream into them and asked for it to pump up the power in their legs, giving them the strength to climb out of this grave themselves. After leading them home to their caskets, I returned for a final act and sent light down to where so much despair had lain, so it could burn away the remnants of the chains that had kept them bound there.

Done, I felt sure our work was over, and I was more than ready to say good job to the other women and goodbye to Egypt. But they knew there was still more to get through. Not D, she was in agreement and wanted to get back to making her twin's healing a primary focus. But T, who hadn't unearthed her story, said she was still buried in the rubble with a group of souls we had yet to uncover. And M was adamant that, while what we'd done was necessary, we still hadn't found and combatted the darker entity behind everything, not to mention the shaman.

Still, I resisted. Telling myself that T only had to open her eyes to whatever had happened to her then, so she could face the fear that consumed her now, I didn't believe there were other souls left to save. My own fear of losing what little normality was left in my life, as well as that of going forward into a battle without any structured strategy, was keeping me from facing the fact that we still weren't done. Instead, I tried to end it by taking the initiative and going back to the ground that had been desecrated by darkness, to perform a healing on it.

Starting with the visible signs of what had doomed us, I shined a light down to clear away the souls of the men who had died there while killing ours, as well as the dark entities that all this death had drawn there. Then I cleared away the rubble of the pyramid that had been brought down on top of us. With my tired body throbbing, I asked for a broader healing for all of the twin couples that had been stationed there, so the men could be relieved of the delusions that were keeping them from seeing their souls' truth. Knowing that job would take more effort on the part of their own women, I did what I could and left the rest for them to clear, once they were ready to uncover it on their own journeys.

Then, turning the two new pyramids and all the tombs and caskets within them into a transparent glass that would let light in, I asked Archangel Michael to place his blue dome of protection above, around, and below the entire area. I filled it all to the brim with the shine of the brightest sun, the one that existed further out in the center of the galaxy. With the darkness that had once resided there disintegrated and the sun shining its brightness down, I asked for the domed space to be filled with a flourish of life in the form of the most vibrant grass, trees, and flowers imaginable. Set to grow across eternity, I packed the earth they were sprouting from with enough nutrients to sustain them. This burial ground that had once absorbed so much death and destruction was now a sacred memorial to those that had lived, loved, and died there.

Feeling more than confident that even if the work wasn't over, I'd done more than enough of the heavy lifting, I sat back and waited to see what the others would say needed to be done. But before we could get there, we had to deal with each other. The beauty and harmony I'd just created didn't follow me back to my current location, and the climate between the four of us soon deteriorated.

Not with M. If anything we'd become closer across a few private messages sent amid our work. It'd been in one of those that she'd brought to light what I hadn't been able to feel for myself. Telling her about the message I'd received from my man a few months earlier, she'd tuned in to what lay behind it and said his energy had been begging me to not make him look at what was too painful to remember. Surprised to hear that it hadn't been pure annoyance towards me, she went on to tell two things that made my heart beat harder from the beauty of them. The dog I loved unconditionally had belonged to my golden man in a previous life. Sent to love and protect me while he wasn't able to, our dog loved my man as much as I did. She'd also felt the love that my man and I held for each other and said that once brought together we'd be a powerful force that could heal and raise the vibration of those around us without doing anything other than loving one another.

I loved hearing these messages, especially coming from this woman whom I'd grown to admire. I knew she could see and understand me, and that she saw the world through the same type of lens I did. One that was focused on harmony, but was able to see the deeper wounds inside that led everyone's actions and reactions. That lens was enabling us both to pick up on the wounds within D, whose negative reactions were growing with intensity and starting to impact us.

A line was being drawn that I was firmly planted on one side of, and although M was secretly there with me, she was wording her replies softly, so the other two still heard her as a neutral voice of reason. I hadn't, as of yet, learned the lessons that had repeatedly tried to teach me the importance of that touch. My truth, as it had been in previous lives when it'd gotten me in trouble, was being declared with the strength of my convictions.

Even though my tone was tempered to not tromp on anyone's feelings, I wouldn't stop wording one reply after another, which was starting to rile D up. I believed we knew enough of the story and had done enough of the healing to let the broader group of women join us in the last round of this battle, the one we'd scheduled to do face-to-face on the following Saturday, a few days from then. The team was divided down the middle. T's fear over what she was going to have to face, and D's pain over a perceived attack by one of those women, who hadn't intended to trigger a wound with a post she'd written, was keeping them from agreeing to what I believed was in the highest good of all.

In truth, this division between D and me had been there from the beginning, before I'd squelched my dissent so I wouldn't create a divide that was impossible to work through. It'd started when T nominated D, who had then elected herself as our team's voice in respect to any messages sent to the master couple. Decided before M and I had had a chance to read or respond, it'd seriously irked me. There was an erratic nature to D's messages that had worried me from the beginning. The quickness of her retorts that read as if she hadn't taken in anything said before she responded, had warned me I didn't want her voice to be the one representing mine.

With a lightness I hadn't been feeling, I'd immediately suggested we discuss this team decision. No flares had gone off, and even though I'd felt that D was offended, I'd been satisfied when all four had unanimously agreed that M would speak for us while including everyone on each message. Then, for the sake of harmony, I'd chosen to let it go when D had written two days later to tell us, nonchalantly, of the response one of the masters had sent her to the message none of us had known she'd written.

Having already healed enough of my wounds that this would have once triggered massively, I'd been annoyed, but not to the point of breaking. Then, the almost daily requests she'd sent, both to the group and privately to each member, asking us to tune in to see if her anxiety, at any given moment, belonged to her twin, had started raising an eyebrow.

Telling her it didn't matter, I'd explained that even if she was picking up on his, it was triggering an anxiety that was hers, one that needed to be uncovered so she could clear it. Typing back, she'd told me that I didn't understand because life was different for her since she was working and had to stay in control. I had smiled at the fact that if sent six months earlier, my unhealed wounds would have riled at the implication that my unemployment status didn't measure me up to her. Instead, with a simple ok, I'd let it go, but had kept my eyes open so her wounds wouldn't lead me somewhere I didn't want to go.

Knowing what I was doing, I'd chosen to buckle when necessary to maintain the group's harmony, but what I believed in never changed. I'd first advocated coming out in the open and telling everyone everything right at the beginning, so they could help with this healing, but had backed down and followed the team's differing, unified decision. Worried that it was too heavy for them, they hadn't thought the broader group of women were ready to go into the depths of this kind of darkness. Feeling sure we were all equal in strength and that our work would be stronger with more numbers, I'd brought it up again after the Egyptian burial ground had been sanctified.

M, who agreed with me wholeheartedly, spoke alongside me but kept her words light to not create a hard divide we wouldn't be able to come back from. The other women couldn't see what I felt, no matter how carefully I crafted my words. It felt demeaning, to all the other women who were being affected by the work we were doing, to assume we were stronger than them. The exchange between D and me became heated, and I didn't win my case, nor was it right to say, when I declared that her ego was coming into play. For the most part, T stayed out of it, and while she was trying to hear my side, it was apparent she was too overwhelmed by fear to focus on anything other than that.

We'd been told the darkness we were going up against would try everything to turn us away, and that one of its tricks would undoubtedly be to try to divide us. I could see its efforts to trigger all of our wounds were working, so I finally decided to step back from my position. While I believed in what I wanted, I didn't want the darkness to win before we even reached our last battle. I could also feel an eternal struggle for power playing itself out between D and me, which I didn't fully understand but wouldn't let interfere with this healing. So even though M and I had agreed we would keep fighting before she'd turned in for her night, I relented.

After waking and catching up on the messages, she questioned what had happened and then put up her own quiet fight, off to the side, with T. M convinced her to change her mind and let the others in, but even with our numbers outweighing her, D wouldn't budge. Analyzing the situation, M and I agreed that the wounds D still hadn't cleared, those standing in the way of her seeing what we were saying clearly, weren't going to be resolved any time soon. We agreed to let it go and have the team's overall decision be a no-go on this one.

Over on the wall that the greater group of women were writing on, I soon noticed a message posted by a woman whose name I'd never read before but had heard in my head earlier that week, and I realized spirit had stepped in to give us the support we needed. Knowing nothing of what we were planning, she was sending out a request for a group meditation, to be held at the same time and day of our work. She'd been guided by a power that wasn't struggling, and thanks to her the majority of the women would send their light and love out into the world, to fight the darkness working against all of us, at the exact moment the four of us would be going up against it head on.

Only, darkness wasn't done trying to detour us through division. The hundreds of daily messages had been tough for everyone, especially T, to weed through. She may have been hit hardest because of her struggles at home, but M and I had felt bombarded by the litany as well. D hadn't said it bothered her, but regardless, the overall communication between all of us was faltering. It was evident in the number of messages sent that seemed to completely ignore anything said a handful of lines earlier, adding to the number of lines written because almost everything had to be explained twice.

M, to solve for it, had created a new page for our group so we could organize, through separate postings, what we each uncovered and believed was behind all of this. It'd been done to help us work together more smoothly while we planned our pending battle. M had started posting her knowledge on it as soon as it was up. Detailed explanations of what she uncovered with her intuition, as well as what she unearthed in the books she was reading. The ones that held more in-depth explanations on how to call on the light forces in the universe to combat the dark ones positioned against them.

In all fairness, the posts had been overwhelming, but I'd taken them in since I'd known that not to would just lead to more erratic messaging and healing. What I pulled out of everything felt simple, and I could feel its truth resonate. The only weapon we needed was love. We had to go in with it firmly implanted within us, holding it up as a shield so we could then drench the darkness with what our souls had sent us to do. Love was the key. I was sure of it.

M understood what I said deeply, but felt we needed to go in armored with more tactics than that. Neither T nor D followed everything posted, and this simplicity was hidden amongst more messages than they were able to weed through. With new contention kicking off over who had and hadn't read everything, which I'd started in my annoyance, we all called a time out and agreed it was time to stop adding more details. At the appointed hour the three of us would show up to assist M, who with her expertise in rituals would lead us wherever we had to go and through whatever we had to do to fight our way through the last of this.

REBORN

CHAPTER 18
CREATING A CLEAR BEACON
MONTH 6 OF YEAR 3 - CONT'D

Before we arrived at our appointed hour, I would have to fight off a fresh attack on my faith in my goodness. As I rushed back from yoga, I was bombarded with the fear that I wasn't who I wanted to be, and I never would be because of whatever darkness resided within that I couldn't exorcise. It seemed obvious. If I was good then why was I starting problems amongst this group of women?

The disappointment I felt in myself over this led to an adamant proclamation, stated silently, releasing any ties linking my love to me. Not that it was possible to do that, since we were bound at a higher level, but I went ahead and told him I knew I didn't deserve him. My mind sent the message that I was sure the woman he was with had a good nature, one he deserved to be coupled with since his spirit was so golden, and I hoped he would find lasting happiness with her in this relationship.

Almost as quickly as it came up, I reeled myself back in, realizing I was being led astray in an attempt to shake the love I needed to have a solid grasp on across the hours ahead. Clearing any new blocks my words had inadvertently created, I hurried home to face the darkness that had raged a battle inside of me since before I knew where it came from, or how to fight off the fear it wielded so expertly.

Home, surrounded by the sage I'd lit and sat next to the crystals I'd laid down, I looked at the three faces lined up on the screen in front of me, and we initiated our healing. All tension laid to rest, I felt the gratitude I held for these women and was thankful the darkness hadn't succeeded in killing our connection. We started with M leading us through some group work to clean our energy.

Envisioning a scorpion positioned at each of our seven chakras, starting at the root and finishing at the crown, we thanked it for teaching us our lessons. Each of us silently repeated M's words, declaring its darkness had no hold over us any longer. The intensity I felt when the scorpion was at my heart, then my throat, confirmed I had barriers in those chakras that still needed to be worked through, but this wasn't the time to deal with them. That work would come later. For now, we released the scorpion and watched as it transformed into a positive symbol. Everyone had a unique one pop to mind. Mine was formed from two curved lines, joined together to create one innocent heart that looked like it'd been drawn by the hand of a small child.

Moving on, we spoke of the broader healing that needed to be tackled, and we were all in unanimous agreement. The day was going to center around T and what she'd been too afraid to look at previously, but had tuned into earlier in the week on her own. Her hands rose to cover the face she was ashamed to have us look at, as she tried to bring herself to recite, through her tears, what she'd done and then buried. Positive that I was right, I chimed in that I didn't think she was the only one responsible. My gut, which was filled with guilt, was screaming that I'd played a part in whatever had been done. She disagreed and took all the blame for what she'd been too afraid to tell us in front of the larger group of women.

Her story was stopped short before it started. The attack I'd felt earlier picked back up, but this time it was aimed at the other women. First, it hit T through the child who couldn't protect himself. Pulled away from her focus for a few moments, she was forced to answer a knock on the door from a neighbor who wanted to tell her he'd knocked something over while playing outside their apartment. Then for longer, after he came in and knocked her off our connection by kicking the cord that ran into the wall of their home. Once we got her back, I tuned in and felt a frenetic energy overwhelming him. I did what I could to clear the chaos working through him to try to stop us. Done with that, we moved on.

Only to be immediately sidetracked by D. A massive pounding in her temples was keeping her from focusing her full attention our way. After we cleared that, she thought it essential to tell us that I could still betray them. Fearing her words, I silently questioned myself, and despite knowing I would never want to betray anyone, doubt filled me. I didn't know for sure that I wouldn't justify her accusation. Trying to set her words aside, we heard that M, as always, was feeling fine, but T was still being hit heavily.

Tuning in, I picked up on something that brought us full circle when I realized the shaman was watching us through T's eyes. My revelation wasn't a surprise to T since she'd already figured out that they were connected in the deed she'd done. The one she deemed the worst ever committed. Keeping that story on hold, we cleared all the vows and contractual obligations that had been made between them, so she could finally be free of this other woman that had been tracking us this entire time.

That's when I felt the shaman clearly. Nearly crying with compassion for her, I voiced what she was telling me. She was lonely and only wanted to be included, so she could help do whatever needed to be done to end this. Our leader quickly jumped in to combat that bit of trickery and said she was sure this woman was trying to manipulate me. Despite my faith in M, I felt the emphatic call to ignore what was said and invite her in anyway.

Pushing my compassion aside, I listened to the woman I trusted and agreed this other one was playing on my good nature. That's when I understood the truth that had eluded me. I, like everyone, would always face choices, which if made without connecting to my inner wisdom could lead my life into darkness, but that wasn't going to happen in this reality. I'd already proven I would almost always choose wisely, and if a mistake were made, then I would always rectify my actions, returning to the light as quickly as possible.

With this newfound confidence in myself, I voiced that we needed to all vow that none of us could invite this woman into this circle of our own volition. She could only enter if we voted and came to a unanimous decision. Everyone agreed and made a silent vow we trusted would work. Finally clear of her attacks, M led us into the work this shaman was trying to stop us from starting.

Going back to the fear that we'd all inhaled in the beginning, we picked up that it had to be cleared from our lungs, where it was still choking us. While doing that we realized our fears had given it form, turning it into an entity that had grown more massive with every new fear we'd fed it. Then, our faithless actions had opened the door that had let it loose into the world, to contribute to the negativity that plagued the collective. Each of us that had lost our faith in love, and instead had sunk into despair, had allowed more fear to enter the world. Calling on our trusted team of high beings, we asked for this dark cloud, which had weighed on everyone for centuries, to be vacuumed out of us, our men, and everyone we'd shared breath with at the time of its first inhalation, hoping to remove the fear it'd wielded over everyone since then.

Clean of it, but knowing there was still more to do, M led us to imagine we were standing at the top of a sun-soaked hill together. Guiding us down a path, we walked towards an old manor planted at the bottom, waiting for us. After entering through its enormous double doors, we saw rooms lining the hallway in front of us, each with a name engraved on its door. M told us to enter the one that held ours and pick out one of the books shelved on the endless rows covering its walls. Landing on whatever page it opened itself up to, the words written there would tell each of us what we had left to do.

Mine opened in the middle, and while there were words to be seen on the pages before and after, the spread I was looking at held nothing but whiteness. There wasn't one thing left for me to actively do in this healing. Despite hearing the word "done," I feared I was being lazy, so I felt in to see if this was really the right direction. That's when I saw what lay ahead, after that day's healing ended. A pair of heavy boots, the type worn by a workman, appeared on my feet, and I was told – "Stomp out fear." Then I heard what would come after – "LOVE."

Elated, thinking that meant my man would be standing by my side soon, I waited for the others to tell everyone what they'd read. Our lead guide explained she was only meant to support us, which felt right, but D's direction didn't resonate, and I silently questioned if we really needed to do it. Having already cleared and created life around the ground where we'd died, what she said needed to be done there, which I was having a hard time tracking, didn't feel like a fit.

I decided to go along with it anyway since shining light up the sides of the pyramid and laying stones down at each corner didn't seem like something that could hurt the brightness I'd asked to shine there eternally. But that was to be done last. First, we needed to get to what our work on this day had been geared towards – it was time for T to tell us the truth she'd been afraid to face.

Apologizing profusely, she laid out what was tormenting her soul. She'd cursed every one of us that had been stationed there. Her grief over the womb she'd lost that she hadn't been able to let go of had given the darkness an opening to manipulate her. Grief had turned the beauty inside of her bitter and had drawn out a resentment that led her to vow that none of us would ever have that which she'd lost. Banning every twin couple from ever birthing or raising a child together, she'd given the dark forces precisely what they'd wanted. Her words, laden with vengeance, had ensured each couple's unconditional love wasn't passed down to the next generation, across every incarnation that had existed since that one.

My womb was struck with a heavy sense of loss by her revelation. Having already accepted that I'd lost children, both my own and the one belonging to my man, I was shocked silent. Hearing about this curse that had caused all that grief gave me a feeling of relief since my fear for his son could finally be released, but it also brought on a faint sense of bitterness. I refused to go there and shook off the resentment that was trying to find its footing within.

Putting the pieces together, I saw the connection and realized the guilt I'd felt earlier, for T's actions, had come from the life when I'd been held responsible for removing her womb. Knowing that one action triggers the next, I knew there were lifetimes of earlier acts shot back and forth, and I was determined to end my part in this cycle. Telling her she wasn't to blame and was forgiven by me, but more importantly, needed to forgive herself, we all took turns trying to make her feel better.

Setting her guilt aside, she went on to recant the curse that had doomed our love from multiplying across the centuries. She had to be the one to do it, and I finally understood why all of my requests to the high beings had never left me feeling like my man's son would be safe once we came back together. Lifted, I was relieved I no longer had to worry about this threat, which had been energetically felt from the moment our separation started and was one of the major blocks to our reunion.

Then it led to a natural thought. I wondered if this meant I would no longer push away the idea of having a child of my own in this life. My conviction that I wasn't meant to have one, which had come on when I was young and then been fortified by that psychic's prediction, could be expunged from my system. I now knew it had been this curse creating a pattern felt by me and seen by her.

With this emancipation, I was ready for our next move. It was the shaman's turn for salvation. With M leading, we combined our energy to clear her of all the darkness she'd let in, and asked that all contracts and vows she'd voiced, which weren't in her soul's highest good, be removed from her records. Finishing off, we asked for any soul fragments, which had been torn from her, to be cleared of the chains impeding them and lifted up into the light. Hopeful, but not sure if this would do the trick, we went on to remove, for each of us and our men, any contracts or vows we might have once unwittingly made to serve her, ensuring we could move forward clear of her influence.

Reciting an incantation of rebirth, M closed off with what she'd read that had once been said by Isis, before we added what D instructed us needed to be placed by our tombs. As M voiced the ancient Egyptian goddess' words, I first saw and then felt a stream of white light coming straight towards me. Entering through the center of my chest, in the spot where the energy of the heart chakra rotates, it rose up and rushed out of my crown. The remaining souls, whom T had known were still in need of saving, were escaping their entrapment straight through me. My light had done what it was meant to and acted as their beacon home.

Ending, we spent a few minutes speaking in awe of what had been accomplished and then said our goodbyes so we could all rest in the current time we lived in. I knew I still had more fear to stomp out, so my man and I could return home to one another, but for now, my body, which was aching in complete exhaustion, needed to shut down. I was done with Egypt and more than ready to turn my back on this part of my past; leaving it behind to rest in the eternal peace we'd created for it.

REBORN

CHAPTER 19
STOMPING OUT FEAR
MONTHS 7-8 OF YEAR 3

Our break from each other only lasted a few days. Then we made a half-hearted attempt to come back together before we broke off for good. The high from what we'd done drove me to initially say that I would participate when D spoke up about another lifetime; this one in Scotland, where we'd all shared an experience that needed to be dealt with. I wanted to go on another adventure, but I didn't want a breakdown in our group's communication to strain our relations, as it had while we were in Egypt.

Deciding it was better to discuss it before we got into it, I spoke up after a day that carried another storm of half-unread messages across the line, mostly pertaining to the physically exhaustive effects of our last battle. Equally exhausted by the thought of continuing on in this fashion, I sent a private message to D regarding the topic weighing on my mind.

Trying to gently explain what I'd noticed, I pointed out

that her style of hitting send, before a sentence was fully written, was tripling the number of messages and leading to a staggering number of pings. She seemed to listen and agreed that we could communicate better. Pleased by the response, I decided to continue and added it only seemed fair, to everyone, that if we had an adamant disagreement over a decision, then we should put it to a vote and let the majority rule on the direction to be taken. Voicing her agreement on that as well, I was heartened. Then disappointed the next day when she went right back to the same type of erratic writing that I believed was overwhelming everyone.

Thinking she hadn't understood what I'd meant, I approached her again privately and pointed out the recent tirade of messages as an example of what I'd been trying to explain. That led her to let loose a fury of words, the likes of which I'd never seen prior. She let it be known in no uncertain terms that she wouldn't be told what to do by anyone, myself included, and was suffocating under the control I was levying on her. I had no right to tell her how to communicate, and she would do whatever she wanted, whenever she wanted since this was my problem, not hers. Knowing it was everyone's, I responded that T had told all of us how difficult the number of messages were to weed through and it had also come up in private conversations.

Not hearing anything other than that she'd been spoken of behind her back, she moved us over to the group thread and voiced anger that words had been exchanged about her. Directing a finger at me, she added the accusation that I'd been trying to silence her from the beginning, so that I could become the group's leader. The viciousness of her words sickened me, but I understood her pain, even though none of the conversations, which were few, had held any malice towards her. This rage was coming from the wounds my words had hit, so I let it slide and didn't send a response I couldn't be sure wasn't a reaction to what felt like an attack.

Hoping her anger had cooled off and having worked through the negativity our exchange had brought up in me, I wrote an apology for having hurt her on the group thread the next morning. I stood by what I thought, and I voiced that but admitted my handling of it could have been better. I shouldn't have brought up the group communication without everyone listening, and I definitely shouldn't have spoken on behalf of the others. My words, which came from the heart but didn't back me down to a spot I didn't believe in, drew her immediate ire. A second tirade, fueled by the same anger as the first, came over.

It was a flood of thoughts streamed together to point out her rights and my faults. Unapologetic, she had and would continue to unleash her Kali – a goddess who fought her battles full of wrath – whenever she had to. Her words screamed that she didn't know who I thought I was, with my messages that read like reports and my insistence on a majority rule. She didn't have to and never would succumb to anyone. She intended to defend herself and slap me down whenever necessary. Closing off her rant, she ended with the line – Oh, and you did this in Egypt too!

Shocked silent, I had no response. Feeling attacked, I still wasn't angry, but I wanted nothing to do with this situation that had turned so ugly. With no response from T, who I knew would steer clear of so much negativity, I was touched when M spoke up to defend my actions. Done in her harmonizing pattern of speak, she tried to diffuse the situation by explaining to D that I'd only been trying to improve the way the group worked together.

The initial reaction to that was more anger, and she argued that our messages, written in English, were hard for her to track, but we didn't see her complaining. Wanting nothing more to do with any of us, she threatened to take herself out of the group. With no desire to continue either, I stayed silent and waited to see how this would play out. Within minutes a message with a new, softer tone displayed itself. Retracting her words about leaving, she wrote with a hope that we could all get past this and start over from a place of unconditional love for one another.

Taking the day to get my bearings, I wrote a few lines later that night to say I needed some time to figure out what the right, next move was for my life. I left it at that and went off to think through everything we'd done and everything that had been said. Conflicted, I couldn't see how we could continue, but didn't want to let the world down. Unsure if this was a divisive attack by negative forces intent on separating us, or if this was merely an unhealthy relationship I was meant to let go of before it drowned me, I went back and forth on it over a few days. Needing a sounding board for the thoughts I couldn't work through, I turned to M for counsel.

Intending to only speak about myself, I asked her for advice about my personal situation. While I wanted to do good deeds that would help the world around me, and I was excited by what we'd accomplished, I needed to kick my own life back into gear. It seemed like the confusion and now strife, which came with our work, would take me away from that. She understood and agreed, and then we softly broached the subject I'd meant to avoid.

D's wounds, which couldn't be talked through to resolution, made her susceptible to the dark energies we would come up against if we continued. Making us all vulnerable to attacks launched through her. Knowing I had to let this group go, I left it up in the air for a few days longer. My final decision was made on the day I went up higher to connect to my team and ask for their guidance. That's when I heard it clearly – "Stay away. You can't help her. She's dangerous."

I'd drowned myself too many times trying to save others, so I decided to let her and the group's work go but kept my personal connection to M, who by that point had become someone I counted a friend. Leaving with a lot of respect for T, I knew the friendship we once had wasn't meant to be resurrected, but that the two of us would be there to help one another whenever either needed.

I wasn't the only one who chose to leave. T decided it was best for her to focus her attention on the life that was too hectic to add this group to. M used her day job and energy training, both of which were starting back up now that the holidays were over, as her reason for leaving. But in truth, I knew she was tired of the strife, which she worried would lower her vibration. Our end drew itself out over a couple more weeks. Having exchanged a few kind words with D, after the shock of the venomous ones had faded, I left her behind without saying it was final. Instead, I sent her my wish for her life with the words – Good Luck. I hope you can figure out where the anxious feelings are coming from.

Only, our connection hadn't been completely severed. We remained part of the larger group of women who continued to share their words of support across one wall. Steering clear of D's posts as much as possible while on there, I thought I was safe from any further attacks. But then, after hearing that M had set her weariness aside and the two were working together to heal what had happened to them in Scotland, I came to find out that it wasn't going to be that easy. Through her I learned of D's residual resentment towards me. It came out on a night M messaged, asking if I'd felt any negativity strike me. Answering no, her response to my query, wondering why she was asking, was distressing.

While working on clearing the Scottish life together, M had seen a dark entity trying to work through D to attack me. Pointing it out in the moment, she hadn't believed her. With its influence manipulating her, D had claimed I was the one all darkness was originating from so they had to protect themselves from me. Her effort to do that had sent an attack my way, but M had flung a load of protection out around me to block it. What she did worked, and I followed it up by rescinding the yes that had once invited D into my field, as well as cutting any cords of energy between us that were still giving her access.

Hoping I'd barred her forever, I became curious. Wanting to know more, I asked and found out some of the details of what had transpired between all of us in Scotland. The story they'd uncovered was that everyone from Egypt, both the women and their men, had been part of a spiritual order. To control us the heads of it had used the order's vows of loyalty to wedge a block in-between our love so it wouldn't undercut their leadership. Going in further, I learned they'd manipulated us through our fears and implanted devices to track our every move. Their programming, which focused our minds on the missions they outlined, had kept some, but not all in check. A rebellion had risen, and it divided everyone. While M saw that the rebels had been the righteous ones, D believed the order was good and had been wronged by the ones who fought against them.

I instantly knew I'd been the one who'd instigated it. Wanting to lead everyone to freedom, I'd denounced their rule, but not everyone had been able to hear the truth, no matter how carefully I'd tried to craft my words. Both couples and friends had been divided by what they'd thought was true. In my case, neither my words nor our love had been able to convince my man to turn his back on his loyalty and obligation to this order, and he hadn't left with me. I didn't know the outcome, but knew we'd been separated and that that pattern was repeating itself in this life with his loyalty and obligation to his family.

Remembering the words of the master couple, I realized this was the spiritual programming that had once divided us, which they had cleared some of in our last session. I now knew there was more of it that needed to be gotten rid of. Tuning in to the two of us in the present, with this new information in mind, I cleared the implants I found that were whispering their divisive words to both of us, with the intent of making us see each other as the devil.

The next morning a new understanding hit. Never having been able to see what I'd done to them in that first Egyptian life clearly, the blame that had overwhelmed me when I'd first heard about it had convinced me that my jealousy had killed all of them. But it had been a trick triggered by this dark force working through D, to weaken me through the energies of guilt, self-blame, and shame. Not only had I not done that to them, but I could now feel clearly that my whispering, which had led to D's downfall, hadn't been done with any ill will in mind.

Voicing the truth to our ruler in that time, I'd led him to see what was driving her destructive actions that were impacting everyone. He'd seen and believed me, but not able to clear her of the darkness leading those actions, her death had been his only solution, and I'd placed the blame for that squarely on my shoulders. With this realization of how events had really unfolded, I felt the truth rise up – I'm a good person, and no one is ever going to convince me otherwise again.

Within a few days of freeing myself from that, I was attacked. I sensed it coming while out walking my dog one evening. The fear of someone trailing me overcame my senses. Then, upon returning and locking the door behind us, the image of someone breaking through it popped to mind. Pushing it aside with the belief that my walls could keep me safe, I laid down for the night. Only to be woken with the feeling that something was floating in the upper left corner of the ceiling above me. With my awareness settling on it, its weight quickly came down and landed on my back, which was facing up, and pressed me down into the mattress below my body. Trapped, I couldn't move a muscle.

Hearing a multitude of mumbling voices in my ear, I couldn't make out what they were saying, but knew it wasn't anything that would lead to anything good. Pushing through the green fog that had enveloped me, I stumbled through the words of protection I could barely manage to get out and a short, intense battle ensued. With mere minutes passing and no idea of who had won, they faded away and left my body free to move of its own volition.

Continuing to voice what I knew would clear anything they had left behind, I felt some fear, but nowhere close to what I would have felt a month earlier. Without having to be told, I knew that this attack, which had been dramatic in its physicality, had been staged to scare me. Fear of it would only give away my power, so I worked to clear myself of as much of it as I could uncover. Their desire to control me would only succeed if I allowed it, and I wasn't going to do that, so I brushed it all off and went back to the sleep that had been interrupted.

Wanting to ensure there was nothing left behind that could harm me, I messaged the master couple the next morning and told them what had happened. Their response was immediate. Expressing compassion for what I'd gone through, they indicated that there was still some residue, and I could eradicate it by asking the high beings to run a fear matrix removal program on it. I did, and I felt the shift that told me more fear had been removed from my system.

Informing M of what had transpired, in case they went after her in the same manner, we jumped on a call to discuss the situation. I let her know I'd made a conscious decision to not fight this order that was still in existence since it felt like an enormous task that would only serve to take me away from the life I wanted with the man I was holding out for. I wouldn't find out for months to come that that wasn't an option since they already had their sights set on me and my man, as they had across the centuries we'd gone up against them. They had and still were throwing everything in their arsenal at us, to try to stop us from reuniting. Setting them aside, for now, I asked her to tune in and clear anything between D and me that was enabling dark forces to turn her against me. We agreed to both look into each other since M had already decided to put distance between the two of them.

Starting first, M gave a small gasp at the number of curses D had made, across lifetimes, with the intent of keeping me from finding peace or happiness in any life. Layered on top of them were curses to keep my man and me from coming together. All stemmed from what she felt I'd done to her in Egypt. That wound had never been forgiven, nor forgotten. Even in the life when she'd been my mother, there had existed a fierce jealousy towards me in regards to the amount of space I occupied in her husband, my father's heart. I wished I could help her let go of it, but knew the only thing to do was let go of her, and I re-voiced the words that severed any cords that still existed on any energetic level.

Tuning in to M, I saw that D was jealous over her. With a fierce desire to keep her to herself, she hated the friendship we'd formed. With an energetic cage placed around M to block me, she truly believed she was protecting her. Already having sensed this, M had done some work to clear those bars, and I put in some more effort towards their removal. Moving on,

I asked for all cords still attaching them, which were inadvertently siphoning M's energy, to be severed. With all that cleared, we agreed the only way to protect ourselves from future attacks was to remain positive and hold nothing but compassion for D since darkness and negativity could only reach us if we lowered ourselves to its level.

Spirit then guided me to reach out to T. Ready to move forward, but unable to see what was coming, I asked her to open my Akashic Records, which she'd just learned how to access, so I could get some answers. Hearing their guidance through her, my guides told me I might be faced with my next worst fear – running into my man with another woman. The devastation of that scene struck hard in the moment, and tears welled up instantly. Leading me to question them – "Haven't I been through enough? Why do I have to see it?"

They then reminded me, through her, that when a twin pair came into either physical or verbal contact with each other, their love was triggered, and each would feel it intensely. A face-to-face would show us both that no one else could ever compare, which was something we both might need to see to believe. Turning to my resistance, they asked T to guide me through it, and we discussed how it might go and why the idea was devastating.

I knew. I was afraid to see him with someone who might be better than me and would make me feel as unimportant as I still felt. Reminding me, they said everything we were both enduring was set up to empower us. I knew what this meant. I needed to believe in my own worth and realize it didn't depend on anyone other than me. That would be my gain if this situation unfolded, as well as to strengthen my faith in our love. Adding to their explanation, I heard that I might be hurt by what I saw on the surface, but would feel our truth hidden below it. I knew what I had to do to move myself forward. Besides continuing to battle what was inside of me that was blocking my self-worth, I had to work through the negativity I felt towards the other women that he'd loved in this life. If I'd been made to love, and I knew I had been, then I needed to love everyone.

Getting to work the next morning, I started with his ex-wife. While meditating, I requested for our souls to meet, and I proceeded to ask hers for forgiveness. It didn't come easily. While feeling the pain and resentment directed at me, I continued to tell her repeatedly – "I'm sorry. I love you. Please forgive me. Thank you." I then went on to thank her for everything she'd done, across this life, to press my man to empower himself. I knew her soul didn't want to keep this cycle going. She was only doing what all three of us needed so we could experience the lessons that would lead each of us to stand up and reclaim our true power.

Initially refusing to relent, her rage came forward to yell her claim on him – "He was MY husband!" Continuing to apologize for us having kicked off too early, she let that go and moved on to their son. Blame for the pain he'd gone through was thrown my way, which migrated on to the shame she'd felt for having lost his father to me, across all of our shared incarnations. Once all that lifted, the fear that I would come in to take on an important role in her son's life, which might draw him away from her, emanated out. Continuing with my soul-level apology through multiple rounds that held 108 incantations each, she eventually softened, and I felt a hint of gratitude for the fact that my presence had helped her end a marriage she hadn't wanted to be in any longer. That's when my vision shifted to the two of us hugging.

Then, I turned to the woman who was standing in the spot I wanted to occupy. With less negativity stuck between us, this one was easier, and I dove in by thanking her for being there for him when I couldn't. For being a shoulder that he needed when mine wasn't the one he wanted. For drawing him out of his pain when I wasn't the one who could do that for him. For bringing laughter back into his life when my words couldn't reach him. For pausing on her path to love so she could help him get back to his. Letting her know I loved her, I continued to say it and send it until I felt it.

Thinking I'd thoroughly beaten away this fear, I told the women on the wall about it, in case doing the same would help them in their situations, and then I headed out for my daily workout. On my way there, and while standing on a corner, I turned abruptly and looked straight into the face of fear. A tall, beautiful blonde stood behind me, and my heart was gripped with the painful thought – What if that's her?

In an instant, I knew I hadn't cleared enough. Realizing what I had to do next, I got up the nerve to perform a feat of courage. Not having done it once in the years since I'd last seen him, out of fear, I looked him up. Both his profile and cover photos showed him traversing a rocky, barren patch of dry land, looking completely isolated while doing it. My heart ached open for him. Then I scrolled down the wall that was in complete lock-down and saw the only other photo that had been made public. One of him with another woman.

He was standing, and she was sitting. With his arms on her shoulders, he was looking up and off to the left, while she faced forward. There was an apple in her mouth, and neither of them was smiling. Understanding that this was a moment when they had been joking, my heart leapt with what I felt. Not having seen his face in ages, since out of the fear of the pain it would bring on I hadn't kept even one photo of our time together, I instantly recognized the man I still loved. And I felt his love for me, deep below the surface that looked pained and thoroughly exhausted.

Focusing on her, I felt that she was a nice person and thanked her again for helping him, but could also see that what existed between them, while good, was a friendship that had taken a turn into more. Not to say he didn't love her, but I knew whatever existed between them couldn't take away from who I was or what we still shared. Of that fact, I was sure. Turning away from what I no longer needed to see, I left them to whatever it was they were learning from each other. With this fear confronted and released, I could move on and past the suffering the unknown had been causing.

These fears weren't the only things I felt myself moving past. I no longer felt drawn to the master couple's style of healing. Still believing in their power, I decided it was time to stop listening to the calls they sent out. Their help, while immense, had started to feel too detailed in its precise pinpointing of past life traumas. It'd been essential to learn about our repeating patterns, but I now wanted to get to the core issues more quickly, without looking at each story individually.

One of those issues, that repeated clearing hadn't succeeded in squelching, was his shame, which I kept intuitively picking up on. So I took a few straight hours out of one day to root out as much of it as I could get to. Without knowing what I was getting myself into, I laid down and filled each of us up, along with the space and cords between us, with St. Germaine's violet flame, and intended for it to burn away this emotion that was crippling our lives.

The pain that ran through every cell, with the release of what he'd held on to for far too long, was agonizing. I knew it was more his than mine because of how every inch of my body tensed with pressure when I directed the flame into his field, then loosened when I guided it back to mine. Wanting to give up at plenty of points, I refused, determined to rid us both of the shame that had been sprung on him for having been with me while he was still married. I only stopped once it'd disintegrated enough that the tightness in my body lifted.

With that done, the next morning brought my mind the most exquisite sense of freedom. I felt it the second I woke and with eyes still shut, rejoiced as my thoughts leapt with spontaneous joy. My brain, which felt lighter than air, was bouncing off the sides of the skull that surrounded it. My entire being lifted higher than anything I'd experienced since before his decision to leave me so his wife and child could return. Positive that what I was feeling was coming from both of us, I broke the promise I'd made four months earlier and reached out to share my thoughts on this feeling with him.

Vowing I wasn't out to hurt anyone – him, the woman he was with, or myself – I explained why I was writing. With no idea that his shame had been weighing me down so heavily, the clearing that had led to so much joy told me that he needed to know what I knew, so he could help himself if he chose to. Sending him the latest recording, I let him know once again, only more clearly – I have been feeling your pain (amongst other things) for over two years, and I hate to think of you this unhappy. Please, for yourself, your son, whomever you love, and me – even if you don't do it for me – find a way to help yourself. That afternoon brought his response through a feeling. Shocked to the core and struck senseless, I heard him realize – "It's all true." And I knew, the early morning joy had been felt by both of us. Hearing of mine experienced simultaneously had confirmed our truth to him.

Content that he now knew, I left him to work through his life and continued on with mine. While reading my records, T had pointed me in the direction of another healer, a female minister that created audios, which went exactly where I needed to go, straight to the root of everything that was causing my suffering. Purchasing plenty of those, I listened as she voiced and sung her light language, channeled from her guides to heal the exact point, in whichever lifetime, the core wound had first entered one's system. Loving this new help, I focused on myself but continually asked that everything be shared with my man to the degree that was in his highest good.

From suppressed sadness, anger, and shame, to feelings of unworthiness and self-doubt, she helped me clear a lot of each. With no need to hear where they came from, I was ready to be rid of what didn't register with my soul. Focusing on fear, which I had plenty of, she broke it down to the fear of both abandonment and commitment, as well as the fear of change, disappointment, rejection, and loss. The audios were short, but the release lasted for hours, sometimes days after I listened to each. I could feel it working with every ounce of each feeling that first riddled and then rose up and left my being. And I soon realized, due to the intense length of each clearing, I wasn't just clearing all of this out of us, but transmuting these negative emotions out of this world for the entire collective.

Then on a random day that started off like every other, a new fear rose to the surface, triggered by something I wasn't expecting. While standing off to the side in the dog park one morning, chatting with a fellow owner, fear grabbed me when my dog and another one got into a scuffle. Running full sprint to the two whose teeth were locked in on each other, all thought was directed at what wounds he might be receiving.

With the help of the other owner, we pulled the two dogs apart, more easily than expected, and I sat mine down for an inspection.

Two slashes of red skin, marring his beautiful black snout, jumped out at me. Worried that they might get infected, I walked past the concerned faces of everyone watching so I could rush him to the closest vet. The second we exited the park's entrance, my eyes welled up, and tears started gushing, while I choked back the sobs that were making my chest heave. Knowing he was fine, I still couldn't control this overwhelming fear for him, even after the vet's technician sent me away with instructions on how to clean it myself and not to worry.

The rest of that day was spent in tears, with fresh ones erupting every time I glanced over at him. I felt a tremendous fear that he would lose his innocent, loving nature now that he'd been in a battle. Seeing the similarity to myself, I realized that what had happened to him was triggering wounds within me that I hadn't seen before, ones related to the loss of my innocence, so I cleared for them. Deciding to go deeper into what was causing this intense emotional reaction, I felt a raw fear that I could, once again, lose what I loved most in this world.

Trying to clear for that throughout the night and into the early hours of the next morning, I finally stopped. No matter whom I called on or what I asked for, it was apparent this fear had to be faced if I wanted to get past it. Walking us both back to the scene of the trauma, I wobbled the whole way, afraid of a repeat occurrence. Pushing past the fear that was trying to scare me away from the place we both loved to go, I brought us inside and let him loose, while initially watching his every move. Forcing myself to stay for an hour, I soon stopped watching him so closely and feeling the fear dissipate, I knew, I'd won yet another round.

All of this healing was bringing about a change in me. With every day that passed, less and less worry rattled my brain. The peace I craved was overcoming the fear that had pervaded my system. Despite still needing to find a way to make more money, the fear of losing my way of life through the potential loss of my home was no longer making a dent in my positive mode of thinking. A faith that I would be alright, no matter what happened, was forming. I knew I would survive all of the lessons the universe provided and once ready everything I'd been holding out for, that was in my highest good, would come to me.

Pleased, but exhausted by my efforts and tired of doing this work without my man, I craved a partnership where the two of us could grow together. I couldn't have that just yet, but the universe heard my plea and delivered what they could. I connected with one of the other twin women off of the page that had brought us all together. The post about finding my love for my man's ex and current woman had resonated with her situation. She was fighting her fear and jealousy of seeing the man whom she'd told was her twin with another woman. So we decided to help one another by exchanging healing sessions for our men, as well as one another.

Our first session, which was interlaced with laughter, won us both over to this collaboration, and we decided to do them weekly. Living on the west coast of Canada, this woman, who was around my age, gave the twin flame moniker the mainstream credibility I was craving. Cool in her appearance and demeanor, she had a sarcastic twist to her language and a twin who was the lead singer in an indie rock band. Speaking like everyday people, we chuckled as we uncovered one tragic feeling after another. Getting rid of each for all four of us, we agreed – "Fuck this. I don't want to hold on to that any longer!"

Woven in with the laughter, I felt bouts of sadness over what she uncovered within me that was still blocking us from moving forward. Looking into my womb, she cleared the remains of numerous miscarried babies that had been held in there across my many incarnations. The disappointment fueled by their deaths, as well as the fear of losing what I cherished again, was energetically stuck inside of me, stifling my power to create and birth anything new in this life. Causing everything to be stillborn time and again, the energy she cleared had been hindering my life from taking off in the direction of my heart's desire.

Then there was the shock that came with what she told me was coming up to be cleared for my man. All information came from his higher-self, whom she would call in at the start of each session, who soon started to appear the second we connected, eager to tell us what needed to be done. With no words being vocalized by my man, I now heard from this higher and wiser version of him routinely, as she received the messages I still couldn't fully believe when I felt them for myself.

One piece of information she relayed was stunning and completely resonated with what I'd been feeling. Not having let myself believe it since it's what I wanted, I'd been sensing that he was either in the process of ending it or that it was already over with this other woman he wasn't supposed to stay with any longer than his personal growth deemed necessary. A few weeks before she announced this, I'd heard clearly – "She doesn't need to know" – which had felt like it was related to me, then – "I need some time alone." Since this was what I wanted, I hadn't let myself believe in what I was hearing or feeling. With her confirmation, which I hadn't asked for, my heart soared. Then it dropped when she told me what I had to do for him. He was going through a tough period, and his higher-self wanted me to reach out to him with a lighthearted touch.

Dismayed, I attempted to protect myself with a sarcastic edge and questioned – "What am I supposed to say? Hey, know you told me to never contact you again, but here's a good joke I heard?" This direction I'd been given sounded utterly asinine, and I seriously doubted I could do it. The feeling of rejection, which had come up with each unanswered message, had become too difficult to bear after he'd replied with the one thing I'd feared more than anything. Even if it was over, how did I know that he wasn't going to cut me down? The thought completely terrified me, and that's what made me realize I had to do it. It was the only way to overcome the fear that was still in control. So soon after that call, I began my campaign of lightness.

The first message came to me out of nowhere, inspired

from above one night while I was watching television. It was the end of a day where the media had been flooded with the story of another woman who had been warned, given an explanation, and yet persisted. Typing quickly and hitting send before I could chicken out, I felt the side of me he hadn't seen in years come out. Later that night I felt him laugh at the short note that said – I think we can both agree, I'm a little like Elizabeth Warren. Just saying. Still here. Still open. I signed my note off with a tweak to her hashtag and made it my own by declaring – #StillPersisting.

Happy in that moment, the fear that came the morning after was petrifying and pushed out every ounce of laughter I'd felt. Crawling deep under the covers, I hid, afraid that his wrath, which I'd never seen, would come down on me. The fear grew to include the woman he'd told me was his girlfriend. What if she was still in his life and upon hearing of my message hurled words of recrimination at me? I couldn't handle the fear that came with the thought of that type of attack.

Turning to the wall of women for support, I received what they perceived to be help, but what felt more like a battering. Those who responded listed out a litany of wounds they sensed I still needed to work on. All of which only succeeded in triggering my fear that I would never be healthy, which added itself to the fear that my note had raised, and drove me to fear that all this fear would manifest the outcome I feared the most. I spent the day working through all of it, slowly and thoroughly, and finally came to realize – no one's words could hurt me. Clearing the fear of his (or her) reaction, as well as the opinions of these women, left me feeling freer than I'd ever felt before. I had the right to act how I saw fit for my life, without accepting anyone's judgment of me. A belief I was only just beginning to attain.

Then, a couple of weeks later, I was told it was time to up the ante, and I went even further than I thought I was capable. Listening to what my fellow healer told me his higher-self wanted me to do, I asked my man if he'd like to meet for a coffee. Promising that it wouldn't kill him, I added a wink with the words – I already cleared for that. I didn't hear back, so I knew he wasn't ready for it, but I could feel his energy lighten towards me, as much as mine was towards him. Which I was starting to realize was his higher-self's intention with this outreach.

What these messages gave me was unfathomable. Finally attaining a true detachment to any outcome, I was freeing myself of the fear that came with consequences that were out of my control. And the work I was doing for this other woman, who was beginning to feel like a friend, had diminished my doubt in myself and was adding to the growing faith I had in my own intuitive power. Letting me know everything I picked up on for her was spot on, I continued to go deeper into healing what was hindering her man from coming back to her. As well as nudging her to look at the darkness in the universe that I thought she was avoiding, out of a fear that her attention would allow it to grow stronger.

Her preference was to focus on the issues that were less scary, which resided within, rather than look at what was hitting us from outside. Which was good, since I'd recently focused my own healing efforts on that and spent less time on what was holding my man and me up from the inside. Together, we worked through it, and she let me know, with each new session, the inner struggles that he couldn't voice, but that his higher-self wanted our assistance in combatting. My golden man was ashamed that he had hurt me and couldn't release the feeling that he didn't deserve to ever speak to me again, which she was able to clear some of for him. He was raging against everyone that had kept him from me for so long. There was a lot of anger, and she helped him let go of what she could, but there was more for him to work through on his own. He felt helpless, like a victim in his own life, unable to break the patterns that entrapped him. The last one she tried to clear repeatedly, but I knew that in the end, he was the only one who could empower himself by choosing to let go of all victimhood. Then the one that I felt so acutely, that filled my heart with the feeling of his tears — he missed me.

Feeling his longing, along with the inner struggle between his desire to and fear of contacting me, I sent a third note. It was prompted by my twin friend's mention of a vision she'd had of him while we were speaking. He was sitting in front of his computer, struggling, starting and stopping a message he had no idea how to write to me. What she saw stuck with me, and when I heard – "help him" – a few days later, I decided to craft a new note of my own. One that reassured him, I understood everything and would never hold this separation against him. His joy after it was read skyrocketed, and then the next day, his emotions dropped with the seesaw action I'd grown to know too well. With fear and anxiety returning, I knew no reply was forthcoming but hung on to my patience in the process. I'd sensed plenty that what would come if I held out was worth the wait, even though I could barely remember the feeling of the time we'd spent together in this life.

Despite all this, which seemed positive since it meant he was facing his true feelings, I started to grow despondent. Then his higher-self told her to reassure me with the message – "There's a desert period in every life." Not having told her about Egypt, I felt personally touched by this message that held no meaning for her. Then I realized that meant that I needed evidence that the messages I was receiving were true, which pointed to the doubt I still had that I needed to continue to clear for, so my faith could become steady.

Fighting off the sadness of our separation when it hit, I routinely requested that our higher-selves stream light and love between their two hearts up above. Then drawing it down from where they were joined together by it, love would flood my system, and I'd ask that it go from my heart to his on the plane our bodies occupied, to fill him up as much as possible. Then, I committed an act that led me to feel that love tenfold. Another one instigated by his higher-self when he let me know through my friend – "It's time to call him."

Devastated by the thought, my new friend had to perform a lot of healing to get me to the point where I could do it, then she held my hand throughout this step that petrified me to the core of my being. After a few days of both my own and her efforts to clear for it, I realized this was another fear that would never lift unless I found the courage to commit the act that was petrifying. With her words of "do it" ringing in my ears, I hung up one of our calls and dialed his number. Hearing the hello that sounded strange to my ear, the realization that he hadn't recognized my number or my voice spiked fear, and I hung up as quickly as he'd picked up.

I called my healer-friend back, and while my entire body shook from head to toe, she tried to reason away my fear. Everything she said was a blur, and all I could think about was that I had to immediately call him back, otherwise be boxed into a corner of fear that it would be difficult to work my way out of. Hanging up and dialing again, relief flooded when the sound of his recorded voice answered. Off the hook, I voiced my sorrow and explained that fear had led me to hang up on him. Keeping it short, I ended with the reason for my call – to see if he was open to having a conversation.

Lying in bed after, I expected to be rattled by regret. What came instead was a boundless joy that radiated throughout and around my entire being, filling me with the most intensely beautiful love imaginable. Every second of fear had been worth it to feel this bubble of bliss once more, and I knew I would do it all over again – every fear-ridden moment – to have us back again. Hoping he was experiencing the same feeling, I drifted off to sleep sure that my dream of our reunion would come true.

Feeling him try to call me back the next night, his fear and anxiety were tangible. Slightly annoyed, I turned in his direction for a second and told him that he could do it. Then put my focus back on the show I was watching, without realizing that my fear was keeping me from aiding the call by clearing the energy between us. He didn't get past it and the weekend that started the next day was filled with one word repeated incessantly in my head – "Call."

Unsure if it was a message for me, or a command he was giving himself, I chose to believe the latter since I couldn't imagine placing another one myself. Then, later that night, the series I was watching clarified it, through a sign that was hung on the window of a door in one of its shop windows – Please Call Again. Sighing, I told him I would, but I knew I couldn't just yet. I wouldn't fight this call, but I needed to clear more fear before I could unearth more courage.

A realization came with this. The arduous process of me going after him, while he gave no logical sign of interest, had been necessary. I already knew it was intended to help me find my faith, but I finally understood the second reason. It was pushing me to break free of the energetic binds that had been suffocating women for centuries. Those that continually pressed women into the pattern of the helpless victim that needed to wait for the man to come forward and save her. With my actions, I was creating a new paradigm – one in which the girl believes in who she is, despite everything, and in her power to save herself, the boy, and the world. Not to say that the boy didn't have to believe the same on his end.

But, if instead, my man had followed stereotype and come for me, then we would have fallen into the same antiquated pattern that had to be eradicated so men and women could exist and thrive as equals. This shift was one of the services all twin women were performing for the collective. Reassured by my realization, I let go of my need for him to contact me, which had been shaking my faith with every day that it didn't happen. I knew I would find the courage to place another call, with faith in the divine timing of this plan our souls had laid out, and hopefully without any fear of the outcome.

REBORN

CHAPTER 20
THE POWER OF DREAMS
MONTHS 9-12 OF YEAR 3

Wanting to take things deeper, I decided to book a private, half-hour session with the healer who called herself a minister, the woman whose audios had cleared multiple layers of my core wounds. She started it off by calling in Archangel Michael, then smiling when she heard him say – "I'm already here. You don't have to call me in." Laughing, I confirmed – "Yeah, he knows me by now."

As he watched and listened, I heard that my dream had come true. Not in this life, not yet, but in a parallel one where different choices had led my golden man and me to already be reunited. Elated that there was a world in which we were together, my joy rose when she said we were working together, in that life over there, to create projects that both entertained and filled the world with inspiring beauty.

Tempering that joy, but handing me hope while doing it, she brought us back to this life. While she could sense that he now knew he could both hear and feel me, he was overwhelmed by the knowledge. Healing some of the disparity between us, so we were on more of an equal level, she warned it would take him more time to get to where I was. Which wasn't to say we weren't linked despite this unequal footing. Confirming something I'd been guessing for a while, she agreed that my life, along with his, was tracking on a timeline according to the choices he was making.

Not to completely disempower me, since I was affecting it with the healing I was doing, but the link between our souls was so strong that upon meeting, my life's trajectory had become tied to his decisions, whether or not he was in it. I'd known, just as surely as I'd known that my choices were impacting him. Feeling relieved that I'd been right, and not crazy, I then heard what I'd already figured out on my own when the *me* on that other timeline piped up – "She's going to have to call him again." Relieved by the news that had been delivered, I left the session pleased that my energy felt strong to this woman.

Enjoying these positive messages that made me feel closer to the man I couldn't see, I soon realized a negative consequence to the healing sessions I was still doing weekly. Working with this other twin woman, who mirrored both my style of daily living, as well as my twin struggles, had given me a much-needed break from working alone, but I had started to rely on what she told me, instead of what I could feel into on my own. My mind was becoming dependent on the messages she was giving me from my man's higher-self.

It was time to take a step back from healing with others. Weary of searching outside of myself for what I knew I could do as well as anyone, I wanted to continue to clear what came up, but only what my intuition told me needed my attention. With that in mind, I decided to let our sessions fade out slowly, but I didn't want to completely cut them off since I enjoyed having her as a friend.

So it hurt when she wrote a few days later and in the nicest terms possible, said she was severing our connection. Her reasons were personal and had to do with the amount of time she had to spare, but it still felt like a rejection. Surprising myself, I did something I'd never done well before. I let it go, trusted it was in my best interest, and didn't take it personal.

Instead, I started to fill my days with something I loved. Bringing back the dream I'd worried couldn't support me, that I'd laid aside when the news of his relationship had ruptured its beauty momentarily, I started to write the story of what I'd lived through. With every word, my faith in the love that was in my heart grew stronger. And my nights started to include something my higher-self had insistently told my healer-friend that I had to do. I let my dreams heal my man and me while we slept. Each night, an intention was set down in writing, calling on a high being to enter both of our dreams and heal us on a deeper level.

Each healing was drawn from an intuitive hit I received during the day and was then worked on across each night. From the fear of facing one another to blocks against our faith in ourselves, each other, and our love. To the fear of getting what we wanted only to lose it again, to believing that we didn't deserve our dreams to come true. To our fear of being controlled by our love, to the fear of being made vulnerable. Layer after layer of each fell away, while I slept and dreamt about it all.

The dreams that came were vivid, startling me awake every few hours. The feelings that were wrung out from deep within would shoot through my senses for the first few hours after I woke each morning. The most intense dreams brought scenarios forward from lives we'd once lived. One of those proved to be the most excruciating to face. Seeing myself alive as his wife, I saw a time when my man had been overcome with jealousy over me, which had been coupled with the fear that I didn't love him. This had destroyed both of us when it drove him to force himself on me and choke the life out of the body lying underneath him.

Waking, knowing that in that life he'd succumbed to the darkness that was trying to come in-between love, I forgave him of everything. The release was massive and lasted across the entire day, leading me through the feelings I imagined a rape victim went through – utter despair, loss of all hope, and rage. Then there was the blame we both held towards him and the one I aimed at myself for having been weak enough to allow it to happen. As well as the fear in each of us, that screamed he had to stay away, otherwise, risk hurting me again as badly as he once had. It was difficult but necessary to go through, to release more of the feelings trapped inside and between us, which were blocking our reunion.

I decided at the end of that day, for no reason in particular, to share what had happened with one of the women I'd met on the wall. Having left the larger group to focus on my life, I'd kept a few connections I'd made across different private messages, and she was one of them. More of an acquaintance, I hadn't previously shared anything private with her, despite her words that had given me a window into her trials. Her response came straight from my man when she wrote – High Five! Letting her know that those words carried a special meaning, she laughed and said that while writing them she'd questioned where the phrase was coming from since it was such a departure from her usual mode of speaking.

A second confirmation of the benefits from this healing came through soon after. Seeing myself in the same hospital bed as the previous vision had held, I watched as my personal bouncers, once again, pushed away my golden man as he tried to approach me. Only this time he didn't retreat as quickly. He fought them to get to me and only turned away after it became apparent he wasn't going to get any closer. My defenses, which I was trying to lower, were still too strong of a barrier, but I could tell they were weakening and it was only a matter of time before they came down.

Then came the night where the dreams ran back to back. Starting with a past life, I went back to another time when I'd been silenced for speaking the truth, which those in power hadn't wanted me to voice, loudly and repetitively. The outcome had been torture, which I knew had happened, but luckily wasn't forced to re-live. What I did see clearly was the pain that had filled my eyes as an iron mask was lowered over my head, with the intent of keeping me hidden in silence for the rest of that life.

After waking from that terror, I slipped into the confusion of a dream where my golden man was the broken boy I'd once dated. Looking on the surface like the one who had hurt me, but knowing he wasn't, my fear of having a broken life again was blocking us from moving forward. As his mirror, I knew my man felt the same about me in regards to his ex-wife.

Waking momentarily to that understanding, I fell back to tossing through a different dream. One in which I wouldn't let myself depend on anyone, out of a fear of being let down by them. The next dream, illuminating in its ridiculousness, put me at a party, being drilled by a man who wanted to know every intimate detail of my life. I answered every question despite my growing discomfort until I realized that I was making myself vulnerable by handing over all of the information that he could use to hurt me.

I woke for a few moments and understanding dawned that we both blamed ourselves for not having made wiser choices at the beginning, ones that wouldn't have led to the excruciating pain endured with this life's separation. I knew our blame was ridiculous the second I sensed it. There would have been no scenario in which we could have stayed away from the bliss we had brought each other, as well as the fact that everything had worked to the plan our souls had set in action so I would be triggered to uncover what needed healing. Glad to be rid of that nonsense, I moved on.

Each dream was more vivid then the last, from one night to the next, and I started to take nights off in-between, so my mind and body could get the rest they needed. The days passed by in a fury of typing out our story – the one I'd been incapable of writing before I'd reached this point in my healing. Working through every memory, I then burned every page written to release the energy of everything that had occurred to, by, and between us across the three years since we'd been a couple. Write, burn, dream, write, burn, dream, write, burn, dream – these daily and nightly releases became my new routine.

At times my daily hits came to me through other people's writing. Walking one day, I glanced down and saw a sign stenciled into the ground at my feet – If only waiters could talk. Remembering the dream I'd had of him as a waiter, it dawned on me that I needed to heal for whatever was keeping him from speaking his truth to me. I kicked off what would turn into a night of endless dreams with the words – Lords of Karma and Archangel Michael, please enter our dream bodies and heal whatever is blocking us from voicing our truth to ourselves, each other, and the world. And so it is. Thank You. Thank You. Thank You.

The first dream that came brought a torrential downpour, the pounding of which scared me beyond measure. Repeatedly questioning if I'd left anything out in it, even though I knew I hadn't, I cowered under the covers. Feeling completely EXPOSED and VULNERABLE, despite the safety of the walls that surrounded me, FEAR rose at what this ATTACK would do to me. Tumbling straight into another scene, I saw my man strapped, spread eagle, to the bed of a wooden cart I was pulling and knew he was afraid of becoming TRAPPED by our love if he came forward.

Leaving him for the moment, the next scene to cycle through put me in a boutique with members of my family, one of whom had been busted for shoplifting. Walking over to the sister who was in handcuffs, she shooed me away out of total EMBARRASSMENT for what she'd done. Not wanting to be REPRIMANDED by me, I understood her and then myself in the next dream that made me feel afraid of being JUDGED. Told I would have to go to a family party, worry over what others there would think of my life, which wouldn't be considered successful by their terms, kept me from going.

The next few that came were forgotten, but the feelings remained. Worry over if we would have anything to talk about was followed with the question of if we would share any common interests and was closed out with the fear that it was too late for us. The morning after those were had was heavy, but with a new understanding of all that was keeping us apart, I felt more clarity and less sadness. I vowed to continue to work through these emotions and alleviate the dense energy that was keeping us from moving forward. We would get through this.

Thinking I'd cleared every misperception that the best thing he could do for me was to stay away, I was surprised by the dream that brought a new trauma to light. It showed him scurrying through cobbled streets in a time I couldn't pinpoint but knew was filled with persecution. Trying to return to me, he couldn't because he was being followed. Sensing them behind him, he'd turned away from our haven so he wouldn't lead them back to where I was hiding.

He saved me, but couldn't save himself. They caught him. Torturing his mind through his body, they eventually hung both and wrung the life out of him. He'd died protecting me. Upon waking, this scene called to mind a memory from when we'd been together in this life. Making a joke that hadn't made sense at the time, he'd once texted a reply that was entirely out of context to our conversation – I didn't tell them anything, even though they were pulling off my fingernails!

Tired of the torture in this life and all the others, a dream finally came through that shocked me awake with its beauty. I hadn't been expecting it or its message, which made it even more incredible to receive. I could feel, as it was unfolding, that it was representative of this life. We were together as a happy couple before my golden man stumbled across a scorpion that bit him.

Seeing the gash of red cut across his leg, my fear of the poison that was entering his body was compounded by the men who came in and grabbed him. Pulled away, they kidnapped my love, and everyone said to move on because he was lost to me forever. I screamed at those who voiced this repeatedly, and I adamantly refused to give up on him. But, despite trying everything I could think of to find out where it was that he was being held, I couldn't locate him.

Without knowing where to turn next, what I'd been hoping for finally happened. He walked in and came to stand in front of me. Twenty pounds lighter and with all of his beautiful golden hair buzzed off, he looked like he'd just gotten out of prison. But it was definitely the man I loved who was looking straight at me, more vivid than in any vision had since I'd last seen him in person. He didn't flinch once as he gazed down at me, and I recognized every detailed line of his face as if I'd seen it yesterday. Every move and gesture made was reminiscent of the ones I'd once seen live.

We stood there and looked at each other without moving or speaking. Starting to embrace, we moved slowly and with trepidation, unsure, after all this time, if the other was real. As we grew comfortable in each other's solid presence, our arms tightened until we were holding each other in a close embrace. Then, with a deep emotion that made my heart quiver, he told me – "I'm home."

The feeling that filled that moment was visceral and went beyond what any dream could. It was similar to the one felt after I'd called him, but even more brilliant in its profound depth and beauty. Surrounding us, it placed our spirits in a protected bubble of bliss, and I felt our golden love engulf our entire beings.

It faded sooner than I would have liked but replaced itself with a scene that brought me a different type of elation. A white trash bag appeared in a corner, crumpled up and waiting to be taken out. Walking over to it, I pulled the top open and looked in to see a pair of dusty old work boots that had completed their assignment. They were ready to be released from the task of stomping out all fear.

Disintegrating, they were replaced by another vision. I saw the little girl who wanted to be born to us. Standing there silently, looking to be about age seven, she had his blue eyes and my wavy dark hair, and she looked like she was ready to exist. Apologizing for not having wanted her sooner, I assured her that I did, in fact, want to be her mother.

I woke as a deep knowing rose. The time had come to draw on my courage and place another call to him. I let it all sink in and process across the next couple of days. Then, on the second night, one that held a full moon in the sky above, I dialed his number. The call went straight to voicemail. I didn't let that deter me and did what I had to, which I hadn't done to date. I asked how he was and shared the hope that he would return my call.

The desire to not intrude on his privacy by asking a personal question had always stopped me from inquiring about his life before. I'd only ever written or said what I was thinking, and I'd never asked him to share anything that he might not be ready to in return. Taking this leap forward brought on a backlash of emotion.

Hanging up, wondering if he'd blocked my number, doubt tried to grip my mind into believing I'd been crazy to believe in any of this all this time. But I fought it and grabbed for my faith. Questioning what I could possibly do next, my guides cut me off mid-sentence with an answer – "Nothing." Relieved, I questioned if this call had been the right move. Three words were rattled off with clarity – "Yes. Energy. Powerful."

I then felt my faith, which had continuously faltered throughout this separation, solidify within and throughout my system. Playing the part my soul had written to perfection, the only thing left to do, for now, was hold on to what had finally been found. I'd done what was needed and healed what I could for both of us. Believing in him, I knew he had the strength to fight the last of the fear he had of me and find his faith in our soul's truth, so he could return to our love in this lifetime.

I knew the next stage in this cycle would arrive when it was supposed to, and until that time, the love I'd been holding space for would remain safe and pure within me, now that it was cleansed back to its immaculate innocence. We'd speak to each other when we could, when he could chose to of his own free will, because we were worth it. Then the words he'd held off from saying until he could commit to me could be offered up and received without any struggle – "I love you."

REBORN

APPENDIX

1. Gary Zukav (1989) The Seat of the Soul. New York, N.Y. Simon & Schuster Paperbacks.

2. Rick Hanson, Ph.D. (2009) Buddha's Brain. New Harbinger Publications, Inc.

3. Don Miguel Ruiz. (1997) The Four Agreements. San Rafael, California. Amber-Allen Publishing.

4. David R. Hawkins, M.D., Ph.D. (1995, 1998, 2004, 2012) Power Vs. Force. Hay House Inc.

5. Michelle DesPres (2012) The Clairvoyant Path. Woodbury, Minnesota. Llewellyn Publications.

6. David R. Hawkins, M.D., Ph.D. (2012) Letting Go. The Pathway of Surrender. Hay House Inc.

REBORN

ABOUT THE AUTHOR

Cristina Costantino has been on a tremendous spiritual ride since she met her Twin Flame and her mainstream life exploded into a multi-dimensional existance in 2014, triggering her to leave everything behind, including a 15-yr career in Advertising, to focus on healing her heart. In 2015, she wrote and published a memoir – *Who Broke The Girl?* – which narrates a 30-year cycle of self-propelled broken patterns from the perspective of the soul. She went on to become an Intuitive Energy Healer and Guide. Evolving, she now paints the HEART, to show and heal more deeply for what's held within all people, to help everyone let more love into their lives. She actively posts on IG as @LoveSquaredAlcheme, and has created numerous HEART paintings available in various forms – Alcheme Kits, HEART Prints & Custom HEARTS. All that she's created to help bring more love, beauty, and healing into this world can be found on LoveSquaredAlcheme.com.

www.ingramcontent.com/pod-product-compliance
Lightning Source LLC
Chambersburg PA
CBHW060149050426
42446CB00013B/2737